IN THE SHADOW
THE RISING DRAG

STORIES OF REPRESSION
IN THE NEW CHINA

EDITED BY
XU YOUYU AND HUA ZE

INTRODUCTION BY
ANDREW J. NATHAN AND
FOREWORD BY JEROME A. COHEN

TRANSLATED BY STACY MOSHER

First published in Hong Kong as *Close Encounters with the Chinese PSB* by Open Books

First published in English in 2013 by PALGRAVE MACMILLAN® in the US—a division of St. Martin's Press LLC, 175 Fifth Avenue, New York, NY 10010.

Where this book is distributed in the UK, Europe and the rest of the world, this is by Palgrave Macmillan, a division of Macmillan Publishers Limited, registered in England, company number 785998, of Houndmills, Basingstoke, Hampshire RG21 6XS.

Palgrave Macmillan is the global academic imprint of the above companies and has companies and representatives throughout the world.

Palgrave® and Macmillan® are registered trademarks in the United States, the United Kingdom, Europe and other countries.

ISBN: 978–1–137–27879–1

Library of Congress Cataloging-in-Publication Data

Zaoyu jingcha. English.

In the shadow of the rising dragon : stories of repression in the new China / edited by Xu Youyu, Hua Ze ; translated by Stacy Mosher.
    pages cm
    ISBN-13: 978–1–137–27879–1 (paperback)
    ISBN-10: 1–137–27879–X (paperback)
    1. Political persecution—China. 2. Internal security—China. 3. Political prisoners—China—Biography. 4. Human rights workers—China—Biography. 5. Human rights—China. 6. Civil rights—China. 7. Political culture—China. 8. China—Politics and government—2002– 9. China—Social conditions—2000– I. Xu, Youyu, 1947- II. Hua, Ze. III. Title.

JC599.C6Z36 2013
323'.0440951—dc23   2013009900

A catalogue record of the book is available from the British Library.

Design by Newgen Knowledge Works (P) Ltd., Chennai, India.

First edition: October 2013

10 9 8 7 6 5 4 3 2 1

Printed in the United States of America.

CONTENTS

CONTENTS

PREFACE TO THE CHINESE EDITION

Xu Youyu and Hua Ze

A DEFINING CHARACTERISTIC OF LIFE IN CHINA TODAY IS THE OMNIPRESENCE of the police. They interfere in the everyday activities of ordinary citizens and violate human rights to a degree not seen since the Cultural Revolution. The reality of the police state stands out in surreal and darkly comical contrast to the official slogan of a "harmonious society."[1]

Over the past few years, the Chinese authorities have increasingly relied on police power to preserve what they term "stability," first in response to the publication of Charter 08, a manifesto calling for major political reforms launched by well-known activists and intellectuals on International Human Rights Day in 2008,[2] then after the awarding of the 2010 Nobel Peace Prize to dissident intellectual Liu Xiaobo, one of the drafters of Charter 08, and again during the series of Jasmine Revolutions in North Africa in late 2010 and early 2011. Having lost confidence in the legitimacy of its rule, the government has developed a pathological sensitivity toward these recent trends. Convinced that prairie blazes are just waiting to be sparked throughout China, they are determined

---

[1] Translator's note (TN): "Harmonious society" is former Chinese president Hu Jintao's vision of a Chinese society stabilized by emphasizing social justice and equality over economic growth. The term became a catchphrase after it was introduced during the 2005 session of the National People's Congress, China's legislature.

[2] TN: A full translation of Charter 08 can be accessed on the website of Human Rights in China: http://www.hrichina.org/crf/article/3203 (accessed May 27, 2013).

to nip in the bud any "destabilizing factor." The authorities have devoted massive national resources to monitoring and controlling society under the rubric of "social management," i.e., comprehensive social control. Coming at a time when totalitarianism has retreated from the global stage and China is forging ahead toward a market economy, this perversely reactionary attempt to restore total control over society lacks popular support and is doomed to fail as it intensifies internal conflict and smothers social vitality. While undermining China's image, the government disingenuously dismisses as a "foreign plot" the international concern and protests its actions have aroused regarding China's human rights situation.

Police violations of citizens' basic rights as well as ubiquitous surveillance, control and suppression are the distinguishing characteristics of a totalitarian or post-totalitarian state. After the Berlin Wall fell, various records (exhibitions, museums, films, novels, memoirs, etc.) that depicted life in the former Soviet Union and Eastern Bloc enabled people to learn of the full gamut of suffering experienced under a police state. Likewise, we need to create a record of China's everyday police surveillance and human rights violations so that future generations can understand and study this period of "policification."

It should be pointed out that this record of Chinese citizens' encounters with the police is just one aspect of historical truth, and falls far short of representing the entirety. The omnipresence of the police made commissioning articles impossible, a difficulty reflected in the varying length, style and flavor of these essays.

While well aware of the situations of major rights defenders such as Gao Zhisheng, Guo Feixiong, Liu Xiaobo and Ai Weiwei, we were unable to include contributions from them or to ask their friends to describe their experiences on their behalf. A number of our personal friends were also the victims of police torture and abuse. We did not seek them out, however, because we learned that upon their release from prison they were sternly warned and even forced to sign guarantees that they would not speak of their experiences. Rather than risk sending these individuals back to prison through inclusion in our book, we were obliged to abandon this valuable content.

We firmly believe that the time will come when historical truth can be revealed in its fullness.

The intention and emphasis in compiling this book is not to reflect the severity and ruthlessness of human rights violations in modern China. Rather, what we wish to reflect is the omnipresence of the police throughout social life, and how public and routine police activities have become.

Unlike the secret police in the former Soviet Union and Eastern Europe, the Chinese police are in no way mysterious or sinister, nor are encounters with the police fortuitous, rare or exceptional to Chinese citizens; rather, they are frequent and routine, occurring not in dark corners but in broad daylight. The police can make a phone call and arrive at your doorstep, or appear without prior appointment, becoming regular visitors over time. They can invite you to tea or coffee, take you to restaurants and become your drinking buddies. They may pitch camp in the doorway or neighborhood of their surveillance target, and when manpower is short they often enlist the help of private security guards, urban management officials or migrant laborers, paying as many as eight people a monthly stipend of 1,000 *yuan* (about US$160) or more to monitor a target in shifts around the clock. Under these circumstances, the police become labor contractors, and the motley crew of casual workers they pull together can be expected to have little in the way of professional pride, standards or ethics.

The police resort to such measures because the government's emphasis on stability requires controlling and surveilling more people than the police are staffed to handle; even the worst of China's laws provide no justification for the long-term detention of these individuals—nor are there adequate facilities to hold them. Compelled to abuse their authority due to a "not on my watch" mentality or under orders to "ensure peaceful passage through a sensitive period," the police sometimes employ "soft" measures: De facto arrest and detention take the form of scenic tours during which the target is booked into a suburban guesthouse or held in a resort town. This purportedly "humane" tactic is actually a means of evading legal procedure. Against the vast majority of targets, however, the police unleash their full ferocity, beating, berating, humiliating and physically abusing even those who are physically disabled or injured.

Most of the people describing their personal experiences in this book have some legal awareness and knowledge, and some are even lawyers. They can therefore make full use of the Constitution and current laws to defend their rights and liberties during their encounters with the police. These episodes reveal the legal ignorance of modern China's law enforcers, who nevertheless feel free to trample on these laws, even after being instructed by their victims. Unlike the humble "subjects" and "abjectly compliant citizens" of old, the writers of these essays boldly employ and defend the Constitution and laws in a reasoned and restrained resistance.

What this book refers to as the police is merely one branch of China's immense law enforcement ranks. These are the political, thought and cultural police—the equivalent of the Russian KGB or East German "Stasi"—which should not even exist in a modern, civilized society. Although China's police are riddled with shocking corruption and squalidness, and it is no secret that the police are often in league with criminals and organized crime, ordinary Chinese people still generally regard them as protectors of their personal safety rather than as a force that threatens and violates civil rights. The Chinese people have full respect and admiration for the traffic police toiling on the public thoroughfares, the narcotics police risking their lives in the border regions and hinterlands, the investigators devoting their energies to apprehending criminals, and all other police officers who steadfastly preserve the normal workings of society. The political police, however, are regarded with fear and loathing as an alien species that impedes the progress of civil society.

Sometime in the future, when genuine political reform is on the agenda, and "establishing a country ruled by law" is a genuine political program instead of merely a slogan, the first order of business will be to disband the political police. In the long view, China's political police are destined to become a relic of history.

FOREWORD

LAWLESSNESS IN CHINA

Jerome A. Cohen

ALTHOUGH CHINA HAS MADE GREAT STRIDES IN ERECTING A FORMAL LEGAL system on the wreckage of the Cultural Revolution, there is widespread agreement that implementation has lagged far behind lawmaking. Thus, inevitably, one of the obvious themes that emerges from this important book is the extent of lawlessness in China.

Lawlessness can take many forms. Under the leadership of the Communist Party's political-legal commissions that operate at every level of government, the police have mastered the range of lawless black arts, and the procuracy (prosecutors' office) and the courts have too often proved accommodating.

The nation's "law enforcement" agencies, in plain view of the National People's Congress and the country's lawyers and law professors, have even stood on their head key provisions of major legislation designed to protect the rights of criminal suspects and defendants.

How long, for example, can police detain a suspect before seeking the procuracy's approval of an arrest? The 1996 Criminal Procedural Law (CPL) in most cases gave police only three days. In certain circumstances they were allowed four more days, and in only three relatively rare instances were they permitted to hold the suspect for as long as 30 days before requesting procuracy approval. Yet in practice the police turned the rare exceptions into the rule by taking up to 30 days in every case, and no legislator, lawyer, prosecutor or judge has been able to cure this distorted application of the law.

Similarly, the 1996 CPL provided for witnesses to testify in open court against an accused and subjected them to cross-examination by the defense, an immensely significant reform in principle. During 16 years of practice under the 1996 CPL, however, witnesses almost never appeared at trial, so the newly-enshrined right of cross-examination usually proved worthless.

The illegal 2011 confinement of the celebrated artist/activist Ai Weiwei for 81 days of incommunicado "residential surveillance"—not in his residence but in a police facility—is a notorious illustration of how law enforcement twists the law. Ai's detention not only violated the CPL but even a published rule of the Ministry of Public Security that warned its subordinates not to convert authorized "house arrest" into unauthorized police detention.

Will the newly-revised CPL that went into effect January 1, 2013, fare any better? One of its most controversial sections now authorizes the public security agency to detain persons incommunicado for up to six months of "residential surveillance"—in police custody, not at home—if they are suspected of terrorism, endangering national security or major corruption. How broadly will the police, including the secret police of the Ministry of State Security, define these three legislated exceptions to the demands of ordinary criminal procedure? Will the exceptions once again defeat the rules? Will the procuracy, which in the system the People's Republic imported from the Soviet Union is supposed to be the "watchdog of legality," effectively monitor the exercise of police discretion? Under the new CPL will the judiciary develop into an institution for controlling police and prosecutorial misconduct?

Until now, the courts, of course, have often had difficulty fairly applying the CPL in what has been their relatively narrow bailiwick—the criminal trial. Party interference, corruption, local protectionism and social networks have all led to distorted applications of the law. Farcical trials have been legion, especially in cases deemed "sensitive" for a variety of reasons. Yet the new CPL for the first time provides opportunity for the courts to review the legality of pre-trial police and prosecutorial investigative practices, including endemic use of torture to obtain confessions during interrogation of suspects. It remains to be seen how judges will interpret the new rules allowing them to summon investigators to court in instances where there are indications of coerced confessions and to exclude from the evidence illegally-obtained statements.

To be sure, good faith interpretation of the CPL is not the only challenge presented by lawlessness to China's criminal justice system. In practice, in a perceived crisis, the CPL has in effect been suspended wholesale as well as in individual cases. In such instances the functional division of labor and checks and balances called for by the CPL since its first enactment in 1979 are ignored. Police, prosecutors and judges, in conjunction with other government and Communist Party officials, are then expected to act like "a single fist" in carrying out investigation, prosecution and criminal punishment. On some occasions, when local law enforcement cannot be trusted by the central government, central authorities organize and dispatch law enforcement work teams from Beijing to jointly dispense criminal justice in the troubled area.

Punishment is also often imposed outside the scope of China's criminal legislation. Since 1957, a series of administrative regulations has authorized police, supposedly in conjunction with other officials, to subject people to what can now be three or even four years of "reeducation through labor" without requiring the approval of either the procuracy or the judiciary. The targets of this widely-feared "administrative punishment" are allowed virtually none of the protections afforded an accused by the formal criminal punishment system under the CPL. As this is written, Chinese supporters of civil liberties are waging a determined, mostly behind-the-scenes, and uphill political struggle against the Ministry of Public Security in an effort to persuade the Party to permit the National People's Congress (NPC) to adopt legislation that will end, or at least substantially reform, "reeducation through labor" and the minimal substantive and procedural norms that govern its application.

"Black jails," in which tens of thousands of would-be petitioners for justice have been arbitrarily locked up in Beijing, although even less transparent than "reeducation through labor," presumably also have some basis in local administrative regulations. Perhaps the same can be said of some other types of administrative detentions, such as those that have been imposed on the families of women attempting to avoid forced abortion and sterilization. Yet, even if authorized by regulations, such violations of personal freedom plainly violate China's Constitution, despite the fact that at present the government offers no effective means of enforcing constitutional protections.

Party members, especially officials suspected of corruption, often suffer their own form of literally lawless punishment. They are subject, totally without legislative authorization or any type of government supervision, to indefinite, incommunicado detention by the Party's Central Discipline Inspection Commission (CDIC) in accordance with the Party's own largely non-transparent rules. After long interrogation and investigation, the CDIC decides the suspect's fate. If the CDIC concludes that he should be criminally punished, it will send the prisoner to the procuracy to initiate prosecution, as in the current case of the deposed leader Bo Xilai. Or the CDIC may turn the matter over to government supervisory officials so that the case can be disposed of via administrative sanctions, such as demotion in rank or removal from office, and, of course, the CDIC itself can mete out Party punishments, including the termination of Party membership that usually precedes criminal prosecution.

Yet the worst kinds of lawlessness are those that are totally unregulated by any norms, whether inscribed in criminal legislation, national or local administrative regulations or Party rules. This book is rife with examples of surveillance, threats, intimidation, coercion, kidnapping, beatings, psychological oppression and many other cruel and degrading techniques carried out against "dissidents" by various police organizations and their hired thugs. The shameful misconduct to which contributors to this volume and other human rights activists and lawyers have been exposed is particularly appalling.

My own experiences in China testify to the protean nature of the problems portrayed here. I recall, for example, unsuccessfully trying to call upon Shanghai lawyer Zheng Enchong in 2006 after his release from a three-year prison sentence that grew out of his representation of victims of forced housing demolition. The local police who barred me from visiting Zheng had no legal authority to do so and, when repeatedly questioned on that score, simply said, again and again, "We are the police," implying that no greater legal authority was required, even in sophisticated Shanghai.

The Shanghai police were at least polite and apologetic, unlike the large band of rural officials and hoodlums who illegally blockaded the Shandong Province farmhouse of the blind "barefoot lawyer" Chen Guangcheng for many long months before and after his imprisonment for four years and three months. They not only harassed and assaulted Chen and his family but, in order to ensure the family's unlawful isolation, also used force against anyone who sought to visit them.

One can only hope that the splendid efforts by the editors of this volume and their contributor-colleagues will bolster the pressures that appear to be growing, both inside the country and abroad, for curbing China's contemporary lawlessness in all its forms. Genuine political and social stability depends on their success.

INTRODUCTION

Andrew J. Nathan

DOMSEC—IN CHINESE, *GUOBAO*—IS A MYSTERIOUS ORGANIZATION INVISIBLE to most Chinese but all-intrusive in the lives of those whom it selects as the objects of its attention. DomSec's full name is thought to be the "Bureau to Guard Domestic Security." It is part of the Ministry of Public Security, China's main domestic security organization, which handles everything from household registrations to traffic and fire-fighting to criminal investigations. DomSec must be this ministry's most important bureau as well as its most inconspicuous, for it can be found in higher-level public security offices behind the doorplate that reads "First Department."

But no private citizen enters that door. What we know about DomSec comes from the accounts of its victims, among them the people who tell their stories in this book. They do not visit Dom-Sec; DomSec comes to find them in their homes and neighborhoods. If it wants to talk to them it takes them to local teahouses or police stations, or it detains them in safe houses that it keeps in hotels and apartment buildings around the country. DomSec at first appears in the form of muscular young men in black sedans, who may stand guard outside a target's apartment in shifts all day and night for weeks or months at a time. If a target is detained, the younger men are joined by graying superiors who come and go, act full of authority, and alternate threats to their victims with appeals to what they believe is common sense and higher ideals. If the detainee is a woman, female agents keep watch at night and help with private functions.

DomSec agents do not wear uniforms or badges. They do not call in advance to set up appointments. They do not show laminated ID cards, and their cars do not bear license plates. They never explain where they are taking a person, why, or for how long. They do not allow their wards to call a lawyer. Their freedom from legal procedures—the flexibility with which they do their jobs—reflects the supreme importance of their mission: Stability Maintenance (*weiwen*).

The regime of course has always had domestic and external enemies. Mao's era was virtually defined by the purges of political rivals inside the Party, the mass campaigns against class enemies in society, and the restless hunt for spies and foreign sympathizers thought to be hidden among the cadres and the masses. The leaders after Mao allowed wider liberties and targeted fewer enemies. They also bureaucratized repression. In a series of reorganizations conducted in the early 1980s, the Ministry of State Security was created out of departments gathered together from other Party, state, and military organizations. The People's Armed Police was detached from the larger body of the People's Liberation Army to serve as a civil-order force.

It may have been the Falun Gong event of April 25, 1999, that alerted the leaders to the gaps these changes had opened up in the work of the Ministry of Public Security. On that date, tens of thousands of practitioners of the mystical health-and-martial-arts movement gathered in a silent demonstration in front of the central Party offices at Zhongnanhai, seeking to protest a burst of media criticisms of their sect. What alarmed the Party leaders more than the demonstration itself—which they promptly dispersed—was that their security agencies had known nothing of the planning for the demonstration. This seems to have been when the leaders decided to put more resources into the bureau then known as Pol-Sec (Political Security). Changing the name to DomSec may have been intended to signal the post-Mao emphasis on social stability rather than political struggle.

One must admire DomSec's precision. It selects just those people who need to be controlled in order to protect the regime, and it does so in a way that is hardly noticeable to anyone else. Its main targets are the few remaining Falun Gong practitioners, people who seek justice too persistently in the country's petitioning system, ethnic minority and religious activists, dissidents promoting constitutional democracy, and "rights defense" lawyers and activists who try to help citizens who have been oppressed by local officials. DomSec removes these nonconformists from society for a harsh kind of talk therapy, then returns them quietly to their normal lives after some period of weeks or months.

These latter-day enemies of the state—these threats to the security of a regime that is creating a cosmopolitan middle class, diversifying the media, promoting sports, fashion, and art museums, building "rule by law," a "harmonious society" and "modern socialist civilization"—are paradoxically the products of the regime's successes: filmmakers, lawyers, journalists and academics; creative people, thoughtful and patriotic. They are a privileged group of detainees because of their social status as intellectuals. In a book about ordinary workers and peasants taken in by the regular police, there would be fewer dialogues and many more instances of violent abuse.

To deal with this small group of security threats, the police have infinite resources and infinite patience. They would rather save them than punish them. The sessions are more like arguments than interrogations. The police alternate mundane banter with pointed political debate and seem to enjoy matching wits. The police take an interest in the fates of their charges. They urge the detainees to consider their parents and children. One policewoman pleads, "Whether you want to hear it or not, I'm saying it. I have to fulfill my duty to pull you back from the precipice." Their curiosity is bottomless; Tang Xiaozhao—an unthreatening person who lacks political connections or ambitions—must report every detail of her thoughts and actions, down to the level of which parts of Charter 08 she agrees with and which not.

Nor do DomSec's attentions wane after a detainee is released. Gu Chuan is asked to send an e-mail every day and report his activities and thoughts, and the police are not satisfied if these do not show agreement with the Party's goals. DomSec also "invites to tea" students and scholars who are about to go overseas to study or who have come home temporarily to visit family, and asks them to report on other students and scholars who are outside the country. The agents typically request an overseas scholar's phone number so they can check up from time to time on his or her activities and those of acquaintances. DomSec or some allied agency also seems to surveil the e-mail of Chinese students, scholars and activists in other countries.

Intellectuals themselves in the Chinese understanding of that term, DomSec agents show little entrenched hostility toward their victims. Instead, they often seem puzzled by their victims' motives in challenging the regime. The officers believe in the urgency of public order and the system's vulnerability to threats. How can intelligent people, patriotic Chinese, public-spirited citizens be so simpleminded as to insist on individual justice when national stability is at stake? How can persons born and bred in China not understand China's special "national conditions," which dictate the necessity to tolerate at least for now an authoritarian state? As one of the agents tells Liu Shasha, "It's good that you want democracy. But China's situation is different; we can't just indiscriminately imitate the West."

An odd comradeship forms. Teng Biao listens sympathetically to an agent's complaints about his child's school problems. In return, the agent expresses respect for Teng Biao: "No one but your wife and immediate family understands you as well as I do. You're a person of high caliber and good character, and you're a good writer...."An agent tells Liu Shasha, "[Another activist] is no coward; he has a lot more spunk than you! He can spend days and nights bent over his computer! He could debate with us all night!" A DomSec officer helps Li Xin'ai take her sick baby to the hospital and another policeman lends her the money for the deposit the hospital requires. When elderly detainee Ding Zilin is in the hospital in a city outside her hometown of Beijing, she calls her Beijing security team to come protect her from a local security agency that is harassing her.[3] The officers who come from Beijing to escort her and her husband back home make sure they have medicine and are warm, because they are elderly and are professors.

---

[3] TN: In this case, Ding and her husband are monitored by State Security (StateSec), which unlike DomSec is mainly responsible for security matters relating to foreign countries. Some individuals suspected of involvement with foreign affairs or international organizations are sometimes put under simultaneous surveillance by both StateSec and DomSec.

Of course, the police also make threats and use violence. Wu Huaying is tortured in retribution for seeking justice for her brother. Teng Biao is forced to ask himself what cause is worth enduring physical torture. Violence may be limited, but it remains a constant threat. When the police courteously urge Hua Ze to contact them if she ever comes back to their province, a pretense of care and friendship masks a frightening warning.

The detainees feel fear. But it falls short of the hopeless terror experienced by victims beaten, enslaved, tortured and killed in the Mao period. Hua Ze laughs in the face of her tormentors. Liu Shasha quotes another person telling DomSec, "Someone like me would have been put before the firing squad in the 1950s, and in the 1960s would have been sentenced to life in prison. Now I can sit here and debate with you—that's the progress of China's democracy!"

Eroding fear is a sign of weakness in an authoritarian system. In that sense, the threat posed by DomSec's victims is not in the relatively trivial substance of their demands—an end to the abuse of a blind rights advocate, or a call to implement China's constitution—but just the fact that they dare to make demands. All Dom-Sec wants is for its victims to shut up because if they do, so will everybody else.

The decline of fear is partly attributable to a rising legal consciousness that affects the police as much as the victims. China still has no independent legal institutions that effectively protect citizens' rights. But for over 30 years the regime has been "constructing rule by law," promulgating laws and regulations, training lawyers and judges, and educating the public in "legal knowledge." It has done so for its own purposes, like attracting foreign investment and creating procedural fig leaves for acts of repression. But the idea of law has developed its own momentum based on people's commonsense understanding of what law is. The simple idea of rights is enough to drive some citizens and their advocates to demand them. Some do so naïvely, thinking their own idea of law is the regime's idea; others do so courageously, knowing that their idea of rights is not an idea the regime is prepared to recognize. Between the naïve and the courageous, a cadre has formed that makes trouble for the regime.

What is more remarkable is to see the regime's agents also becoming entangled in the idea of law. Even though the police believe in the necessity to defend the state by all possible means, they also know that they are violating any coherent concept of legal procedure. They often describe their own actions as outside the law. They seem to fear that what they are doing now may later be considered wrong, that their victims today may become their accusers tomorrow. "What you're saying is that someday you'll be judging us," Gu Chuan's interrogators assert, to which he replies, "You said it, not me." Between the lines we seem to witness the police and their victims agreeing more than they disagree about who is going to end up on the wrong side of history.

This leads to a subtle inversion of the balance of power between DomSec and its victims. We find police agents pleading for understanding and seeking to preserve "human feelings," and activists feeling sorry for their persecutors. As Teng Biao puts it, "[P]erpetrators are also victims. . . . [T]he people . . . who could only mechanically follow orders and had no ability to distinguish between right and wrong also faced their own hardship, embarrassment and pain." One is reminded of the popular Chinese saying, "If you don't do shameful things, you won't need to fear the devil at the door."

In this sense, DomSec is right. Fearless citizens do present a threat. But they do so only because the regime is afraid of them. The security state has no problem with those who have no problem with it. If the security state did not exist, neither would its opponents, and then the security state would no longer be necessary. DomSec perhaps should heed the wisdom of the ancient Daoist philosopher Laozi, who said, "The more you make prohibitions, the more you make violators."

DUE NORTH

MY PERILOUS ATTEMPT TO VISIT CHEN GUANGCHENG

He Peirong

He Peirong (online name Zhenzhu, meaning "Pearl"), a signatory of Charter 08, was born in the eastern city of Nanjing in the 1970s. A former website developer, she became a volunteer helping victims of the 2008 Sichuan earthquake, and then in 2009 launched a Twitter campaign to raise funds to support the families of China's prisoners of conscience.

In January 2011, He attempted to visit the blind legal activist Chen Guangcheng while he was under house arrest. She was one of a number of people (including the British actor Christian Bale) who used such failed visit attempts and the resulting abusive treatment by police to raise awareness of the plight of Chen and his family. After Chen managed to escape his home under cover of night in April 2012, He was involved in helping him reach the US Embassy in Beijing. Chen has since gone to the United States as a "visiting scholar."

ON JANUARY 10, 2011, I DROVE ON MY OWN FROM NANJING TO DONGSHIGU Village, Shuanghou Township, in Yinan County of Shandong Province's Linyi City, hoping to visit Mr. Chen Guangcheng, who was being held under so-called "soft detention" in his home. What follows is a description of the violent obstruction I encountered during this attempt.

Many people were deeply worried about Chen's living conditions. Following his release from prison, the local authorities had kept him under virtual house arrest, refusing him access to medical treatment and preventing his children from going to school. Outside aid organizations were monitoring the situation, but they knew little about the conditions under which he was being held. No one knew what kind of cooperation existed between the village government and the police; we were all in a muddle, and no amount of effort provided the kind of firsthand information needed for planning a "tour." I also wondered what kind of people were watching over Chen, whether they were local bullies and deadbeats or villagers, as well as who was paying them, whether there was some kind of formal agreement, and if so, for how long.

At one point I considered finding an online friend with either police or investigative experience to go along with me. After further thought, however, I decided it would be safer to go on my own. First of all, people who had previously tried to visit Chen had been met with violent attacks, some life-threatening. I had no way to ensure the safety of anyone who accompanied me, much less to free someone who might be arrested. I was willing to take the risk myself, but I would not require a similar sacrifice of another. No one wishes to cavalierly risk her life or subject herself to senseless beatings by police, but sometimes this is the price that must be paid. As my Twitter friend @yinys says, "When the time comes, I'll use my body as a battering ram." I felt this was just such a time.

I believed that the violent obstructions facing Chen's visitors weren't a spontaneous reflection of a hostile local mindset, but rather meticulously planned and rationally decided. It was on that basis that I planned my own action.

Gandhi once said, "If we can only develop our willpower, we will find that we no longer need armed force." The way I saw it, if I couldn't match the brutality of those who were backed and incited by the authorities, I must resort to weakness. If someone raised their club, I must present my head to receive the blow; if someone struck my left cheek, I must turn the other to him as well. In any event, I had to show my unshakeable determination not to be driven away, and to pay any price for the sake of seeing Chen Guangcheng. I would use my own actions to tell those thugs that their terroristic methods were useless. Laozi said, "Nothing is softer and weaker than water, yet nothing is more effective in attacking what is firm and strong. The soft overcomes the hard, and the weak the strong." I refused to lose faith in human nature, and was determined to summon goodness with goodness.

Before setting off, I "Googled" the telephone numbers of the local DomSec police. These people were used to carrying out their villainy under cover of the system, and I wanted to publicize their names and telephone numbers, and even their addresses, so that if things went wrong, individuals could be called to account for their crimes.

I believe that the power of China's civil society is steadily rising and that popular surveillance is changing China. A little bit of luck would also help.

DUE NORTH

On the morning of January 10, I set off on my own for Dongshigu Village. Bumped and jostled the whole way, I arrived in Linyi a little after 6:00 that night. I had no navigation system and was unfamiliar with the roads, but by heading due north I located National Highway 205. Upon reaching the end of the highway, I was obliged to stop and ask for directions, and found that I'd already passed by the lodgings a Twitter friend had recommended. I suspected that word was already out on Twitter, and that once I checked in, Shandong's Finest would show up in the middle of the night and see me home. Twitter enthusiasts are especially active at night, and attention was focused; by the next day it would be much more difficult to sustain interest. I decided to make my move that night.

All I'd had that day was a cup of coffee in the morning and a cup of hot water and an egg at noon, and after the 12-hour drive I was parched and famished. I had no way of knowing when I'd get another chance to eat and drink, so I found a small restaurant, and as I ate I sounded out the proprietor on the local situation. I learned that I was now 30 kilometers outside of Linyi, which meant I had about 50 kilometers to go before reaching my destination.

I no longer had internet access through my cell phone, so I went to an internet café next to the restaurant to send out an update. My planned five-hour trip from Nanjing to Linyi had taken twelve hours instead, and I had missed the prearranged times to report my safe arrival by cell phone and Twitter. I could only hope that the Sina.com blog would carry my news to the other side of the Great Firewall.

Along the way, I noticed that most shops lacked air conditioners and were heated with coal stoves, and that people seemed simple and honest rather than cunning and vicious. This made me more confident of my course of action.

Once back on the road, a little after 7:00, I was ecstatic to find that I could once again access Twitter from my cell phone, and I quickly tweeted, "Heading due north, not stopping for rest." An hour later I received a phone call from lawyer Jiang Tianyong, who asked my location, and shortly thereafter I received a call from Piaoxiang,[1] who urged me to be careful and set a time for the next call.

I turned on the video and audio recording equipment in my car, and set the video camera for sound activation so it would automatically shut down after two minutes of silence and then resume filming when the sound level reached 60 decibels. I tested the function several times with my car radio.

Entering the hills before 9:00, I guessed I was near my destination. I pulled my car over to the side of the road, tucked heat pads inside my jacket, wrapped a muffler around my neck, zipped up my jacket and was ready to face the winter wind. I tried the recorder one more time. All was in order. Driving due north once more, I still saw no sign of Dongshigu Village. With exhaustion setting in, I finally asked a truck driver how to get to Dongshigu, and he cheerfully informed me that I'd just passed it. I managed to miss the spot two more times before I spotted the village.

Not daring to drive straight in, I stopped my car on the next road beyond it and tweeted my arrival before I drove in the back way. Finally I spotted two houses and the wall of yet another, and as I sat gazing at them, a man in uniform standing by a van walked over with a flashlight.

I stuck my head out the window and asked, "Is this Xishigu Village?"

---

[1] TN: The pen name used by Hua Ze.

He said, "No. Turn around, and the road on your right will take you to Xishigu Village"

I asked again, "So where am I now?"

He hesitated, then said, "Dongshigu Village."

DIRECT ENGAGEMENT

I was so happy that I didn't immediately know what to do. Turning my car around, I drove several meters, then stopped along the road and dialed Piaoxiang's number and told her I'd managed to stumble onto the village. As I spoke, I looked in my rearview mirror and noticed the flashlight beam of the village sentry advancing toward me.

I asked him if all villages had sentry posts, and if I could find a sentry at Xishigu Village who could give me directions. The villager looked somewhat embarrassed and said no, not all villages were like this. Then he told me to telephone my contact and have him or her come out and receive me. I asked him to join me in my car so I could talk with him, while at the same time reaching into my handbag for my wallet, where I had about 1,500 *yuan* prepared. But the villager refused to enter my car, and standing by my window he bent down and asked me to quickly tell him what I wanted. After a moment's thought, I asked him straight out, "Is this where Chen Guangcheng lives?" At the sound of that name, the villager jumped as if jolted out of his shoes, then ran back and grabbed his walkie-talkie, which began squawking. I clicked down the lock on my car door and turned on my tape recorder, and seeing the video camera indicator light in sleep mode, I switched the camera back on as well, preparing to face the inevitable.

In a twinkling I was surrounded by four or five villagers, who asked me what I was up to. I cracked open my car window and told them I wanted to see the village head. I said, "You're not responsible and I don't want to cause you any trouble. I understand you're just doing your duty. Please have the village head come out. I want to talk to him." The villagers scurried about, pounding on my car and telling me to leave. I sat inside my car and watched. There was nothing they could do.

Just then a light flashed up ahead and a police car arrived. I immediately opened my car door and jumped out to block the police car. I was joined by the villagers, who asked who was inside. The people inside the car said they needed to get into the village. I said I wanted to go along, but a uniformed man in the car refused, and the car drove into the village. One of the villagers reported this development on his walkie-talkie, and I wrote down the license number and reported it to Piaoxiang over the phone. "If things don't go well tonight, contact the police officer using this car." I purposely said this loudly enough for the villagers to overhear.

I then went back into my car and refused to come out, cracking open the window just enough to repeat my demand to see the village head. I told the villagers, "When the police come, I'll leave." Just then, a man in his thirties wearing round glasses came out of the village and roughly ordered me to stay put, asking my business and demanding to see my identity card. I was on the phone with lawyer Jiang Tianyong just then, and Jiang told me the villagers had no authority to examine my ID. All the same, after hanging up, I decided to let them see it. I turned my car toward the entrance of the village and told the villagers, "I'm not leaving." Then I put my ID card up against the window. They shined their flashlights on it, after which the man in the glasses said, "We can't read it," and told me to push the ID card out the window. When I refused, he said he was the village head, and that he wanted to come into my car. I told him to show me his ID, but he refused. Just then a call came from Piaoxiang, and I told her to quickly telephone the commander of the Shuanghou police station and file a complaint.

The man in the glasses kicked my car. "She's a thief," he said, and told the others to grab my car windows. I said, "I'm employed, I'm a teacher, so let's see who has credibility. I've been transmitting everything that's going on, and whatever you do here will be broadcast for the whole country to hear." The man with the glasses asked, "What are you up to?" Then he told the others I was an enemy agent, and directed them to grab my car and shake it back and forth, planning to flip it over. I pressed down on the accelerator, giving them a scare. I was angry and shouted out of the window, "I've been very restrained, I haven't been aggressive, and when you grabbed my car windows I didn't even pinch your fingers in them. I want to see the village head. If you raise your hands to me, I won't let you off, or anyone in your families. I hear you're all ex-cons and that you're prepared to do anything. Then you'd better just take me away in pieces, because you can't scare me. I'm not an American journalist or a lawyer who can be run off by the likes of you. I'm a born and bred Chinese—I've been raised on intimidation. Who hasn't seen thugs like you before?!"

The villagers began piling rocks around my car. Just as a call from Chen Yunfei[2] came through on my phone, the man in the glasses came over carrying two poles. "I'll show you," he said, then bashed in my windshield and my window on the driver's side, after which he reached into the car, pulled out my car keys, opened the car door and began yanking me out. I kept describing to Chen Yunfei what was happening until they took my cell phone away.

I was flung to the ground but quickly stood up and dusted myself off. Down I went again and then back up. I was kicked three or four times, and then the men just cursed at me and left me alone.

As they ran into the village, I jumped back into my car and stepped on the accelerator, the chassis scraping over the pile of rocks as I drove toward the village. The men rushed to pile rocks in my path and I was tossed out of my car again. The villagers wanted to tow me back onto the highway, so I said, "All right, I'll sit there and block your National Highway 205." After thinking for a minute, the villagers sent two people to walk me to a road about 20 meters from the village, and the three of us stood there in the cold wind.

Whenever a villager passed, I would grab him and say, "Do you know Chen Guangcheng? He's blind. Have you seen him?" Those people always bowed their heads and dashed off.

During this time I saw someone who looked like a village head come out, and I tried to grab him, but the villagers quickly said, "He's not the village head."

I said, "If he's not the village head, why do you trot around him like dogs with your tongues hanging out until he waves you away?" The villagers laughed. I went on, "Your township head says Chen Guangcheng has a good life and his children are going to school. Is that true?"

---

[2] TN: A Chengdu-based activist and blogger.

A villager twisted his head around and snorted, "Says who? Go ask him!"

The cold of the northern winter night was oppressive, and after a while I simply couldn't take it any longer. I said, "I need to rest." The two villagers disagreed with each other and almost began fighting. Just then another man came out of the village to relieve them, and when I repeated my request, this one agreed. I climbed into the back seat of my car and lay down. The villagers turned on the light inside my car so they could keep an eye on me, but I was so tired that I eventually drifted off to sleep.

POLICE AND CIVILIAN COLLUSION

I was shaken awake by police officers, who told me, "You're safe, come with us." When I got into their car I asked to see the time. They said to wait until we reached the police station, but they never did let me see a clock.

After we arrived at the police station, they took a written statement. The police interrogated me about my work, my educational background, how I had gotten here, whether I had an accomplice, whether the car was mine, when I bought it, and sometimes interrupted their line of questioning to revert to my work experience. Suddenly I understood: "So you think I'm an enemy agent, and you're investigating me." A policeman off to the side tittered.

The policeman questioning me blushed and assured me, "Not at all. We're just asking exactly who you are; we're responsible for you."

I said, "The Nanjing police have me on file. You can carry out an ID check. As to whether I came on my own, you can view the surveillance footage. Don't ask such stupid questions, all right?" Finally they had me hand over all my receipts from bridges and toll booths, and after working out the sequence, they no longer concerned themselves with this line of questioning.

They went on to ask, "Is it appropriate to go to the village this late at night?"

"I couldn't help it. That's when I arrived, and in Nanjing no one sleeps that early—the night life is just beginning!"

The policeman said that in northern villages, everyone's asleep by that time of night, and it was only natural that someone trying to barge into the village would come under attack by the villagers.

I said, "I was there to visit a friend. If that friend doesn't mind, what business is it of anyone else?"

The policeman insisted that my timing was inappropriate, and I watched him until he was done, then said, "Since you're being such an idiot, I might as well put it plainly: If I come back next time in broad daylight, will I be allowed into the village?" Then they questioned me in detail about the video equipment in my car, and I told them everything. One police officer observed, "It looks like you came prepared."

"Nonsense," I said. "If I'd been killed, how would you have cracked the case? I prepared all that equipment to make it easier for you police to investigate and arrest a suspect and solve the case faster."

The police also interrogated me about what had happened at the village and asked if I'd tried to run down the villagers. I said they were trying to tip over my car, so that's when I tried to run them down. I said I'd showed them my ID card and had repeatedly asked to see the village head. Finally I had the police listen to the audio-tape and look at the video footage so they could see whether it was me or the villagers who were telling the truth. After listening, the police explained that their ranks were thin in the countryside, so public security depended heavily on the villagers' self-organized efforts, and so on.

Basically, no one, neither villager nor policeman, was willing to mention Chen Guangcheng's name. The police used "that person" to refer to Chen, and what they always asked was, "Do you know who he is?" The next day in the car, I once again brought up how Chen had filed a lawsuit in Beijing for the rights of the handicapped. The policeman snorted, "How do you know it was him who did it?"

At the police station I mentioned the novel *Red Crag*, and asked the police officers if they remembered the character Little Radish Head.[3] Instilled with "red" education from our youth, we'd been taught that the incorrigibly evil Kuomintang society would

---

[3] TN: In this iconic revolutionary novel, nine-year-old "Radish Head" is imprisoned with his parents and eventually killed by the Kuomintang.

not spare even a child. I said, "If you think Chen Guangcheng is a counterrevolutionary, then go ahead and execute him. But his children are innocent; why should they be confined to their home and deprived of schooling? Why should a man's whole family be punished? Even the Communist Party now knows better than to execute a counterrevolutionary on the spot." I said, "You're police officers, you must have social connections and status; you've been through the Cultural Revolution, you know how people with the wrong family backgrounds were labeled 'sons of bitches.' Now times have changed and they've been rehabilitated. Think how things were back then and have a little empathy."

Finally I said, "We Chinese have an old saying, 'Never take things to extremes.' If you keep breaking through the ethical bottom line, not letting a person see a doctor when he's ill and depriving children of their education, people will become indignant and use all kinds of methods to try to see Mr. Chen."

Throughout the interrogation, apart from my being allowed one phone call and to send out one approved tweet, my cell phone remained under the control of the police, and from where it was placed just a meter away I could hear it ringing non-stop. Sometimes the police would shut it off, other times they'd just ignore it. Finally one of them took it away. I said that if they were searching my cell phone, they needed a search warrant.

The police had initially promised to mediate with the villagers and escort me back after my car was repaired. But after they searched my cell phone it was another story; they said we'd go to Linyi the next day and return when the car was repaired. I again demanded an explanation or a search warrant, then lay down to sleep and ignored them.

At daybreak the following morning, my statement was stamped by the officer who appeared to be the leader and who the night before had told me to make a telephone call reporting I was safe. Later, a female police officer brought me two meat pies to eat. I asked, "When can I leave? If I'm not allowed to leave, I want a lawyer."

Soon after that, the police officer who had taken my statement appeared, but his attitude had changed, and he very politely said, "I'll take you right away. Your car is at Linyi because there wasn't the right kind of window glass available around here. I'll take you to fetch your car, and then you can go."

Four police officers drove me to the repair shop. We had to wait for a very long time, and I fell fast asleep in the police car. After getting my car, two police officers drove it up ahead, with me in the back of the police car. After filling my car with gas, we kept driving around for quite a while. The police officers with me seemed anxious to get me on my way, and drove up to the other car and exchanged words with those officers.

When we reached the highway, the police returned my cell phone and urged me to tell my friends that I was safe and that they needn't come to Shandong. Upon hearing that the "tour group" that had set out to visit me had turned back, they asked where I wanted to go now, and were relieved when I replied, "Back home to feed my cat."

At the border of Shandong and Jiangsu provinces, we all got out of our cars, and the police had me take photos of my car from various angles. I found that the glass had been replaced, but asked, "What about the sun shade? And there are still a lot of dents in the car door. And what about my clothes and shoes that were ruined? The equipment was expensive—it wasn't damaged was it?"

A policeman said, "Oh come on, you're not that short of money, let it go. We don't know whether or not the equipment's been damaged."

When shaking hands with the police, I got a "poke" of static electricity, and the plainclothes officer escorting me said it meant we shared a destiny. I said, "Yes, first time strangers, second time intimates; if this problem isn't resolved, I'll be back."

Having returned home safely from Shandong, I am even more worried about Chen Guangcheng's situation. He lives in an economically backward and relatively closed-off area, an old revolutionary region with a dense ideological atmosphere. Calling someone an enemy agent is almost enough to strip a person of his human rights. Neither the police nor the villagers seem aware of basic humanitarian concepts.

What I learned from this trip is that every telephone call, every postcard, is useful. Sending Chen Guangcheng a postcard tells villagers that he's a good man, not an enemy agent, that their actions are being monitored, that no wrongdoing will be ignored and that sacrificing conscience for petty reward is irredeemably disgraceful. The local mood in Shandong is simple and unsophisticated; people are likely to be influenced by reputation. The people who bribe villagers to commit violence are therefore the most shameless and unscrupulous of all.

NEVER GIVE UP

RECORD OF AN ABDUCTION

Teng Biao

A lawyer and signatory of Charter 08, Teng Biao was born in the 1970s in China's northeastern Jilin Province. He became a public figure in 2003 for campaigning against Custody and Repatriation, a system that allowed police to detain people lacking an urban residential permit and send them back to their place of origin. Teng Biao was one of a group of lawyers who challenged the legality of the system following the death in custody of Sun Zhigang, a university graduate working in Guangzhou as a fashion designer. The public outcry, combined with the lawyers' campaign, led China's legislature, the National People's Congress, to abolish the Custody and Repatriation system, and also resulted in "rights defense" replacing political democratization as the main focus of China's activists. Soon afterward, Teng, his law school classmate Xu Zhiyong and others established the Open Constitution Initiative Consulting Co. Ltd., also known by its Chinese abbreviation, Gongmeng, through which lawyers such as Teng provided legal representation for many cases involving religious freedom, freedom of expression, family planning, forced relocation for urban redevelopment, equal access to education, forced confessions, torture, the death penalty and other social issues.

Due to Teng Biao's involvement in these sensitive issues, the government has routinely subjected him to surveillance, beatings, shadowing, abduction and prolonged disappearance, one instance of which is described in the essay below.

AT 8:25 ON THE EVENING OF MARCH 6, 2008, AFTER BUYING SOME BOOKS at the All Saints Bookstore,[1] I telephoned my wife and said I'd be home in about 20 minutes.

At around 8:40, just after I had parked my car and was locking the doors, I found myself surrounded by four middle-aged men, one of whom clamped a hand on my shoulder and said, "Are you Teng Biao?" Without waiting for my reply, they shoved me toward a black sedan, and it took me a moment to realize that I was being abducted. I began shouting and struggling as if my life depended on it for at least three minutes; the residents and watchmen of nearby buildings must have heard me, but not a soul emerged. I was hopelessly outnumbered and quickly immobilized with my arms handcuffed behind my back. Once they had stuffed me into the car, no one could hear me, so I stopped shouting.

I'd lost my glasses during the struggle, and the car was pitch black inside. Two of the men pinned me in the back seat and pulled a black hood over my head. As we drove, the man on my left kept pressure on my arms, while the one on my right crushed my head against the seat with his back. Any resistance provoked a stream of filthy and abusive language, especially from the man on my left.

I began wondering who these people actually were and guessed they were probably Domestic Security. The circumstances were very similar to lawyer Li Heping's abduction the previous October, in which case I should expect physical torment: being taken to the outskirts of the city, stripped of my clothing, pummeled, kicked, shocked with an electric baton, tossed in a ditch and left to find my way home.... Over the last two years I'd witnessed two instances of abduction by the authorities: One time was the day before Chen Guangcheng went to trial in Linyi, Shandong Province, and a key witness, his cousin Chen Guangyu, was abducted; the second time was when Shandong police abducted Chen Guangcheng's mother and child from the lower floor of my building. There were many more such cases: Chen Guangcheng himself had been abducted on September 6, 2005, Gao Zhisheng on August 17, 2006, Li Heping

---

[1] TN: Beijing's All Saints (Wansheng) Bookstore and its attached Thinkers Café, located in Haidian District, are popular meeting places for independent intellectuals, and are sometimes shut down during government crackdowns on dissent during sensitive periods.

on September 30, 2007, and Qi Zhiyong on January 14, 2008.[2] Abductions of defendants, witnesses and lawyers had been routine in the cases I'd handled.

I could tolerate a light beating, but this gang seemed particularly thuggish, and that meant trouble. Some of my cases had irritated officials and police, and if they wanted to get back at me, I could end up with a broken arm or leg, or paralyzed like Fu Xiancai.[3] At this point, I could only accept my fate.

After 40 minutes or so, the car stopped, and the sound of dogs barking indicated that we were in some rural village. Everyone climbed out of the car, and I was escorted into a house. From beginning to end, I never learned any of my assailants' names, so I will refer to the anonymous thugs as A, B, C and D.

After removing my hood, they ordered me to stand in the middle of the room as they surrounded me, glowering. One of them said, "Strip down!" I thought, "Oh no, here it comes!" and remained motionless. To my surprise, he said again, "Take off your coat, it's hot in here."

Someone began hectoring me. I couldn't tell if he was one of the original four, so I'll call him E.

"Do you know why you're here?"

"Who are you? What do you want?" I shouted back.

"Relax! We're from the 'municipal bureau,' not gangsters."[4]

"Do you have identification?"

"This isn't the time. We'll show you ID when we need to."

My left wrist ached from their twisting, and I rotated it like a boxer warming up in the ring.

"What's this, you want to fight?" E said. "If you keep that up and a gun goes off, what then?"

"We've been waiting for you all day; if you keep provoking us, do you think you can take it?"

---

[2] TN: Gao Zhisheng and Li Heping are prominent rights defense lawyers. Qi Zhiyong lost a leg after being shot during the Tiananmen crackdown in June 1989. Since then he has campaigned for official accountability and compensation for the families of victims of the crackdown.

[3] TN: Fu Xiancai, a rural activist calling for better compensation for villagers displaced by the Three Gorges Dam project, was rendered paralyzed by unknown assailants in June 2006 after he gave an interview to a German television station.

[4] Meaning he was a police officer from the Beijing Municipal Public Security Bureau, rather than one of the ruffians the authorities sometimes hire to intimidate "troublemakers."

I suddenly recalled my mother-in-law coming to our home that morning and saying there was a suspicious car downstairs. Thinking it was just Changping DomSec looking me up as usual before the Two Sessions,[5] I wasn't worried, and when I looked down and didn't recognize the car, I decided it had nothing to do with me. Now I realized whose car it had been.

I just stared at them and said nothing, then looked at the ceiling to keep my head up. The room held two long tables and several chairs, and curtains covered the windows. There were also two lamps and a radiator, and the lamp in front of me was aimed at my eyes, but it wasn't turned on. I recalled a Shanghai petitioner's description of a "special interrogation room," and guessed the lamp was for video recordings. In any case, this was neither a guesthouse nor a residence, and was definitely an interrogation room. The next day, when they opened the door, I caught a glimpse of several other such rooms across the hallway.

"We have our rules here. If you don't answer truthfully, don't blame us for what happens."

My greatest worry was for my family, but I was also tired and hungry after spending all afternoon at the bookstore. I said, "I'll answer your questions, but under two conditions: First, let me telephone my wife, and second, let me eat."

They said, "The rules say you can't make any phone calls, but we'll think it over." Then they started in with their badgering. These were professional brainwashers who loved to talk, but all that came out were the usual clichés, empty and illogical.

After an hour, someone came back and said, "You can't make a telephone call, but you can send a text message. Do you know what you want to say?"

"I just want to tell her not to worry."

"Write that you're discussing something with friends."

Taking my cell phone, I texted, "My dear, don't worry, just look after our child. I'm discussing something with friends. Your loving husband." They looked it over, and after deciding there was

---

[5] Referring to the sessions of the National People's Congress and the Chinese People's Political Consultative Conference, held every March. Police typically visit, and sometimes detain, activists and dissidents around this time as a safeguard against social unrest.

no hidden message, they let me send it. That was at 10:45 p.m. on March 6.

Even without knowing whether I'd sent the message myself, my wife would guess I was in trouble, since I never wrote "look after our child" or "your loving husband" while on routine business.

About an hour later, they brought me a rice box. The fried vegetables were cold, wilted and skimpy. E said, "Eat it up—what you get inside is even worse." By "inside" he meant the detention center, my next step, as they repeatedly told me, and where things would be much harder for me.

———◆———

"If you're sentenced to ten years, you'll come out an old man, and what can you do then?" E said. "Don't go up against the government. It wouldn't take much for us to deprive you of a living." I knew other prisoners of conscience had been prevented from finding work or housing before and after their imprisonment.

E went on, "You're going to be here a while. My colleague will explain the rules to you." F was a burly man in his thirties who I later learned was leader of the watch guards.

"First, up at six and exercise. Second, stand up and greet police officers when they enter or leave the room. Third, answer questions truthfully and clearly."

The second item was clearly an affront to a prisoner's dignity. There was certainly no natural justice in standing respectfully for secret police who were the enemies of free thought.

Two thugs sat on either side of me, watching for any reason to hit me, so passive resistance was best. I was also sure I was being videotaped, so I had to stay calm and confident.

Later two more men came in. G and H were responsible for questioning me and taking notes, and probably came from the interrogation division. When they entered, I didn't stand up, and E said, "Have you forgotten the rules?" I rose languidly, but didn't greet them. (I continued to refuse to greet them or to stand up when they left. When they entered, I slowly made as if to stand, and in most cases they immediately motioned for me to sit back down.

Sometimes if I was eating or writing, I pretended not to notice them entering and they did not object.)

E and F went out, leaving behind G, H, me and two guards, I and J. Six guards rotated in three shifts around the clock. Whether I was eating, sleeping, using the washroom or thinking, two pairs of eyes were always watching, bringing to mind the electric screen in Orwell's *1984*. From what I could see, there were three reasons for maintaining a 24-hour watch: preventing escape or suicide, and reporting a person's every action, including his living habits, health, mental condition and any emotional changes. The police were said to have brainwashing experts who used these details to identify a person's weaknesses for psychological attacks, altering their tactics as necessary. To have someone staring at me less than a meter away while I used the toilet was ridiculous and humiliating.

The interrogation began, with G mainly asking the questions and H taking notes. Mixed in with the questions were clumps of "ideological and political education." The core questions on the evening of the sixth were: "You came from a village and were admitted to Peking University, obtained a PhD and now you're a lecturer and a lawyer, you have a nice home, so why are you bothering with these other things? Why pick at the government's faults and write essays that are published overseas? Why not use normal channels to report problems? Why don't we see you coming out with praise when the government does something good? Do you give any thought to your country's welfare? What is it you're after?"

When G spoke of publishing articles overseas and of patriotism, H became agitated and interjected, "You worship foreigners, you stinking traitor." I looked at him contemptuously without speaking. But these brainwashers are themselves the victims of brainwashing, and we should pity them.

G was not devoid of humanity. He spoke of similarities between his experience and mine: brought up in poverty, entering the university in 1992, experiencing China's failed 1993 bid to host the Olympics. He said, "The fact that the first thing you wanted to do was telephone your wife shows you're responsible, and that's good. But have you considered showing more responsibility for your country? Westerners don't understand China in the first place, and when you talk about nothing but the bad side, how does China look to Western eyes?" (At other times, he used the opposite tack: "Forget about democracy and rights defense; you need to think about your own family. If you go to prison, how will your wife and child manage?")

After they finished, I spoke up: "I grew up in an impoverished village, so I know all about the life of the lower classes. After studying law at the university, I became more concerned about China's human rights situation, and I realized that flaws in the political and legal systems were the root causes of the people's suffering. After the Sun Zhigang incident, I gradually became a so-called public intellectual, and felt even more responsible for doing something concrete to promote rule of law. I'm a legal scholar and a practicing lawyer, so I feel the least I can do is take responsibility as an intellectual for telling the truth and being an honest person. But under the present circumstances, telling the truth is dangerous, and I feel this risk should be borne by those with reputations, knowledge and resources, rather than by those who are helpless and miserable.

"On some occasions and in some articles I've also acknowledged China's progress in human rights. Although I feel this is largely a result of struggles by citizens and at great cost, I don't deny that some individuals within the system have contributed to it. As an independent intellectual, there's no way I'm going to spend all my time singing praises and flattering the government. I find that whenever the government does the least bit of good, there are plenty of writers, journalists and scholars willing to serve as eulogists, so I won't be missed. The role of an independent intellectual is to find fault; even good social systems have their problems.

"As a husband and father, I'm also responsible for my family. Neither social nor family responsibility can be abandoned, but over the years I've found this a hard balance to maintain. Of course I don't want to go to prison, but I'm not afraid of it, either."

They did their best to use my articles as grounds for Article 105 (2) of the Criminal Law, "incitement to subvert state power,"[6] but I

---

[6] TN: "Whoever incites others by spreading rumors or slanders or any other means to subvert the State power or overthrow the socialist system shall be sentenced to fixed-term imprisonment of not more than five years, criminal detention, public surveillance or deprivation of political rights; and the ringleaders and the others who commit major crimes shall be sentenced to fixed-term imprisonment of not less than five years." (English translation provided by the PRC National People's Congress, http://www.npc.gov.cn/englishnpc/Law/2007–12/13 /content_1384075.htm.)

said, "I love my country and my people; I always have and I always will. I feel that pointing out the flaws and errors of our country and our government and helping them improve is an even more profound love. The truth hurts, but concealing the truth and lying is what really harms China. Because our professional roles are different, intellectuals are most likely to know of malpractices in our system, and keeping silent would be irresponsible. Loving my country as I do, how would I incite others to overturn our government? I've studied law and have represented cases of incitement to subvert state power. I know very well that my articles don't constitute this crime."

———◆———

It wasn't until after 2:00 a.m. that they let me sleep. (During a previous abduction on January 18, 2008, DomSec police from the Beijing Municipal Public Security Bureau had interrogated me under sleep deprivation.) They brought in a bed, and I fell asleep straightaway.

The lights were kept on, and two guards sat there watching me, even less at liberty than I was. They didn't get me up at 6:00 a.m., and when I finally awoke and saw how fatigued the guards looked, I said, "You've had a tough night." I wasn't being sarcastic; I felt for them. While depriving others of their liberty, these thuggish guards lost their own freedom, and while beating others, how could their own humanity not suffer?

I made my bed, washed my face, ate breakfast and waited for them to continue their interrogation. That morning, the seventh, it was G and H doing the questioning again. They brought photocopies of around 15 of my articles and interviews, including "China on the Eve of the Olympics," "We Can't Sit and Wait for a Better Society," "What Does Hu Jia's Arrest Imply?" and "Civil Ethics and Civic Responsibility in the Post-Totalitarian Era." Some sentences were underlined, indicating where they thought I'd "gone out of bounds." They had me sign each document and then questioned me on each sentence.

G said something along the lines that there were two roads before me; one road might lead to the judicial process—detention, arrest, trial and prison—while the other was one in which I would be shown lenience for a good attitude, and would eventually be released. He had a good impression of me and said I was the kind of high-quality intellectual China needed. Before leaving, he said in an almost imploring tone of voice, "Teng Biao, just say a few words admitting error, even if you don't believe it, just as a favor to me." This was partly for my sake: A good attitude would get me off lightly; but at the same time, if the record showed no "ideological transformation" on my part, he would also be faulted.

The more time I spend inside, the more I hate this system, and the more sympathy I feel for the system's enforcers. Some people lose their freedom in order to fight for their own freedom, and also for the freedom of those who have deprived them of their free-dom. Havel once said, "We are all—though naturally to differing extents—responsible for the operation of the totalitarian machin-ery. None of us is just its victim. We are all also its co-creators."[7] In other words, all perpetrators are also victims. The people before me who could only mechanically follow orders and had no ability to distinguish between right and wrong also faced their own hard-ship, embarrassment and pain.

Now there was only H taking the record, along with the two guards and myself. I felt embarrassed to be part of a scenario in the twenty-first century in which some Chinese were brainwashing another Chinese. It made me think of the writer in the German film *The Lives of Others*,[8] whose life moved and even changed the man who was carrying out surveillance on him. From their questions, I could tell that these people had carefully read my articles, and I felt this had to have some effect on them. If they were moved, my effort would not be wasted; it was for this special audience as well that I must keep writing, and must continue striving to write even better works.

Around 2:00 p.m., H finished his questioning and left, and I had a chance to rest.

---

[7] TN: Vaclav Havel, "New Year's Address to the Nation," January 1, 1990, http://old.hrad.cz /president/Havel/speeches/1990/0101_uk.html (accessed January 2, 2013).

[8] TN: *Das Leben der Anderen*, 2006, directed by Florian Henckel von Donnersmarck and winner of the 2006 Academy Award for Best Foreign Language Film. Among the film's many awards, Ulrich Mühe, a former Berlin Wall border guard who performed the role of Stasi captain Gerd Wiesler, won the gold award for Best Actor at the German Film Awards and 2006 European Film Awards. Although not shown in Chinese cinemas, the film has circulated in mainland China through DVDs, and many Chinese intellectuals have written essays praising it.

Even without the interrogators present, it was possible that I was being videotaped, and I needed to show them that I was calm and not fearful, depressed or remorseful, and that there was no possibility of my capitulating or bargaining. A prison can hold the body captive, but it can't incarcerate the nobility of the soul. I closed my eyes to rest my mind, lightly reciting some Tang and Song poetry I'd memorized, and quietly recollecting my favorite music, Beethoven's Fifth Symphony, "Fate," and Mozart's Serenade No. 13 in G Major, "Eine Kleine Nachtmusik."

The night before I had dreamed of sneaking out of Building 41 at Peking University to telephone my wife, telling her I was being watched and had to find a way out. We dream about what occupies our minds in daylight; I really wanted to telephone her. Building 41 was where I had lived as an undergraduate; perhaps today's imprisonment symbolized my inevitable fate after studying at Peking University. If so, it was likewise the consequence of opening my eyes to the world and obeying my inner voice....

I missed my home and my child. Qiao had spent two days with her grandmother, and I'd been too busy to go see her. How long would it take me to return home—a month, a year, three years? Although these fellows were threatening me with ten years, I thought that impossible. Five years was the typical sentencing interval, and those articles of mine didn't even merit the first five years. It was also possible that appeals from outside would reduce my sentence....

There were many things I wanted to tell my wife. I composed a poem in my mind and memorized it, and in the afternoon I asked for a pen and wrote it down. It was called "To My Wife from Prison." The guards confiscated the poem, but I hope they treated it as a literary work, not as a coded political call to arms.

Now, facing prison walls
I write a poem for you, my love
Tonight, stars flicker as of old in the desolate night sky
And fireflies still blink in the undergrowth.

Please tell our child that I can't make it this time
Tell her goodbye, daddy has gone on a long trip

Every day before she sleeps
And after she awakes, please kiss her for me.

Take her to play with the plantain pods beneath the fence
On some bright, sunny morning
If she sees dewdrops on the leaves,
She'll sense the depths of my love.

After you water the lilacs, please strum the "Fisherman's Song at Dusk"
Believe I can hear it, my love
Please look after those silent and happy goldfish
That silence concealing my rich and restless youth.

I'm walking a rough and rugged road
But I've never stopped singing, my love
The willow leaves along the road gradually change color
The wind carries the faint sound of distant snows.

All sounds are in silence; here the night is extremely simple
When you think of me, please don't sigh, my love
My rivers of suffering and joy have merged
In their long traversing of my body.

Before the rain stops drizzling
I'll be at your side once more, my love
In the rain, in the rain how can I wipe away your tears
—I'll use my rescued soul.

Having a pen and paper was a great comfort, and I practiced calligraphy on Tang poems. I'd always loved calligraphy and the sense of becoming one with my creation. If any of the guards appreciated calligraphy, perhaps they'd allow me to have brushes and ink sent from home....

F stopped in that afternoon: "Since you have so much time to write poetry, how about hurrying up with your ideological awareness statement? I'm only in charge of you and have no control over how they deal with you. This is for your own good. People who've gotten out of here in the past have all written something. In my experience, the better you write, the quicker you get out."

Screw that ideological awareness statement!

All right, better do it. I sorted through what I'd said the day before and wrote it up as "My Thoughts": rejecting lies, telling the truth, concern about human rights, promoting rule of law, free thought, independent critique, the responsibility of intellectuals and so on, signing it "Chinese citizen Teng Biao."

After reading it, F said, "You'd have been better off writing nothing! Do you think this will satisfy the guys upstairs? Think about writing another one. I'll hold onto this one for you." He took it away, along with my poem.

The "guys upstairs" are sure to have read my "ideological accounting" and that poem. F pushed me to write more, but I refused—writing more might only further annoy the "guys upstairs," with even more serious consequences.

After dinner, E resumed his lecturing and then said, "Our leader is coming. That shows how much importance is attached to your case." The "leader," arriving soon afterward, proved to be a tall and solidly built man with short hair, probably not yet 40 years old. I'll call him O.

O loved the sound of his own voice. For the next two hours, he hardly stopped preaching. Anyone who tried to interject was cut off: "I'm still talking." He left as soon as he finished, giving me no chance to respond, like some ideologically ossified professors I know who slink off after a lecture without giving students a chance to challenge them.

After dozens of rounds with DomSec police, I find their ideological work follows the same four or five tacks. O was no exception, as summarized below:

1. Nationalism: Which country has no flaws? Is America perfect? America has even more people like us than China has! What good results from posting articles denigrating our government on reactionary overseas websites? Has it been easy for the Chinese Communist Party (CCP) to achieve what it has? Have you been to the Forbidden City? You can still see knife marks where imperialist invaders stripped

off the gilding. Do you think our backwardness today has nothing to do with imperialist aggression?

2. You're fighting a losing battle: I've come to tell you that the government isn't afraid of you. When has the government ever feared anyone? Don't think you can set yourself against our powerful government. Wei Jingsheng and Xu Wenli[9] are much more famous than you, but did we hesitate to send them to prison? Who are you? Do you think you'll have it easy once you've entered our radar? And don't think you can just run off overseas! I'm telling you, whenever you get out of here, don't think you can go back to your rights defending! Rice mentioned Hu Jia's case when she came here this last time,[10] and do you know what our Foreign Ministry told her? "We have our laws, and it's none of your business!" What about Gao Zhisheng? To tell the truth, I could have him come here and carry out ideological work on you. Do you believe it?

3. Vicious laws are still laws: Some people say we should scrap Article 105 (2) of the Criminal Law on "incitement to subvert state power." Don't bother talking to me about that. Our job is to uphold that law. As long as it's not repealed, it has legal effect, and we have to execute it. If we don't, we're in dereliction of duty. After Gao Zhisheng, Hu Jia came along and we arrested him. Now Teng Biao comes along to "continue Hu Jia's work." Fine, we'll use Article 105 against you, too!

4. Responsibility to family: You're in good shape now—you have a car, a home. You drive a Focus, I drive a Chery.[11] You have a 140-square-meter home, I have 90 square meters. You have a good job, a happy family; you should put your family responsibilities first. Your child is so young.

---

[9] TN: Wei Jingsheng and Xu Wenli are both dissidents who spent many years in prison before being sent into exile. Both currently reside in the United States.

[10] TN: US Secretary of State Condoleezza Rice raised the case of dissident Hu Jia with her Chinese counterparts during a trip to Beijing in February 2008. She subsequently criticized the Chinese government for sentencing Hu Jia to 3½ years in prison.

[11] TN: I.e., Teng Biao can afford a foreign-brand car, whereas his interrogator drives a local model.

Someday when she asks where Daddy is, what will her
momma say?

But O expressed respect for me personally, saying, "No one but
your wife and immediate family understands you as well as I do.
You're a person of high caliber and good character, and you're a
good writer...." Before my release, a friend comforted my wife by
saying that I had a good character, so I was unlikely to be beaten
in prison. I felt this was not necessarily true; not everyone inside
has a good measure of your character, and if there's a principle of
"not beating good people," there should be one against arresting
them as well.

Finally O said, "We can follow formal legal procedure, but it's
a lot of bother, requiring all kinds of proof. We'd rather use the
approach of education and recovery to give you another chance.
We won't only be looking at how you do this time, but also at what
you do in the future."

I went to sleep after 10:00 without having said anything.

Up at 6:00, I washed my face and then exercised in the room.

G came and asked me if I'd thought things through. I responded
as follows:

1. Some of the sentences and phrases in my essays were
   somewhat inappropriate, and I quoted some things without verifying them, matters I'd pay closer attention to in
   the future.
2. From now on I would devote more energy to education and
   scholarly research.
3. I would not write any more articles about the Olympics or
   Hu Jia's case before the Olympics ended. (Beijing DomSec
   had demanded this of me on February 22 and had it from
   me in writing. If I hadn't agreed to it at that time, I'd have
   immediately lost my teaching position, whereas agreeing to it was no great loss. The objective of this abduction
   likewise was clearly to make me write less.)

Compromise was necessary if I was to return to my family sooner rather than later. But I held to my bottom line: I would not harm others; I would not cooperate with the police by, for example, accepting assignments or providing them with information; I would not admit guilt; I would not give up my right to continue writing. The first two were principles I would maintain even at the risk of imprisonment. (However, if someone writes a pledge or statement of repentance under torture or enormous psychological pressure, I completely understand. What shame is there in writing "I dearly love my kidnappers" under threat from those kidnappers? Can anyone be held to a pledge made under threat and intimidation? What cause is worth enduring physical torture? Which belief or ideal will be damaged if someone is forced to renounce it?)

After this I said, "I hope you'll release me within 48 hours, which is before 8:40 tonight, first of all because my mother-in-law has a chronic psychological disorder, and if something happens to me, she may relapse. Second, I need to take my daughter to and from the nursery every day. Third, I have a class on Monday and need at least a day to prepare for it. Fourth, my friends are sure to launch an appeal on my behalf, and human rights organizations will also protest, and there will be media reports that will make the government look bad. Some organizations will also react if someone goes missing for 48 hours. I'm not making a threat, just thinking of the image of the government and the Olympics.

"Finally, if you're not prepared to release me tonight, I'll need some personal items: underwear, a toothbrush and toothpaste, a towel, socks, a razor and some books. If I have books I can sit here quietly and read for as long as you like and I won't cause you any trouble."

G reported this, and a few minutes later he returned with a toothbrush, toothpaste and a washcloth. "You can brush your teeth, but I couldn't get underwear." It looked like they didn't intend to release me.

G came back at noon, and I asked him the reaction of the "guys upstairs." He went on and on, but the gist seemed to be that I would be released.

Lunch was very good. I'd had six meals inside, and each one was better than the one before.

After lunch, two new guards came on shift, P and Q. Q saw my handwriting and asked, "Have you practiced Liu-style calligraphy?" I said, "Yes, but I've practiced Yan-style more, and I've put some effort into Yan's Qin Li Bei."[12] He said he also practiced calligraphy, and at one point when he'd been very depressed, he'd used calligraphy to bring back his emotional equilibrium. I said, "It's true, calligraphy can purge your spirit...."

G came in and gave back items that had been confiscated from me: my wallet, keys and cell phone. He said, "You can't turn on your cell phone yet. Wait until you get home to make any calls."

P and Q pulled a light green hood over my head, G saying, "Sorry about that." I said, "I understand." They led me out and politely directed me: "Lift your foot," "Lower your head," "Get into the car."

On the road, G talked to me about his child's school problems. He had a six-year-old daughter, and her mother had her involved in all kinds of lessons and clubs. I said that wasn't good, his daughter should have more time to just play with friends and take in the natural world. She should be taken to the countryside to count the stars. The most important thing was to give a child freedom. A child's education shouldn't make success in competition the only or most important goal; money, status and fame were not what mattered. It was a rich inner life, a capacity for happiness and a soul that could experience love and beauty that would provide a life of inexhaustible wealth.

He said this made a lot of sense. I don't know if he perceived the hidden meaning in my words.

After about 40 minutes we reached the vicinity of my home. They took off the hood and we said our goodbyes. The car was a black Jetta with no license plate.

———❖———

When Qiao saw me, she was lying happily on the floor. I picked her up, wanting to cry.

---

[12] TN: A famous inscription written by Yan Zhenqing and used as a model for practicing Yan's style of calligraphy.

My wife hadn't expected me to return so soon. She said she'd been getting ready for an afternoon swim to put herself into a physical and mental state for the long process of freeing me.

I looked at my watch. It was 1:40 in the afternoon.

All our friends said she'd performed splendidly, discussing strategies, reporting my disappearance, accepting interviews, all the time maintaining a calm appearance and handling everything as well as possible. She'd recorded every detail since my disappearance: every phone call, every interview and all her feelings:

March 8, 7:20. I woke up feeling calm. I don't dare think too much for fear of crying.

March 8, 7:40. Teacher Xu[13] telephoned and asked how I was doing, telling me not to worry, and I began weeping uncontrollably.

I never again want her to cry because of me, but I don't know if I can be master of my fate.

A friend said to me, "You shouted and struggled downstairs for three minutes, but no one dared to come out and see what was happening. The police investigated, but no one was willing to give a statement. Is it really worth fighting for the freedom and human rights of such people?"

Yes it is.

The system that has intimidated them into apathy is exactly what I and thousands of other ordinary rights defenders are trying to change. Even if only so that my daughter will no longer live in such fear, I can never abandon my dream, my writings, my actions, my love.

I will never give up. Even if it should result in my eventual disappearance, there's no going back.

---

[13] TN: Xu Zhiyong.

UNTIL WE MEET AGAIN

Liu Shasha

Liu Shasha, a signatory of Charter 08, was born Liu Linna in the 1970s in central China's Henan Province. She began participating in the civil rights defense movement in 2008 through a newly developed rights defense tactic known as "popular surveillance" (weiguan). Popular surveillance came to the fore through efforts by the Open Constitution Initiative (Gongmeng) to expose the issue of "black prisons," informal holding centers where local officials detain individuals for extended periods without recourse to normal legal procedures. The Chinese term weiguan, literally "surrounding gaze," originally held a negative connotation, criticized by the great writer Lu Xun as the tendency of Chinese to look on in apathy while their countrymen suffer. In the past few years, weiguan has become a form of activism, similar to the "Copwatch" system in the United States targeting abuses by the police. In China, this has recently taken the form of visiting people under house arrest, or standing vigil outside of detention centers or courts. Such activities have become particularly effective through the internet, which helps activists organize and publicize popular surveillance activities. In some cases, the internet itself serves as a virtual form of popular surveillance as multitudes of postings inform the authorities that the public is actively monitoring certain cases. In a "black box" system in which detention and even trial allow minimal intervention from the outside, open expression of public concern in some cases results in earlier releases or lighter sentences.

In this essay, Liu Shasha describes her attempt in November 2008 to visit Guo Quan, a former Nanjing university professor and government critic who formed an opposition political party and in October 2009 was sentenced to ten years in prison for subversion. Liu has continued to engage in popular surveillance and visit campaigns since then, including one in May 2011 to support the blind legal activist Chen Guangcheng and his family, who at that time were still under house arrest in Linyi, Shandong Province.

AROUND 5:00 P.M. ON NOVEMBER 20, 2008, I WENT TO NANJING NORMAL University to deliver gifts of sympathy to Li Jing, the wife of imprisoned activist Guo Quan. I left the gifts at her building's reception office and then returned to Fuzimiao,[1] where I accessed the internet, ate dinner and returned to my hotel around 9:00. As I approached the counter, a squinty-eyed middle-aged man came up behind me and said, "Are you Liu XX?" (My real name).

When I replied that I was, he said, "I'm from the Nanjing Public Security Bureau. Please come with me."

"Fine, but I have to make a phone call first."

"No phone calls, and turn off your cell phone."

I then saw that he was not alone, and that others were sitting on the hotel lobby sofa, so I sat down beside them with a smile and said, "I was just going to come up for a chat with you."

They smiled back and asked, "When did you arrive in Nanjing?"

"This morning."

"What are you here for?"

I replied frankly with a smile, "To see Guo Quan." They then accompanied me upstairs to my room, and I gathered my things into my backpack. I had purposely left some small change on the table, but one of the policemen helpfully placed it in my bag.

I joined two of the policemen in the back seat of their car. Once the car set off, they asked, "Why do you want to see Guo Quan?"

Hemming and hawing as I usually do when in over my head, I said, "What if I told you it was out of—idealism? I believe that the next step of China's democratic reforms will be to embark on a multi-party system, and Guo Quan has taken this step. So in the end I'm here for my—ideals."

---

[1] TN: A tourist district in southern Nanjing.

The car was silent for several seconds, and I could imagine them dismissing me: Ideals, in this age?

Finally one of them asked, "Do you know Guo Quan?"

"No, but in the QQ groups[2] I've read his essays and the platform of the New Democracy Party."

"So you admire him, worship him?"

"I don't admire or worship anyone; I regard all political figures the same way. I just read his party platform and agreed with some of its content; for example, multi-party elections, rotation of power and so on. Of course there are things Guo Quan says and does that I don't agree with. For example, I think it was silly and rash for him to smash the gravestone,[3] and I think his idea of thousands of parties is ill-conceived."

Another silence, which I finally broke by saying, "In fact, I was planning to look you up today and exchange views on Guo Quan and on improvements to your work methods."

"So why didn't you come?"

I stammered, "Well, I was a bit scared."

The policeman driving the car gave a snort of derisive laughter.

Upon arriving at what I later learned was Nanjing's Gulou District Huaqiao Road police station, I was taken to the end of a corridor, through an iron door and upstairs, then past several offices until they opened a door and said, "Please enter." I stood in the doorway, my head high and my eyebrows raised with keen anticipation. Finally it was my generation's turn to mount the revolutionary stage!

I didn't realize that after sitting down my grand resolve would be gradually eroded by a mild-mannered, diminutive old cop who spent ages asking me basic and trivial questions such as my name, address, occupation and so on, and entering it all into his computer. This was a lesson to me: There's no point in mustering your fighting spirit when a pile of red tape awaits you. In my mind, I named the old cop "Egghead."

---

[2] TN: The Chinese version of an internet chat room.

[3] TN: As part of his campaign to "Defend the Diaoyu Islands" over disputed sovereignty with Japan, Guo in 2005 defaced the gravestone of Wang Zhi, a Ming Dynasty pirate who had assisted a Japanese pirate raid of the Chinese coast. See Human Rights in China, "Guo Quan: A Chronology," http://www.hrichina.org/crf/article/5711 (accessed May 27, 2013).

Once he had sorted out my particulars, he asked genially, "When did you arrive in Nanjing?"

"This morning."

Suddenly, a policeman with a pale, square face who had been looming off to the side sternly demanded, "Who told you to come?"

I immediately shot back, "I came on my own."

He persisted: "Who was it who told you to come?"

I stubbornly insisted, "I came on my own. No one told me to. No one can make me do anything!"

Later we'll see how much this pale-faced policeman, whom I nicknamed Guo Fan, actually admired and respected Guo Quan.

Noting the deadlock, old Egghead pleasantly interjected, "How do you know about Guo Quan?"

"From the QQ groups." This is when the police began showing their annoying side: asking the same question over and over again, first one asking and then another, today and then tomorrow all over again. The idea is to wear you out, and also to see if you give consistent answers. Of course, it was also because they couldn't think of anything else to ask.

I repeated what I'd said about reading Guo Quan's essays, agreeing with his party platform, what I didn't agree with, and so on. They just sat there nodding and grunting, and the atmosphere was becoming more congenial when someone asked, "Do you know Ning Wenzhong?"[4]

"Yes," I said.

"What's his online name?"

"Woodcutter."

"How do you happen to have his phone number?"

"He posted it in a QQ group."

"When?"

I suddenly went on guard; this was no longer a friendly conversation, but an interrogation. I refused to say anything more. Lacking experience, I had spilled on a friend—but this would be the last time.

---

[4] TN: Ning Wenzhong, who blogs under the name "Woodcutter," was sent to one year of Re-education Through Labor (RTL) (an extrajudicial form of punishment) when he appealed online for people to lay flowers on Tiananmen Square on the twentieth anniversary of the June 4, 1989, crackdown.

The toughest part of this "tea session" was the first day, the evening of the twentieth. Lacking experience and off my guard, I gave them too much information—you treat someone like a friend, but they see you as a criminal. What you consider a conversation they see as an interrogation. I set out to shine like the moon, but ended up illuminating a gutter.

—•—

At that point another policeman entered the room and began questioning me from a chair behind me and to the right. I turned and saw a long, sharp face, single-lidded eyes and a sallow, spotty complexion—a ferociously ugly face. I gave him the nickname "Spymaster," for reasons that will become clear later on.

The next part was the worst. First of all, where he was seated obliged me, out of "courtesy," to constantly turn around, which became tiring and distracting. Second, he spoke extremely fast, shooting a new question at me even before I finished answering the one before. Bang! One after another, all of them leading questions. Lacking experience, I was unequal to the task, especially after being worn out by the policemen who had come before.

The dialogue below will give some idea of the pace and rhythm of the questioning. If the "cyber police" take the trouble to get an audio recording from their Nanjing counterparts, they can learn a thing or two.... ~_~[5]

I suspect this cop had received special training—he only needed to hear half of your answer before knowing what the rest would be and moving on:

"Why did you come to Nanjing?"

"To see Guo Quan."

"How did you know Guo Quan was arrested?"

"From the QQ groups."

"Why did you come to see Guo Quan?"

"I was afraid he wasn't being treated right."

"Hey, you're more worried about Guo Quan than his wife is!"

---

[5] TN: An emoticon meaning "embarrassed."

I lowered my face for a moment. "What do you mean?"

After a few seconds' pause he started all over again: "Why did you come to Nanjing?"

"To see Guo Quan."

"Why did you want to see Guo Quan?"

"I was afraid he wasn't being treated right."

"In what way?"

"Being beaten."

"You think we beat people? What evidence do you have?" (He said this in a threatening tone of voice.)

Preferring to give him some face, I decided not to use the term "fascist," and hesitantly said, "I've heard it."

"You think you'll be allowed to see Guo Quan?"

"If not, I'll just visit his wife."

"What for?"

"To ask if he's being treated right."

"If he's not, what are you going to do about it?"

"Appeal on the internet to help victims of injustice."

"Have you seen his wife yet?"

"No."

"Why not?"

"His wife is afraid to see anyone."

"So what are your plans?"

"To go home."

"Are you still going to launch an appeal?"

"No."

"Why not?"

"Because right now I have no evidence that you've been beating him."

"Well, you had no evidence before and you have none now. Doesn't that mean you just made it all up?"

That infuriated me, and I crushed my paper cup on the table. My face stiff, I said nothing more. Is it clear to everyone where my downfall was?

Rising smugly, he stood by my side, and after a few seconds I sighed and said, "I understand, you were using leading questions, and no matter how I answered, I was trapped. In a normal interrogation, leading questions aren't allowed, because that's considered entrapment." At that point, the square-faced cop across from me and Spymaster exchanged a look of genuine surprise and admiration for a worthy opponent.

Then Spymaster stood there and went back to his barrage, saying at one point, "You contradict yourself."

I interrupted him, "If you say I'm making things up and you attack me personally, I'm not answering any more of your questions!"

He started in again: "You didn't have any evidence to begin with, and you don't now, do you? So isn't that fabrication?" Then he started to get nasty and, nursing my wounded ego, I only caught the last few sentences: "What's a woman like you involved in this for anyway? You're just a busybody meddling in things you know nothing about!"

Lifting my chin, I said, "I've heard all that before."

Surprised, both of them sat there nonplussed as I continued, "I've heard the same thing before, in those old revolutionary movies. It's what the spymaster says!" This shut them up for a while as they glanced at each other with embarrassed smirks.

Spymaster muttered, "What's this spymaster nonsense..."

At that moment the mild-mannered old cop came back and handed me a paper to sign. It was a Notice of Interrogation, stating: "Liu XX, you are being interrogated under suspicion of incitement and of planning an illegal march or protest."

I stared at the paper for a long time, disgusted at the words "incitement" and "illegal." Finally I decided, all right, it was only "suspicion" after all, so I signed it.

The next conversation demonstrates another despicable and illogical aspect of the police. This time it was one against four, and I was to tangle with them and their same tactics all over again early in the morning of the twenty-first.

Spymaster: "Why did you come to see Guo Quan?"

"Because I endorse multi-party elections and endorse his establishment of a party. You say he's subverting state power, but he's just a scholar, without guns or cannons, so how can he subvert state power?"

"So you think we go around arresting people for nothing?" (He was already using the public security organ's sterling reputation to back himself and threaten me.)

"Fine. You show me evidence that Guo Quan subverted state power, and I'll promise not to involve myself further in Guo Quan's case. Do you have evidence?"

"How can we show you evidence? It's a state secret!"

"Then I'm sorry, a citizen is innocent until proven guilty."

Egghead took up the thread: "That's why we say Guo Quan is just under suspicion, and we're investigating!"

"Okay, you believe he's subverting the state and I don't believe he's subverting the state. We have the right to organize a protest and express our views."

"Your expression is wrong!"

"How can you say our expression is wrong?"

"Guo Quan committed the crime of subverting state power, and if you protest on his behalf, you're supporting subversion!"

"Not true! Staging a protest falls under freedom of expression!"

Here we can see that when you ask directly what crime Guo Quan committed and whether there's evidence, the police first try to throw you off track with disingenuous questions like "You think we arrest people without evidence," and then back off by saying it's only "suspicion." But then when they want to scare you by saying "rescuing Guo Quan is also a crime," they claim that Guo's subversion has already been established!

Then another policeman standing behind me on the other side asked, "Are you in contact with Falun Gong?"[6]

"No."

"Why not?"

"Because I don't agree with the worldview of Falun Gong. I'm a believer in dialectical materialism; I'm 80 percent a Marxist."

"Eighty percent?"

"Yes, I accept 80 percent of Marxism."

"What part don't you accept?"

"In Marx's socialist theory, regarding democracy...."

Before I could finish, Spymaster cut in fiercely: "When did you arrive in Nanjing?"

I was taken aback: "Weren't you asking me about democracy?"

---

[6] TN: A spiritual movement outlawed in China in July 1999.

"We're here to talk about the facts! When did you arrive in Nanjing?"

"This morning."

"How did you get here?"

"By train."

"What time did you arrive?"

"6:30."

"Which train station?"

"The one at Xuanwu Lake."

"What did you do when you arrived?"

"Grabbed a McDonald's."

"And then?"

"Contacted Li Jing."

"And who else?"

By then I was exhausted, and I protested, "You picked me up at around 10:00, it must be at least midnight" (the taking of my particulars had dragged on so long), "if you try sleep deprivation tactics, that's inhumane. I protest your inhumane treatment and won't answer any more questions." Then I clamped my mouth shut.

At that point, the mild-mannered egg-headed policeman spoke again, "It's good that you want democracy. But China's situation is different; we can't just indiscriminately imitate the West," and on and on and on he went.

This is another thing I hate about them: When they ask you something you actually know and are willing to talk about, like democracy, they cut you off after a couple of sentences and make you stick to facts and break your concentration. When you talk facts, they irritate and confuse you so you won't say any more, then they start in again with theory and insult democracy, teasing more talk out of you.

———◆◆◆———

While I was in the haze of slumber, Spymaster made me shift my legs so he could pass in front of me. After twisting my legs to let him pass, I muttered, "You spy, you spymaster...." He had already sat down at another table, but my imprecations irked him to laughter, and he walked back over and sat at my table. Just as he was opening his mouth, I stopped him: "You're disgusting! I'm not talking to you or answering any of your questions!"

But after I dropped my weary head and closed my eyes, he started in with the questions again. I tried to push him from my consciousness, but this just made him angry, and he said, "What's this attitude you're giving me?"

Without raising my head, I said, "Sister Jiang's attitude."[7]

Incredulously, he asked, "If you're Sister Jiang, then who are we?"

I thought to myself, "Communist reactionaries," but if the word "reactionary" escaped my lips it would require a whole spiel on what is "reactionary," and how the Communist Party could go from "revolutionary" to "counterrevolutionary," and why the revolutionary martyrs cried "Down with the Kuomintang reactionary clique" instead of "Down with the Kuomintang." I was just too tired and didn't have the energy for a long debate, so I kept my thoughts to myself and closed my eyes to re-energize.

He rattled on and on, and when I didn't respond, he got nasty again: "Don't think we can't get you! Your reactionary comments on the internet are already enough to put you away for years!"

This enraged me so much that I stared at the wall with my lips clenched—my vision encompassing the wide world and upholding justice, accepting death by a thousand cuts before submission: "If you convict me it proves I'm right and that you're out-and-out fascists!" I was truly furious and ready to go for broke, proud and disdainful.

From the corner of my eye I could see him staring at me, but still I refused to look at him, and we became deadlocked. After some time had passed and I saw that he actually had nothing more to say, I closed my eyes and slept.

Once I clammed up, the scene became very dry and boring. The six of them took turns nattering away, and of that stale tirade I recall only a few points:

---

[7] TN: In the revolutionary novel *Red Crag* by Luo Guangbin and Yang Yiyan, the character Jiang Zhuyun, known as Sister Jiang, is an indomitable heroine who stands up under interrogation by the Kuomintang intelligence chief and becomes a revolutionary martyr. *Red Crag* has become a literary touchstone for activists who see themselves as heroically confronting autocracy like their revolutionary forebears.

This from the pale, square-faced Guo Fan:

1. "Don't think you're the only one we arrested this time. We grabbed a whole bunch of you! We've been arresting people all over the country! We already arrested Ning Wenzhong and Wu Weimin."

   I didn't open my eyes: Nothing unexpected here.

2. "You left those things for Li Jing in the reception office, but no one's come to get them. She couldn't care less about those trifling gifts."

   I thought: Divide and conquer.

3. "Why are you so tired, so worn out? If you don't have the energy, how can you push for democracy? You're a coward! Do you hear me? A coward!"

   I thought: Six against one. Who's a coward?

4. "Guo Quan is no coward; he has a lot more spunk than you! He can spend days and nights bent over his computer! He could debate with us all night!"

   Through my bleary eyes I saw that when he spoke of Guo Quan, his face was full of admiration. His glowing expression made my heart glow as well: So Guo Quan has a fan in the police force as well.

5. "Democracy can't be built overnight. Guo Quan said something interesting: 'Someone like me would have been put before the firing squad in the 1950s, and in the 1960s would have been sentenced to life in prison. Now I can sit here and debate with you—that's the progress of China's democracy!'"

   I thought: It's not anywhere near enough. Then I thought, Ah, Guo Fan's idol has acknowledged him as "progressive," and look how happy he is!

6. "You people pushing for democracy should be frank and honest. Guo Quan is frank and honest, he says what he thinks. He keeps saying, 'Why don't you arrest me? Why don't you sentence me?'"

   My thoughts were, first: Frank and honest? I can be frank and honest with anyone but you! I can be frank and honest about myself but absolutely not about what my friends are doing! Second: Ugh! Guo Quan Guo Quan Guo Quan—don't you think you've said that name a little too much? And if Guo Quan really said that, it sounds like a case of mutual Stockholm syndrome!

7. "I've had at least ten meals with Guo Quan. Actually, Guo Quan is a good guy, sometimes he just gets carried away...."

   I thought: Is this concern? Love?

8. "Lots of people have come to see Guo Quan, and we've arrested quite a few of them: Wu Weimin from Lishui, So-and-so from Hefei, we arrested them and then we sent them home. Others told us about you, they sold you out long ago!"

   I thought, first: Divide and conquer. Second: You were just talking to me about being frank and honest, and now you're telling me others have sold me out! So if I'm frank and honest with you, you'll turn around and try to intimidate my friends by telling them, Liu Shasha sold you out long ago!

9. "Hey! Wake up! Go wash your face! Don't sleep!" (kicking my chair) "Are you too comfortable? Better get you a different chair!" Next to my leather armchair they placed a hard chair with no arms.

   I looked at it: "Will I be forced to stand and squat next?"

   They all laughed: "You think we're that horrible? Where did you hear that?"

   I closed my eyes, bowed my head and dozed off. Even if they put me in that hard chair, I was going to sleep.

10. "Are you unwell? If so, just speak up and we'll arrange for you to be looked after."

    I wanted to tell them that I'd been suffering from headaches for two or three years, that my heart was weak and had caused fainting spells in the past, and that at the moment I felt a tightening in my chest, but I gritted my teeth and said nothing. I didn't want them to discover my weakness, nor did I want to seek their help or owe them anything.

11. "Why visit Li Jing? Are you trying to pull her into your movement?"

At that moment, a police officer in a black uniform entered (the others were in plainclothes), and this guy was a complete hooligan. I nicknamed him "Thug," and this is what he said to me:

"What work do you do?"

"Oil field."

"How did you end up in an oil field?"

"I passed the exam."

"Why were you allowed to take the exam?"

"The enterprise needed labor."

"Who runs that enterprise? Isn't it the Communist Party? Isn't it the Communist Party that's feeding you?"

As soon as I heard his logic of servile gratitude, I realized that he was utterly beneath me and that I could safely ignore him. Whenever he spoke to me from then on, I just smiled disdainfully at the slave's logic that regarded gainfully earned wages as the Communist Party's grace and favor.

"Why were you allowed to go to the oil field and not someone else? Isn't this the Communist Party granting you a living, just as it did your father and mother? You've been eating from the state's rice bowl and drinking from its cup all your life, and now you want to subvert the state? Do you think that if you follow along with Guo Quan, you'll be given some official posting after the Communist Party is overthrown?"

I just sneered at everything he said, until that last sentence, at which I laughed outright. My disdain deflated him, and he left in a huff.

After that I dozed off again while Guo Fan, Spymaster and Egghead gave pep talks, threatened and soothed me; their faces red, white and speckled in turn—a porridge of blather bubbling away, sometimes near, sometimes far, and in any case meaningless. I just squeezed my eyes and lips shut and dozed, my show of resistance.

Finally they wore themselves out and gave up. "Come on, sign this and then you can sleep."

Opening my eyes enough to glance at it, I saw the record of interview ended at 1:30, and that the content was more or less accurate. Still half asleep, I signed my name in a big, loopy scrawl.

Then an old security guard escorted me out of the office, and I followed him, bleary-eyed and bumping into walls along the way, until we reached the end of the corridor. From behind me I heard Guo Fan's sarcastic voice: "Look how you've run out of steam. You can't come close to Guo Quan!" Mentally I shot back: Shasha doesn't waste her fight on midnight sparring!

The old security guard began walking down the stairs, but I paused, swaying slightly, and from behind me, Guo Fan yelled, "Grab her, don't let her fall!" The security guard turned and looked up at me. I smiled bitterly and descended one step at a time, leaning on the railing.

From behind me, Guo Fan laughed derisively: "Let's see you push your democracy when you're this tired! And this is just the first day!" I thought, it's you who should be ashamed of the state I'm in, not me.

I stumbled blindly around a few more corners into hallways that became increasingly dark and narrow until we finally came to a stop, and I was told, "You'll sleep here tonight."

The sight before me was disheartening: against one wall, three hard, smooth, round stools resembling those used at bank counters or bars, about 30 cm in diameter, part of which tilted into semi-circular back rests. That meant a flat surface of only around 20 cm.

Discouraged as I was, I refused to ask for help and had no energy left to fight. I just stretched myself across the stools and fell asleep with my clothes on.

Looking back, I consider this one of their most despicable aspects, refusing to let me sleep enough to regain the mental agility to argue with them. This was a lesson in the importance of humane treatment—eating, sleeping and treatment of illness. If you're too proud to make demands, you won't have the strength for fights or exchanges with them the next day. Democracy and rights activists must first and foremost fight for their personal rights; otherwise, how can they fight for others?

I dozed in fits and starts, constantly awakened by footsteps and laughter in the hallway. I buried my face in my arms and immersed myself in the depths of the midnight sea. It was then that I began to think, and to fear.

At the outset, I hadn't thought this was more than a casual conversation, and when Spymaster threatened me with his talk of "locking me up for years," I was angry rather than frightened. In the heat of argument, I forgot to fear. But now that I'd been tossed off to the side, with a few roguish security guards joking around nearby as I slept all alone, around 3:00 a.m. I began to feel truly afraid.

I had come here alone, without telling any of my friends or relatives. When the police had asked me, I'd told them truthfully that netizens knew I'd come, but that after dropping off the gifts, I'd sent off a message that "all was well." No one knew that I'd been arrested, and putting it crudely, the police could shove me into a gunny sack and toss me into the river without the least risk of discovery. Who would notice if I got lost in Nanjing? In the words of the blogger Watchful Eagle, "If you die, no one will even know how." And another blogger, Li Hanqiu, had said, "They can burn the corpse and destroy the evidence." Where were the remains of the thousands who had disappeared under Pinochet? I was a tiny insect, a skeleton in some godforsaken gully of history, one of millions, disappearing in silence, a grain of sand in the ocean. How many lives had the democratic struggle consumed without sound or trace?

That wasn't what terrified me—I could steel myself to be tossed into the Yangtze River for the democratic cause. I had no fear of those few seconds during which I met my death, but what I did fear was long, drawn-out torment—what Spymaster had referred to as "locking me up for years." As an outsider, I would be dumped into a Nanjing prison with no one I knew to look after me; I would certainly be beaten by other prisoners, in particular those assigned to the task by the police. Then, to cause such distress and worry to my parents, who were already in poor health,

and who might not be around anymore by the time I got out—
these thoughts were so agonizing that I had to thrust them from
my mind.

But even this fear and pain were not enough to make me yield
ground, at least not beyond my bottom line.

I was not a member of the New Democracy Party and had no
intention of joining. I had come to Nanjing out of sympathy: "I dis-
approve of what you say, but I will defend to the death your right
to say it."[8] It was also a matter of trust; I'd said I would come, and I
had to keep my word and deliver the gifts before returning home.
Being unfamiliar with the conditions for street protests, I had
already abandoned that plan, as I would explain to them tomorrow. That was the extent to which I was prepared to compromise.

As for the rest: establishing a multi-party system for China,
pursuing democracy, my friends—on those matters I would never
budge an inch. To give up all talk of democracy would be so shameful that I would feel I had lost my purpose in life. If I couldn't defend
this bottom line, could I claim any backbone at all, and wouldn't
China's democracy be a little poorer for it?

This resolve allowed me to relax somewhat. The old security
guard had switched on the heat, and I felt a bit more comfortable.
The young guards who had been chattering non-stop had finally
tired themselves into silence, but the noise from their electronic
games still kept me awake. I slept fitfully for probably less than an
hour; my weary, aching brain, the precarious stools and the noise
kept me tossing and turning until dawn.

My interrogators on the twenty-first were Egghead and another
middle-aged policeman. This cop was in his forties, with a rectangular, pale face, level eyebrows and large, double-lidded eyes, refined
and good-looking, like the Kuomintang leader Wang Jingwei in
his youth. He wore a black overcoat that gave him a dignified air,
and his manner of speech was proper, authoritative and logical. I

[8] TN: A quote routinely attributed to Voltaire, but actually written by his biographer Evelyn
Beatrice Hall (under the pseudonym S.G. Tallentyre) to summarize his beliefs (*The Friends of
Voltaire*, 1906).

gave him the nickname "Professor." Of course, the standard of dialectics and epistemology he brought to bear would only have been considered slightly above average in my netizen circles and would certainly not qualify him as an actual professor. But it's also true that a lot of professors nowadays just go through the motions.

Egghead and Professor woke me at dawn: "Xiao Liu, get up and have something to eat. Have you washed yet? Did you bring a toothbrush?"

"No, I was planning to use the hotel's...."

Egghead quickly told Professor, "Go buy one for her."

As Professor turned to leave, I called to him, "I'll give you the money."

"No need."

"Are you spending taxpayer money on me?" (I was unwilling to benefit at the expense of taxpayers.)

He stared at me for a moment. "You can pay me back." Then he went out.

We returned to the upstairs office of the day before, and in a short time Professor returned with a toothbrush, toothpaste and a washcloth, for which I duly paid him. After washing up, I came back and ate with them: a plastic bag containing deep-fried dough sticks, salted vegetables, three rice balls and soya milk. Egghead poured some soya milk for me, but I said, "No thanks, I drink coffee." I pulled a packet of instant coffee from my backpack for my morning wake-up.

The rice balls were hard and greasy, and I abandoned mine after a few bites, waiting for them to finish. Egghead and I sat on either side of one desk and Professor sat at another desk behind Egghead.

After Egghead spent a few minutes copying and pasting my personal information into a new form, I said, "I'd like to start out today by saying three things. First: yesterday one of you said that I wanted to pull Li Jing into the movement, but that's wrong. I've always believed that a husband and wife can't both be involved in politics; otherwise, who looks after the home and kids? Guo Quan is already inside, and if Li Jing gets involved in politics, it will be terrible for the kids. All I wanted was to show her some sympathy, not to involve her.

"Second, yesterday one of you said I wanted to get some kind of official position under the New Democracy Party—that's just ridiculous! I'm not cut out to be an official. I tried two years as secretary of a Communist Youth League branch, and I just couldn't handle all that mundane busywork. I came here out of sympathy for Guo Quan and his right to express himself. I don't endorse his party, but I endorse his right to establish one. I also came to keep my word by offering sympathy, and now that I've done that, I'll go home. In any case, Guo Quan and his New Democracy Party are so far from succeeding that only some tuned-out lowlife would claim I'm jockeying for an official position." I laughed while thinking, this is the claim of a Communist thug, but the two in front of me didn't fit that category, so I kept my thoughts to myself.

"Third, you can ask anything you want about me, what I do, how I think, my future plans, whatever. But if you ask me about anyone else, I won't say a word." The two of them stared at me, surprised by my suddenly decisive tone.

Professor said, "Even if you don't say anything, we can get all the information we need."

"Sure, you have QQ records, you tap phones. So this isn't a matter of evidence or attitude. It's A Matter Of Integrity! If I can't retain even this bit of integrity, you'll look down on me.

"And don't bother telling me that 'others have already sold me out.' It's disgusting. You tell me about others selling me out and then ask me to be frank and honest so you can turn around and tell others that Liu Shasha sold them out. I will not disgrace myself in this way. So if you want to ask me about myself, we can have a frank and honest conversation. But don't ask me about anyone else."

They were stymied, but finally Egghead said, "Fine. Let's start. Why did you come to Nanjing?"

"To see Guo Quan...."

There followed a battle of wits, with our conversation spinning from one topic to the next like fluff in a windstorm, from the question of Guo Quan's guilt to whether street protests were acceptable; from "What is truth?" to "The breakfast this morning was lousy"; from my "prospects for the universal principle of democracy" to their "patience with China's national circumstances." We sparred like pros, but always came to a screeching halt when it came to the subject of "other people."

In the heat of the debate, Professor suddenly asked, "Whose idea was the street protest?"

I said, "I don't know. At the time everyone was talking at once, so I don't know who raised it."

"Let me refresh your memory. Did someone first mention 'strolling'?"

I saw that he planned to look through the QQ records, and quickly put in, "It was me! I suggested it!" I stared resolutely at him. I felt the weight of a multi-year sentence as a secret agent, but it couldn't crush my pride and sense of duty: "If you want to sentence me to prison for planning a protest, I'll consider it an honor!"

He was dumbstruck again for a few seconds, and as he began to speak, I interrupted him: "Don't bother telling me that 'someone sold me out.' I'm not playing the prisoner's dilemma. Even if you show me a statement or let me hear a recording, I still won't sell anyone else out. I'd rather have everyone else owe me than for me to owe anyone else. That's the way I am. It's called integrity!"

The air and the sunlight seemed to come to a standstill in a silence, like golden leaves that only sound when struck—a sound as clear as gold and jade.

After a few seconds' pause, I asked Professor, "Am I an idiot?"

A balloon of pride swelled, awaiting acknowledgment and praise.

Professor gave me a gloomy look, then said sarcastically, "I think you're very smart. All along you've managed to evade one key question."

"Oh."

Punctured, my balloon tumbled with a pop and a squeak. I felt disheartened for a second or two, but "you're very smart" was a consolation.

Egghead asked again, "When did you arrive in Nanjing?"

"Yesterday morning."

"Who did you contact after you arrived?"

"I'm not saying. I already told you I won't talk about anyone else."

In truth, on the morning of the twenty-first, I lost more than I won. Almost every theoretical attack by my opponents ended either with my saying, "Let's leave it at that; we aren't going to convince each other, and we're just arguing in circles," or with my staring blankly at them without responding. I didn't like to admit defeat, even though I'd had less than an hour's sleep the night before. My opponents' reasoning was the usual government line that I'd long ago torn to shreds. Yet here in the police station, I was constantly backed into a corner by one of them, after which the other would jump in and steer my shattered brain onto a new train of thought. Or they'd say something objectionable that my aching head and bleary eyes prevented me from rebutting. They won with an unfair advantage, and I accepted my defeat with pride.

Exhausted beyond endurance, I said, "You're not playing fair if you don't let me sleep."

To my surprise, Egghead and Professor laughed sardonically, "You think we've been sleeping? While you were sleeping we were putting together your file."

Egghead said, "Look at the dark circles under our eyes!"

It was true, and I realized that was an element of Professor's sinister appearance. Just then, Guo Fan came in with his own black-rimmed eyes: "What's up for today?"

"Questioning."

Guo Fan sat down beside me and started in with his nattering. I opened my eyes and listened, but all that sank in was one sentence: "You're a fool—ten people have dug you a pit, and all you have to do is jump in."

"I know."

"You know this and you're still protecting them?"

Professor sneered: "What's integrity to them!" He gave me a ferocious look, but his lips curled into a smile. He was like a head teacher interrogating a group of unruly and uncooperative students, and his anger was almost comical. "What is integrity to them!"

Guo Fan stared blankly at him. "Uh, integrity?"

Everyone in the room laughed. I laughed as I nodded off.

—◆◆—

"You're a fool—ten people have dug you a pit, and all you have to do is jump in."

I knew that. I wished he would read my essay "The Minstrels Will Sing of You Forever" so he could see my lack of illusion about the purity of revolution. Every revolution has its scheming and tawdriness. Your leader is ready at any moment to sell out and run off, and after all your personal sacrifice you're left alone to nurse your ember of democracy.

I knew that whenever I participated in a movement, I'd be the first to be sold out. But I forged ahead, even while knowing someone behind me would betray me.

No regrets.

Inevitably there would be someone to play the fool, someone to be sacrificed, someone who bolted, and someone who survived and climbed to the top by treading on the skulls and bones of his comrades: "Long live the people!"

Every revolution is the same. The Communist Party, Kuomintang, Democratic Progressive Party—no one is untainted, everyone is flawed.

Politics has always been unsavory, and in today's China, it couldn't be only the Communist Party that was dirty; there had to be another competing party, another scheming method to fight dirt with dirt. That's the only way to have a well-matched fight and to force all the parties in all countries to learn something about face and about buying over popular sentiment. Revolution is buying over, incitement, sowing discord, prodding, youthful ardor, mature shrewdness, pure idealism, base unscrupulousness, power games, cannon fodder, spurring comrades to give their all so you can ascend to power—so despicable, so dirty—it's through this filth that history moves forward.

No regrets!

———※·———

Rice boxes for lunch, and after lunch back to the office, where I bent over the table and napped. Professor and Egghead put their files in order.

After a nap, my enthusiasm returned, and as I raised my head, a golden glow radiated before my eyes: "Do you know how I'm feeling right now?"

They looked at me uncomprehendingly.

"What I'm feeling now is—happy! First because you're both smart, and arguing with you is intellectually stimulating; second because it's finally my turn to stand at the frontline of our era and boost social progress. That's very satisfying!"

Professor was seething but also fighting back a smile: "You're so childish!"

Seeing my disgruntlement, he weighed his words and watched my expression: "Don't blame me for not pulling punches. You don't have kids; when you do, you'll realize how infantile your ideas are."

"Oh." I really couldn't see what logical relationship there was between child-rearing and pushing society forward. The problem was that I actually didn't have kids, so I couldn't quibble over this point.

He sat back down behind the table: "We've done our best to help, but you keep up this antagonistic attitude."

"This sounds like a scene from a children's story: A big dog fights with a little dog, and the big dog thinks the little dog is nothing, but the little dog is going 'bow wow!' Scary!" @_@[9]

He laughed again. "We don't mean for you to think we're scary! So how is it in your own experience? We haven't done anything to you, have we? We haven't been too scary?"

I nodded while thinking about Spymaster the day before—a genuinely vicious big dog!

While I napped again, there was another changing of the guard. This time there was a female cop in her forties, along with a young hunk who'd been among those who had arrested me the day before and who had collected my discarded change for me. He had a slightly pudgy, egg-shaped face, fair skin and level brows, with large, single-lidded eyes delicately furrowed beneath, a nice nose and lips—in short, Wallace Chung with more Chinese eyes, or a slightly fatter version of Michael Miu.[10] He looked like he had more beauty than brains, so I nicknamed him "Doofus."

As he and the female cop chatted, I got up to stretch my legs, and looking more closely at him, I couldn't hold back a smile

---

[9] TN: The emoticon has the meaning of the word before, "scary."

[10] TN: Wallace Chung Hon-leung and Michael Miu Kiu-wai are both Hong Kong entertainers.

when I saw his eyes, which looked as if someone had brushed a swath of ink beneath them. "Looks like you've been up all night, too!" I recalled losing sight of him the day before, and he hadn't been present at my interrogation—so whom had he been questioning instead? How many people had they arrested?

He responded pleasantly, "Nice of you to care!"

I replied with a smile, "It's not that I care, I'm just curious...."

I don't care about you, I'm just worried about my comrades.

In this office, the wall between the office and the balcony had been knocked down, and the sun filled the office with light. I sat at a desk on what had once been the balcony, basking and dozing.

After I'd napped for a bit, Wally—all right, even if Doofus was a bit dumb, since I ended up eating a whole bag of his melon seeds, I don't feel right about continuing to insult him, so from now on I'll refer to him as Wally—asked me, "How did a girl like you get involved in politics? Who influenced you?"

"Lin Da influenced me."

"Lin Da?" His pudgy face stiffened. Whenever I talk to someone about something he knows nothing about, and his brain is grinding away, that kind of stupid, stolid look is what comes up. But to be fair, I must have had that expression on my face more than once over these two days. Embarrassing.

After a moment's hesitation, his eyes darted awkwardly as he asked, "Lin Da...who's that?" He thought it was a vigilant look appropriate for detecting a new criminal.

"He's a Chinese living in the United States who's written a lot of articles, and a lot of them have appeared in China, too."[11] Mentally, I sighed in amazement: You haven't even heard of Lin Da? How can you handle political cases, kiddo?

He persisted, "Are you in contact with him?"

I hardly knew whether to laugh or cry. "His books have been published, even in China! I've never contacted him."

Then I quoted, "You can't rely on the President, on Congress, on the public prosecutor or on the Supreme Court; you can only rely on a system with checks and balances between all of those

---

[11] TN: Lin Da is the pen name used by a Shanghai-born husband and wife, Ding Hongfu and Li Xiaolin, who moved to the United States in 1991 and have published many articles and books in China about life in America, earning them the nickname "China's de Tocqueville."

things."[12] Listening to him grunt in response, I couldn't tell if he understood anything I was saying, and in any case I was just too tired, so after those few words, I leaned over the table and slept.

He went out, then returned in a moment and gave the female cop some melon seeds. He called to me as well: "Hey—have some melon seeds."

"No, thanks," I said, and went back to sleep.

He cracked away at them himself, and soon the whole office smelled of melon seeds. Unable to resist any longer, I got up and poured myself a handful of his melon seeds and started cracking.

Just then the female cop came in: "Hey, no more after you finish those. We need to get back to work."

After that, the female cop and Wally sat there gossiping while I basked in the sun, thoroughly bored and flipping through a stack of magazines, stuff like *Phoenix Monthly*, until I fell asleep again. The female cop came over and asked me again about my occupation, address, salary....It was like polite inquiries or a friendly chat, and it seemed rude not to answer. Next came where I lived, my parents, the weather, what books I liked....

I liked reading political history books, the mortgage crisis, currency wars; I wasn't interested in cooking, home improvements, appliances....

The female cop sighed, "Aiya, I guess we don't have much to talk about, then." Back to the weather again: "The plane tree over there hasn't dropped its leaves yet."

"The chrysanthemums in the courtyard are really pretty. I've spent extra time looking at them, since it'll probably be a few years before I see such nice flowers again."

The female cop stared at me. "Why's that?"

"Yesterday wasn't there that one guy who said I'd be put away for years?" Not to mention how I'd cemented my future this morning. But then I regretted appearing anxious over being "put away."

Wally said, "You were doing all right in the oil fields, so why get involved in all this?"

"I was doing all right, but that's not the way to spend a life. Shouldn't I do something more meaningful? That's why I'm pushing

---

[12] TN: Liu Shasha is quoting Lin Da here.

for democracy. And now I get to learn about life in prison," I added, emphasizing the last sentence.

The female cop sounded surprised: "Learn about life in prison?"

"In prison I can observe human nature, the most complicated and profound human nature. That's learning about life." After coming out I could write a book, a Chinese version of the *Gulag Archipelago*, I wanted to add, but then it occurred to me that they might never have heard of that book, so I left it.

In any case, I wasn't afraid of them.

Wally took a phone call, then called me over and asked, "Why do you have two cell phone numbers? Where did you take the train from? Who bought the ticket for you?"

"I bought it myself."

The female cop cut in, "How much did it cost?"

"I forget. It wasn't expensive."

The female cop insisted, "You can't remember what you yourself paid?" I thought, a tacky woman like you would remember, but I'm a romantic, so I don't remember, especially after what I've been through these past two days.

Wally asked, "What were you planning to do after dropping off the gifts for Li Jing?"

"Hang out here in Nanjing, go to Yuhuatai, the Sun Yat-sen Mausoleum, the Nanjing Massacre Memorial Hall, whatever."

He burst out, "This isn't the first time you've come here, is it?" He squinted his panda eyes aggressively at me.

I was taken by surprise. "It is the first time, really!"

"You're very familiar with Nanjing."

I laughed out loud. "I have a map! And anyone who's even slightly well-read knows what the major sites are here." I thought to myself, this kid is too stupid for words.

But he kept on trying to argue politics with me: "Do you think the Communist Party is good?"

I laughed again. "What an infantile question!" Then I continued seriously: "The Communist Party has played an extremely progressive role in history. Ever since the *Communist Manifesto* was published in 1848, it has achieved great historical accomplishments in the pursuit of socialism and equality in the Soviet and

Chinese revolutions. In the 1960s and '70s, Western democracies began adopting a number of socialism's good points on a democratic foundation, and Asian socialist countries, lacking democracy, began taking a back seat in history."

He laughed. "So you're saying the Communist Party has had its good times and its bad times?"

I also laughed. "Yes, it's capable of being both good and bad."

He snorted, "You're never willing to give a straight answer."

I retorted with a smile, "That's because your questions are too childish!"

He turned to what he thought was not a childish question: "So what do you think is wrong with the Communist Party?"

Mentally I thought of several recent cases, but out loud I took a less provocative approach: "It's just a general rule that all people have faults, and parties do too. That's why we need multiple parties to monitor each other."

Wally said, "We have lots of parties already."

"They're just window-dressing."

"How can you say that?"

"I've heard they can only grow to a limited number of members, and one member has to die before they can admit a new one." (That was the best I could come up with for the moment.)

"Why haven't I heard of these limits? Did you know Nanjing has a Kuomintang?"

Now it was my turn to be stymied. "No, I didn't know." After a few seconds I perked up. "Is that true?"

The afternoon's conversation went more or less like that.

After finishing his notes, he asked me to sign off on having "received no interference." I quibbled over that phrase: "You didn't torture me to confess, but you did entrap me."

Wally: "That arose naturally from the process."

We continued to argue until Egghead intervened: "Enough already, just cross it out." Then I signed.

After eating a rice box downstairs, I took another nap on the three stools.

Wally called to me, "Grab your backpack, we're going to a hotel. Your local PSB is coming to take you back."

As we walked to the hotel in the dark, he told me, "The conditions aren't good, and you won't be able to wash up, so you'll have to sleep in your clothes."

We finally arrived at a filthy old guesthouse. Two policemen were already standing at the doorway of the innermost room, where I saw two beds, one occupied by a young guy who had committed some unknown offense. They woke him up and moved him to the other bed, while tossing me a blanket and saying, "Get some sleep."

I shed my down jacket and climbed under the covers still wearing my sweater. With great difficulty I fell asleep amidst their chattering and television programs. Later I awoke and sat up, watching television and listening to them talk. Around 2:00 a.m., I heard several people exchange greetings at the end of the hallway, and then someone came in and told me, "Your PSB officers have arrived. Get up."

Two people came in, a fat man in black whom I didn't recognize—I later learned he was from the factory's security division—and another whom I recognized, our Party secretary. Giving me a look like a big brother picking up his naughty sister and glad nothing worse had happened, he said, "Xiao Ye is waiting for you in the car." (Xiao Ye was my best friend at work.)

Spymaster was waiting in the doorway, but he was no longer so overbearing and seemed unwilling to meet my gaze. He looked like a bodyguard sent to escort a senior cadre, or a child scolded by his teacher. I suddenly felt I might have been too hard on him. He was just doing his job, but I had treated him so derisively.

Professor came forward to meet me, and I bid him a warm farewell as I walked down the hall: "You were more skillful than most of my other opponents. My estimation of the police force has improved."

Behind me he snorted, "What cops have you met before?" I wanted to say that the police I'd met had all been inaccessible, unsightly, inarticulate and incompetent,[13] but I didn't want to speak ill of my native place to outsiders, so I left the question

---

[13] TN: A common aspersion cast on local authorities in mainland China.

unanswered. I had an urge to shake Spymaster's hand with a salute, but he'd dropped to the rear and was saying goodbye to our Party secretary in the darkness. I was always awkward on such occasions, and thought better of rushing over and forcing the issue. By then I had reached my work unit's car, and a light shone through the darkness as my friend Ye Xiaoli climbed out and cried, "Sha-sha!" I ran over and hugged her, and the two of us babbled with excitement. In my heart, though, I kept dwelling on my failure to say goodbye to Spymaster, and on losing the chance to raise my clasped hands to him respectfully and say, "Farewell, my worthy opponent, until we meet again!"

A CUP OF TEA

Tang Xiaozhao

Tang Xiaozhao was born in the western megacity of Chongqing in the 1970s. She currently works in Shanghai as a marketing planner.

Tang is an example of an ordinary person, as opposed to an activist, who felt compelled to sign Charter 08, a manifesto calling for political reform in China. Charter 08 was initially published on International Human Rights Day, December 10, 2008, with the signatures of 303 prominent intellectuals and activists, including Liu Xiaobo, the charter's main drafter, who was subsequently awarded the Nobel Peace Prize. Following publication, the charter drew signatures through the internet from a wide spectrum of society, including Tang Xiaozhao.

In early 2009, when many Charter 08 signatories were called in for questioning by the police, Tang drew particular attention from the authorities because of an interview she had given to a Western news organization. She was one of the first to describe her experiences with the police in writing. After the essay below was published, the police repeatedly harassed and intimidated Tang, causing her to leave Shanghai and live in Xinjiang for a time. In the course of these experiences, Tang's anxiety receded. She says that writing this article is her way of telling others that there is nothing to fear from "drinking tea" with the police.

SHANGHAI, THE AFTERNOON OF FEBRUARY 5, 2009.

I left Dashijie station on the No. 8 Metro line and walked east on Jinling East Road. I was very calm, as if meeting a friend for tea. The only difference was that I had the option of declining tea with a friend, but when the police invited me, I had no choice but to go.

Ever since signing Charter 08 I had been waiting for this day—so many others had gone to drink tea, and there was no reason to expect things would be different for me.

The police had telephoned that morning and asked, "Where are you?" I didn't want my home or office to become the scene of their "law enforcement," so I generously offered, "I'll come up to your office." From what I'd read on the internet, many people "invited to tea" regarded the police station as No Man's Land, but it didn't faze me.

The Huangpu District PSB station came into view, and I saw a police officer in a leather jacket standing next to the guard house. Calling to me from afar, he asked, "Is that Xiao Tang?"

"Yes," I said, approaching him.

Xiao Tang—Little Tang—a friendly form of address. Wasn't I a "class enemy"? Not really, of course.

He led me into a room to the left of the entrance, where another man was already sitting. His face was serious, and spread before him were several sheets of paper for taking notes.

To be polite, I won't reveal their names. I'll call the officer who telephoned me "Leather Jacket." He was around 40 years old and asked most of the questions. The other was a few years older and mainly took notes, so I'll call him "Recorder."

The room was 20-odd square meters, with a huge police insignia hanging on the wall. The sight of the insignia distressed me somewhat; what should have been a guardian angel hovering over me had become a coercion pressing down on my head.

I sat across from Recorder and Leather Jacket sat between us. He was more animated than the stolid Recorder, constantly getting up to pace the room.

Each of them had a cup of tea, but no one poured me a glass of water. I wondered how I could be called in for tea and then not be given tea. Since I wasn't a guest here, I kept my feelings to myself, but once we started talking I became thirsty, and when it looked like the conversation would go on for some time, I asked, "Is there another cup? I'd like some water." Recorder then got up and asked politely if I wanted tea. I said, "No thanks, just boiled water."

"Don't worry, we've just called you in for a chat to get a better understanding of things," Leather Jacket said. When he'd called that morning, I'd brought up Charter 08, so there was no need to beat around the bush.

"I'm not worried," I said, smiling. "I've been waiting for you to call ever since I signed Charter 08 a month and a half ago."

Leather Jacket smiled back. "We knew as soon as your name appeared on the sixth round of signatures. We didn't contact you at first, because your ID card gives a Chongqing address in XX District. Is that correct?"

Hm, so they even knew the address on my ID card. When I'd had dinner with a friend before the Spring Festival, I'd expressed surprise that I hadn't yet been called in for tea. My friend had suggested that the police didn't know where I was, because my household registration (*hukou*) was in Chongqing rather than Shanghai. But I'd found that hard to believe. "I'm not that hard to find. They certainly won't go by my *hukou* when they can trace me through the internet." Who could evade the infinitely resourceful police? When they didn't call me in, I decided that I simply wasn't important enough.

Charter 08 signatories could be divided into three categories: The first was the Notables, people with definite fame and influence who made the government nervous. The second consisted of those whose rights had been infringed: the displaced, the unemployed, farmers deprived of their land. They tended to be emotionally volatile and were prone to creating incidents, and therefore also caused the government considerable anxiety. I belonged to the third group, ordinary people with no influence, whose rights had not been violated, emotionally stable and with no "previous record" with the authorities, and therefore occasioning the least concern. I'd probably have been exempted from this "tea drinking" if I hadn't given an interview to overseas media.

Recorder lifted his pen and began writing, first my name, then my date of birth and so on, and I answered truthfully. Then he asked, "Work unit?"

I said, "My signing of the charter has nothing to do with my work, it's my private business. But I know you can find it out anyway, so I'll tell you." They asked me to write down the name, and when Leather Jacket heard that it was a public interest organization, he said in a laid-back fashion, "It's great that you're involved in public interest work. I know a lot of such people, they're very ardent."

He was plainly laying a trap for me. I grinned, "Don't think I don't know; some of these organizations are very 'sensitive,' for example the ones involved with HIV/AIDS and the environment. But my organization isn't sensitive." In any case, I'd worked in Shanghai's public interest circles for years; I "hadn't eaten pork, but I'd seen a pig run." I knew the heads of some organizations were regularly "teaed," but I myself had never been involved in sensitive activities.

"No, no, I fully support public interest work and the good it does for society. Last time there was some campaign or other at People's Square, and they were there passing out leaflets." I stared at him in surprise. "What campaign? I didn't know about it!"

I guessed that the activity he referred to was one the authorities had kept a close eye on, and if I'd taken part, my "sensitivity ranking" would have gained a star. But I actually knew nothing about it. Public interest organizations were as thick as buffalo hair in Shanghai, and I hadn't the energy to take note of all of them.

Leather Jacket continued talking about the event at People's Square: "I chatted with them afterward, and when I understood more of what they were doing, I was very supportive."

I just listened silently. I still felt he was laying a trap that would let him dig up even more "sensitive material" on me, but the truth was I didn't know anything.

"Where do you get your funding? Do you collect donations?"

"Yes, all the groups do this. We get private donations and also apply for project subvention from enterprises and charitable foundations."

"Some public interest organizations also accept funding from overseas," he said.

Ah, that's what I'd been waiting for! I grinned again. "Don't think I don't know—accepting funding from overseas is also 'sensitive'!"

He smiled and asked me directly, "Have you applied for financial support from overseas?"

"Our organization hasn't been involved in anything 'sensitive.' You can go ahead and check. The city leadership knows all about our organization." I'd accompanied my boss just the previous month to a meeting with the municipal government.

That ended discussion of my work unit.

He went on to ask about my educational background and where I'd gone to college. "My school isn't famous; you wouldn't have heard of it." I was right, and at his request I wrote down the name of the school and the years I'd attended.

"Where did you attend upper secondary school?" I wrote it down. "Which years?" I wrote down my years of lower and upper secondary school and explained, "Upper and lower secondary were in the same school."

One of the years I wrote down immediately attracted their attention. "1989?"

"Don't worry, I didn't take part in any of that, or even see it. I don't know anything."

"How could you not know anything?" Leather Jacket asked incredulously.

Yes, as a teenager, even without participating I should have noticed the ferment, but in fact I hadn't. I explained to them that my secondary school was in a suburban district, not in the city. "The closest town was several kilometers away, and we were shut off from the news. Everything in the newspapers and on TV was what the government wanted us to see. So I didn't know anything. It's only over the last two years that I've learned from the internet what happened back then."

Luckily they didn't ask me "what had happened back then." They'd have to get that from someone who'd participated at the time, not from an outsider who'd been kept in the dark for 18 years.

After they finished with my schooling, they asked, "What's your father's name? Where does he work?"

That angered me. "This is my own business and has nothing to do with my family! Signing Charter 08 doesn't warrant investigating my entire family tree."

Recorder explained, "We won't go to Chongqing and look up your parents, it's just procedure. Everyone has to answer."

"What if I don't answer? If you find it out yourself, that's your business, but I'm not willing to answer this question. Signing the charter was my personal business and has absolutely nothing to do with my family. They don't even know about it."

As I spoke, I couldn't hold back my tears. There was a box of tissues on the table, and I quickly grabbed one and wiped my face.

"I'm sure you can find out whatever you like, but don't count on me to tell you. I hate implicating others! This is the twenty-first century, not feudal times. What a person does is his own business. Why drag my parents into it? I won't cooperate!"

Seeing me cry, Recorder quickly said, "All right, all right, leave it."

Wiping my face, I scolded myself: How can you break down over such a trifle? How humiliating!

My main worry before coming to "drink tea" was whether I would cry. I'd bawled my head off while signing the charter, and when interviewed by the *Washington Post*, I'd cried again, so the photo showed me with swollen eyes and a red nose. I'd all along worried that crying while "drinking tea" would hurt my image; shouldn't I show some courage in the presence of the police? But I was simply unable to control my emotions. "Big girls don't cry," but whenever I feel distress, I can't keep the tears from flowing.

The police continued with their questioning, and I cried several more times right up to the end, making a complete fool of myself. Among the 8,000-plus charter signatories, I'm sure to qualify as "Biggest Bawl Calf."

After finishing with my personal particulars, they turned to the main topic: "When did you sign Charter 08?"

"On the fifteenth"

"January 15?"

"Uh, no, it was December 15."

"So how did you come to read Charter 08? Did someone e-mail it to you?"

"No, I read it online."

"*Washington Post* said it was e-mailed to you."

"They got it wrong. Translated interviews are sometimes inaccurate."

"What website did you read it on?"

"I don't remember."

"How can you not remember?"

"Of course I don't. I never remember where I read something on the internet."

"So how did you learn about Charter 08?"

"Also through the internet. I read that Liu Xiaobo was arrested, and then someone said it was because of Charter 08. I was curious, so I did a search. It had been pulled off a lot of websites, but I managed to find one that slipped through the net."

"After reading it, what did you do?"

"I agreed with its stands, but at first I didn't plan to sign it, because...." I was somewhat irritated, "Because in this country of ours, signing your name like that is risky." Being called in by the police was in fact one of those risks.

"So why did you eventually sign it?"

"I posted Charter 08 on my blog, but after a couple of days my posting was deleted. It made me really mad that I couldn't even share it. And I was distressed over Xiaobo being arrested. Having the misfortune to be born in this country, we're deprived of so many rights, and we all know it, but not even being allowed to express an opinion! I hate this situation and I want it to change, so I signed my name."

"What's your appraisal of Charter 08?"

"Nothing much to say about it. I found it a bit simplistic—I'd already thought of a lot of what's in it. It was just what others had been writing on the internet all along, and some of its content is already in our Constitution. All in all, I found it kind of old hat, but it brought all that content together into an advocacy document and it was published so that anyone who agreed could sign it—the form it took was new.

"In fact," I added, "I don't endorse every article in the charter, and I might be in disagreement with specific parts, but taken as a whole, I agree with it completely."

"Which parts to you agree with, and which parts do you disagree with?" Leather Jacket asked.

"That's hard to say, because there are so many articles in the charter, I can't remember them all. Do you have a copy? I could look at it and tell you."

I was sure they had a copy, but they said they didn't. They probably didn't want to give me a chance to borrow its eloquence. On the internet I'd read a lot of stories of signatories' tea-drinking sessions, and some had taken the opportunity to promote Charter 08 among the police, but I didn't plan to use this tactic. First, I didn't believe the police hadn't read it; second, the content of the charter was clear at a glance and required no explanation; third, I lacked the skills to persuade the police, so why waste my breath?

There was a large envelope on the table, with seven or eight photocopies scattered beside it, the "material" the police had gathered on me. Leather Jacket occasionally picked up these papers and looked at them as he questioned me. I was curious to know what was in them, but of course they didn't show me.

So, from now on I'd have a "secret file." What an honor!

I recalled what an online friend had said: "Xiaozhao, the things you write on your blog worry me a little. If the authorities take notice, you'll be branded for the rest of your life and you'll be limited in anything you want to do. There's a teacher who took part in the June 4th incident, and if he hadn't been protected at the time by a certain old gentleman, he'd have been locked up in prison. Even though he was protected, from then on his career development was tightly restricted. This was a high-level teacher who'd been assistant provost for many years, and who should have been promoted to vice-provost long ago, but he could never pass the political vetting. That mark will stay in his files forever, and at his age he's unlikely to get another opportunity, which is obviously depressing. There are lots of similar examples."

This friend didn't realize that I'm a complete "outsider" and had decided from my earliest years never to enter this system. I don't need the system to provide me with professional evaluations, housing, promotions or opportunities for enrichment. I don't like it and it doesn't like me, and we keep our distance. A mark in my file therefore means nothing to me.

Do you think this situation will last forever and that Chinese face a lifetime of terror? Not a chance! The time we're waiting for is not far off.

Signing Charter 08 and writing essays on my blog are legal, rational and appropriate activities; it's nothing to be ashamed of, but rather it shows that I have courage and a sense of justice, and I should be proud of it. I hope the police will preserve my "material" and not lose any of it. Later, when my hair is gray, I'll sit under the grape arbor and tell my little granddaughter, "Long, long ago, when we Chinese were still fighting for our freedom, your grandmother conquered her fear and signed Charter 08." Then I can show her my file so she knows it's not idle boasting.

Interrupting my daydream, Leather Jacket pulled me back to reality: "How did you sign it?"

"Through e-mail. The charter had e-mail addresses for signatures, and both were very easy to remember."

"Did you read the charter carefully before signing?"

"Yes. I read it once when I first heard about it, and when I decided to sign it, I read it through carefully twice. I always read any document at least twice before signing it."

"You certainly didn't read it carefully," said Leather Jacket decisively. "If you had, you never would have signed it. Didn't you notice that this charter opposes the Party and socialism?"

I shook my head. "I didn't see that."

"You're an emotional person who gets carried away, and you signed the charter without clearly seeing what it was."

How aggravating! Just because I cry easily, I get called emotional. "Of course I have my emotional side, but generally I'm a very rational person. Signing the charter was a rational choice, and it was a decision I made very calmly."

"Your initial decision not to sign was rational, and it was the right decision. But later you signed, according to what you've said, because your posting was deleted. That's impulsive, not rational behavior."

"I signed, first of all because I agree with it—that's the main reason. The second reason was that my reposting of the charter was deleted, which along with Xiaobo's arrest made me feel contrary and infuriated, so I signed. It was retaliation against your suppression."

As the saying goes, "goading is more effective than asking," and if I hadn't been so angry, my name wouldn't have been in the third round of signatures. I'm sure there were others like me who signed out of spite. The government's brutal quashing of free expression has intimidated some people, but it has spurred others to retaliate.

"That's such a childish thing to do! How does signing something change anything? It's completely useless and will only bring you trouble. You're obviously politically immature," Leather Jacket said.

I'd read the phrase "politically immature" in books since I was small, but never guessed it would be applied to me. Well, by the Party's standards I undoubtedly never would be mature. In China's environment, being "politically mature" means losing your humanity and becoming a cold-blooded machine.

I said, "Chinese consider politics dirty and full of scheming and intrigue, deception and conspiracy, and as soon as something is tied to politics, it becomes terrifying. In fact, that's not true. Sun Yat-sen said, *zheng* is the people's business, *zhi* is management, so politics (*zhengzhi*) is managing the people's business. Since it's everybody's business, politics should be open and transparent; everyone should be able to discuss and take part in it."

I had no plans to "participate," but only enjoyed discussing it a bit, and since even this was risky, I signed my name.

"I hope I can exercise the rights guaranteed under the Constitution. Think about it, I'm this old and I've never seen a ballot."

"How could you have never seen a ballot?" Leather Jacket asked incredulously. "We have ballots!"

"Where would I go to vote? Back to Chongqing? I don't live there anymore and it has nothing to do with me. In Shanghai? I don't have household registration here." I smirked. "And anyway, do you think I believe your people's congress delegates really represent the people's interests? Aren't they all just putting on a show?"

Leather Jacket just smiled without responding.

I recalled a friend of mine from Shanghai who had emigrated overseas. He said he had never voted: "Every time the neighborhood committee delivered a ballot, I just tore it up." Why? Because he didn't believe the piece of paper in his hand was a genuine ballot; if it wasn't guaranteed by a fair electoral process, there couldn't be fair results, and he preferred to abstain from this rape of the public will. He made his abstention absolute through emigration.

"I want a real ballot," I went on. "This country belongs to the people, and we have a right to discuss our country's future development, put forward our own views and agree or disagree with the views of others. The government should serve the people, and public power should be bestowed by the people."

"There's nothing wrong with what you say; I also endorse democracy. But we have to take it a step at a time. What you're talking about are ideal conditions, but that's not China's reality now. Since you're living in this reality, you have to play by the rules of the game, otherwise things won't go well for you."

I said coldly, "I know, I'm in the palm of your hand." I used my hand to draw a circle. "China is a big cage imprisoning all of us."

I'm not the least bit interested in endorsing a "reality" that consists of unrestrained public power, people trapped in a cage and citizens living in fear. I only endorse freedom, human rights and democracy, and the hope that our next generation will enjoy "freedom from fear."

"I haven't broken any of the rules of your game. Everything I do follows two principles: First, don't break national laws; second, don't violate social ethics. I signed Charter 08 as a way of expressing my identification with certain views, and this is my right."

Leather Jacket patiently admonished me. "You have that right, but Charter 08 is a serious matter; it's not just a viewpoint as you think. The government has determined that it's a serious 'anti-Party, anti-socialism' political matter."

More than a month ago I'd read rumors of this "determination" on the internet. It looked very serious, but I found it ridiculous rather than frightening. What era were we in that an issue was still resolved by a few people making a "determination" behind closed doors? Could it be that I wasn't living in 2009, but in 221 BCE, when China's first emperor took power? This was a different era!

The matter seemed simple to me: If Charter 08 was a legal issue, it should be handed to the courts (of course, in a fair and open trial with full legal process, not a black box operation like the Yang Jia case);[1] if it was an ethical issue, it should be handed over to public opinion to pass judgment.

---

[1] TN: An employed man detained in Shanghai for riding an unlicensed bicycle in October 2007, Yang Jia subsequently complained of being insulted and beaten by police officers. In July 2008, he was accused of attacking Shanghai's Zhabei District police station, killing six policemen and injuring five others. His closed-door trial attracted considerable public sympathy, highlighting public resentment of police brutality. Yang was executed on November 26, 2008.

I didn't reply to him, but continued thinking: What do you plan to do after this "determination"? Are you going to arrest and imprison thousands of signatories? Go ahead. I pity the Chinese, who call themselves citizens without enjoying the rights of citizens, and who with no power to protect themselves can only resign themselves to their fates.

Leather Jacket went on, "Do you know the Four Cardinal Principles?"[2]

I nodded indifferently: "I know them." It was inexplicable that such stuff had been enshrined in the Constitution.

"In any case, you have to face reality; upholding the leadership of the Communist Party and upholding the socialist path is still the mainstream viewpoint of our country...."

I corrected him, "It's the official viewpoint."

In order to be considered mainstream, it had to be endorsed by the majority of China's citizens. From what I could see, it was democracy that was the mainstream.

He continued, "Fine, it's the official mainstream viewpoint. Now this Charter 08 wants to overthrow the Communist Party's leadership and the socialist system...."

"I don't see where it's overthrowing anything."

"You don't see it?" He looked astounded. "Charter 08 calls for a multi-party system. That's overthrowing the leadership of the Communist Party! It calls for separation of powers, which means overthrowing the socialist system!"

I sighed. "I'm not interested in your '-isms,' and I'm not going to argue with you. I've developed an aversion to -isms after having them shoved at me since childhood; hearing that syllable makes my head ache."

From what I can see, there are just two kinds of countries in the world today: democratic and autocratic. Obviously I prefer democracy, and there was nothing more to say.

Irritated by my constant interruptions, Leather Jacket said, "Let me finish!"

---

[2] TN: Deng Xiaoping's Four Cardinal Principles—upholding the socialist path, the people's democratic dictatorship, the leadership of the Chinese Communist Party and Mao Zedong Thought—are considered beyond debate and were written into the preamble of the PRC Constitution adopted in December 1982.

"Okay, please go on."

He continued with his official mainstream viewpoints, none of which I committed to memory. When he finally paused, I couldn't tell if he had actually finished and was waiting for my response, or if he was simply catching his breath, so I urged, "Go on, I'm listening."

He wrapped up what he wanted to say, and seeing that I didn't even care enough to respond, he went on, "The Chinese Constitution stipulates the Four Cardinal Principles; Charter 08 wants to replace the Constitution, overthrow the leadership of the Party and overthrow the socialist system, and that violates the Constitution!"

"An individual can't violate the Constitution, only a state organ can. Xu Youyu wrote an essay on this question." (In fact, I once read such an essay, but I'm not sure Xu Youyu wrote it.) "And also," I added, "Charter 08 isn't a legal document; it's just a proposal, not a constitution. Amending the Constitution requires approval by a two-thirds majority of the People's Congress delegates." Anyone who wanted to make Charter 08 into a constitution was bonkers and had my deepest sympathies.

Leather Jacket asked, "Do you know who drafted Charter 08?"

"No. Even you don't know, so how would I? You arrested Xiaobo, so aren't you claiming he's the drafter?"

"Who says we don't know? We've known all along that it was Liu Xiaobo!"

It was none of my business anyway, since I hadn't drafted it.

"Do you know what kind of person Liu Xiaobo is?"

"I don't know him. I'd never heard of him until I read a lot of his essays on the internet over the last two years and got a general idea."

"During June 4th, Liu Xiaobo...." He went on with an "official introduction" to Xiaobo. I don't remember all of what he said, but the general idea was that Xiaobo was the behind-the-scenes instigator back then, and that he'd been in contact with overseas powers in recent years; his background was complicated; a naïve and impulsive person like me couldn't possibly understand him, I'd been used by him, etc.

I muttered, "No one used me. I signed the charter of my own accord; no one forced me." Curious, I asked, "I read on the internet that Liu Xiaobo is China's most sensitive person. Is that true?"

"That kind of person is sure to be sensitive, but he may not rank number one."

So, the government didn't like Xiaobo, but in the public assessment, Xiaobo was a good guy! I admired that kind of courageous and knowledgeable man.

They went on: "Were you interviewed by the media?"

I thought to myself, you know very well, so why ask? But I answered, "Yes."

"Which media?"

"The *Washington Post*."

"When was the interview?"

"On the evening of January 19."

"How did you find them?"

"I didn't find them, they found me."

"So how did they find you?"

"My e-mail address was on my blog, and they saw it there and sent me an e-mail."

"So you arranged the interview by e-mail?"

"No, we arranged it by telephone."

"How was the interview carried out? Over the telephone?"

"No, face-to-face."

"Why did you agree to be interviewed?"

"Why?" I stared at him. "I have the right to accept an interview!"

Public authorities are "not allowed to do anything not explicitly authorized by the law," but personal rights are anything the law does not explicitly prohibit. I was well aware that I possessed these rights. Anyway, I'd never been interviewed by foreign media, and I was curious.

"Where was the interview?"

"In a restaurant, while we ate."

"Which restaurant?"

"Somewhere on Huanghe Road. I just followed them in and then followed them back out. I didn't notice the name."

"How many people interviewed you?"

"Two"

"Male or female?"

"They were both women."

"Chinese or foreigners?"

"One was Chinese and one was American, but of Korean descent."

"So the Chinese was an interpreter?"

"Right."

"The American must have looked Chinese. How did you know she was American?"

"I originally thought she was Chinese, but she spoke in English, so I asked her assistant where she was from, and the assistant said she was American but her parents were of Korean descent."

"How was the interview done? Was it tape recorded?"

"It was done in person."

"What kind of questions did they ask you?"

"You know that, it's all in the article."

"Have you read the article they wrote?"

"Yes."

"You can read English?"

"Ha, that's easy enough. I just used Google Translate and worked my way through it." I explained, "I mainly checked to make sure the part about me was accurate. There were some small errors but nothing that mattered. I didn't like their headline, though; to me, the title was exaggerated."

"You mean..." Leather Jacket picked up a photocopy and read out: "'In China, A Grassroots Rebellion'?"

I guessed that what the police had read was a third-party description of the article on a Chinese website, in particular the part about me. They didn't know I had posted a Chinese translation of the whole article on my blog.

"Yes. I felt I was not that intense, and applying that title to me was a bit...exaggerated." I couldn't think of exactly the right word.

It was Recorder who suggested, "A little 'extreme'?"

"Yes," I nodded quickly.

The word "rebellion" could be translated into Chinese as "armed rebellion," "insurrection," "revolt" or any of a number of other words that were very detrimental to me, so when I first translated it, I avoided the title altogether. But when Chinese websites reposted the article using such terms in the title, I broke out in a cold sweat.

In fact, I didn't care what headline someone used. But I was "in China," and to me, that China was not warm like a mother's embrace, but cold and unfeeling as an iron cage; it could at any moment reach out its iron claws and tear me to pieces. If the language you use is too severe, Mr. Wei Guangzheng[3] will lay it on my account, and I'll be left hanging in the wind.

That's why I couldn't approve of that headline.

"You see, the foreign media were using you without your knowing it," Leather Jacket jumped at this opportunity to educate me.

I didn't feel that the *Washington Post* used me. Put another way, if they were using me, wasn't I also using them? They used me to observe China's ordinary signatories, and I used them to spread my views to the rest of the world. The Chinese media had maintained total silence on Charter 08, and the only way to speak out was through the foreign media.

Leather Jacket was especially interested in the content of the interview, and asked me about it repeatedly. I always answered, "It's what's written in the news report." After such a long time, how could I remember? I wasn't a reporter and hadn't taken notes.

"Do you know anything about the *Washington Post*?"

"No. I'd never read any of their news reports before."

"The *Washington Post* is a very major newspaper; it's *world famous*." Leather Jacket particularly emphasized this point and closely observed my reaction.

I was indifferent. "I didn't know. I'd just heard the name." To myself I thought, you built your Berlin Wall to keep me from seeing the outside world, so what would I know?

A few days after this, a friend told me that the *Washington Post* was well known as an anti-China newspaper and I was greatly shocked. No wonder the policemen watched so closely for my response when we were "drinking tea." Kept in ignorance, I had no idea which newspapers were "anti-China" or "pro-China." But even if I'd known in advance, it wouldn't have mattered. I don't believe the American media can be "anti-China," because that would constitute racial bias, which is a minefield of controversy in the United States.

---

[3] TN: A play on the abbreviation for *weida, guangrong, zhengque*—great, glorious and correct—the phrase the Chinese Communist Party uses to describe itself, but which is used with considerably more irony outside of the Party.

"Anti-Communist" was more like it; that only constituted a different political viewpoint, and was normal in the United States. Generally speaking, the mainstream media of Western countries were unlikely to align themselves with the Great, Glorious and Correct.

"Why did you agree to be interviewed by them?" Leather Jacket asked again.

I stared at him. "Am I not allowed to accept an interview from the *Washington Post*?"

All he could say was, "You have the right to accept the *Washington Post*'s interview."

Okay, it's good that you admit it.

Leather Jacket said sincerely, "You shouldn't accept interviews from the foreign media ever again."

I said, "I'm not making any promises."

"What? You want to accept more interviews from the foreign media?" Leather Jacket looked astounded.

"I didn't say I wanted to, I just said I wouldn't make any promises. This is my decision to make."

I have a contrarian mindset, and especially hate to be threatened. When I'm threatened, I retaliate. He didn't have to worry anyway—there wouldn't be many news organizations interviewing me. I hadn't done anything, just signed my name like the others. It was a minor matter with little news value and not worth further interviews.

"In fact, I didn't hope to become famous from Charter 08," I said.

He quickly agreed: "That kind of fame isn't good for you."

Opinions might differ on that point, but that wasn't what I was talking about: "I feel that if I'm to become famous, it should be for my own abilities. I wasn't involved in writing Charter 08 and it didn't reflect my personal capabilities, so I don't want to become famous because of it."

The police wanted me to promise: "Don't involve yourself with Charter 08 anymore."

I replied, "Getting involved is beside the point. All I did was sign my name to express my agreement with its standpoints. My name is signed and, as far as I'm concerned, that's the end of the matter."

We'd been drinking for about two hours and, although hardly "intimate," the atmosphere could be considered cordial and friendly.

Afterward they had me read the written record of interview. I read it carefully twice and changed a couple of words, then signed off on it. I was happy to see that Recorder had included my words "public power should be bestowed by the people."

The record of interview was very simple, but I thought that after I left they would still have to write an "assessment report" about me, like the head teacher has to write for his students at the end of term. They had been observing and speculating about me all along, and I wondered what they would finally "determine" about me.

We all stood up and prepared to leave the room. Leather Jacket warned me, "Don't talk to anyone about what happened today, and don't post it on your blog."

"I'm not making any promises."

"What? You want to write up what happened today on your blog?" said Leather Jacket, staring.

"I didn't say I'd put it on my blog, I just said I wouldn't make any promises. I feel this is my personal business and it's up to me to decide. I don't like other people forcing a decision on me."

"If you go public with what happened today, you'll bear the legal consequences!"

As I walked out I turned and asked him, "Let me just ask, what are the legal consequences?"

"Of course there are legal consequences!"

Tsk! That was no answer. If there were legal consequences, there would have to first be a legal statute to determine whether the law had been broken. Second, what would the legal consequences be? Surveillance, detention, a prison sentence, a life sentence, capital punishment? I really didn't know, and that's why I asked. What I did know was that today's "tea drinking" session didn't constitute any kind of state secret. Don't bother accusing me of "leaking state secrets." I don't buy it.

⇒•⇐

Postscript, February 21, 2009:

In order to bring peace of mind to all who are concerned about Xiaozhao's fate, and in order to practice my principle of "standing in the sunlight," I naturally have to make my "tea drinking" session public. This is a new step in my life and if anything interesting follows, I will certainly share it.

I've said that I won't live like a mouse in a sewer pipe. If I die, it will be under the sun and in the glare of the public eye. Dear friends, I thank you for your concern. Xiaozhao is still alive and well, at least for now. No one can know the future. As long as Liu Xiaobo's freedom isn't restored, the fate of thousands of Charter 08 signatories hangs in the balance. Having had the misfortune to be born in China, I'll just have to grin and bear it.

God bless us, every one. Amen!

INJUSTICE

Wu Huaying

Wu Huaying, a signatory of Charter 08, was born in the 1970s in China's southern Fujian Province. Wu was the proprietor of a clothing business, but after her younger brother, Wu Changlong, was unjustly imprisoned for involvement in the 2001 bombing of an official building in Fuqing, Wu Huaying began to petition the government on his behalf. Her petitioning led her to develop an interest in other cases of injustice. In 2009, she helped produce a documentary about Lin Xiuying, a woman who claimed that police protected local hoodlums who had gang raped and killed her daughter, Yan Xiaoling. After the film was uploaded onto the internet on June 24, 2009, producers Wu Huaying, You Jingyou and Fan Yanqiong were arrested and unjustly convicted, as described by Wu in this essay. An internet campaign garnered them wide public support as the Three Fujianese Netizens, and their case became a galvanizing episode in the rights defense movement.

ARREST AT MIDNIGHT

Around midnight on June 30, 2009, our family was awakened from deep slumber by a sudden pounding on our door. My terrified father and daughter ran out of their bedrooms as I opened the inner wooden door and asked through the metal security grate, "Who is it, and what do you want in the middle of the night?"

From the darkness outside a male voice said, "We're checking your household registration."

"Again? Why are you only checking our house?"

The person outside ignored my inference and continued shouting for me to open the door.

I said, "Please show me your identification."

He claimed to be the commander of the Yinxi police station, and said he'd forgotten his ID.

I was disgusted that they used their disregard for basic procedure as an excuse. Without identification, how am I to know you're a police officer, and why should I open my door just because you tell me to?

In fact, I knew very well that they were police. Over the years, I'd been petitioning everywhere on behalf of my brother, and they hated the sight of me. This kind of late-night harassment had happened countless times before.

I said, "Please go back and get your ID. Once I've seen your papers, I'll cooperate with your 'inspection.'"

After a moment of silence, they left.

I immediately telephoned my lawyer and friends and reported that the police had come tonight to "inspect my *hukou*." I then pulled out my digital recording pen and set it to record the entire "inspection" process.

While awaiting their return, I also telephoned a friend who had agreed to accompany me to the detention center the next day to deliver some items to my brother, and told him the appointment might have to be canceled. Before I finished the conversation, there was pounding at my door again: "We've brought our papers. Open up."

I set the telephone aside and covered it with a cloth, then opened the door, at which point two uniformed officers, one male and one female, charged in with six or seven plainclothes officers close on their heels, one shouldering a camcorder.

At that moment, my cell phone rang. Pressing the "answer" key without taking the call, I asked the police officers, "Did you bring a summons?"

After hesitating, a skinny plainclothes officer leading the group said, "We need to straighten out some things first. What's your name?"

I calmly answered, "Wu Huaying."

Seeing me holding a cell phone, several of the plainclothes cops demanded in unison that I drop it. They then began searching my home, one lifting the cloth off my landline and replacing the receiver. The digital recorder hidden in my refrigerator was also soon discovered.

Watching them turn my house upside down, I asked again, "Why are you searching my house? Have you brought your police IDs, a search warrant and a summons?"

The skinny plainclothes officer motioned to one beside him, who pulled out his police ID and flashed it at me.

I asked Skinny, "Where are you from? Please show me your ID."

Skinny replied, "From the city bureau."

"Which city bureau?"

"The Fuzhou Municipal PSB."

"Since you're from the Fuzhou PSB, you should show me your ID."

My father, standing to one side, burst out, "My son's been in prison for eight years and no one cares. What are you doing here in the middle of the night? This abuse of power is intolerable! Intolerable!"

Afraid that my father's impatience and rage would create an incident, I quickly comforted him: "I didn't break the law, don't worry. If they want to toss our home, let them do it."

Having finished with the living room, they started searching the bedrooms, dumping our clothes and other belongings all over the place. My heart sank as I watched them take my computer. When my brother had been detained eight years ago, the police had searched our home repeatedly and had never given us a list of confiscated items. I said, "Can you leave me a list of whatever you take today?"

A plainclothes officer said, "Don't worry, we're following legal procedures. We'll give you a list of anything we take."

Hearing them repeatedly refer to legal procedures got my dander up: "Don't give me that sanctimonious talk. The things you've taken all these years, my brother's cell phone, our home appliances, our stamp collection and other things, how come we haven't seen a trace of them up to now?"

The policeman said, "If we don't put it on the confiscation list, you can refuse to give it to us."

I laughed cynically, knowing that further talk was pointless.

After searching for more than two hours, they gathered up 13 items, mainly my computer and some documents.

A plainclothes officer with a southern Fujian accent took out a search warrant and asked my family, "Which of you is handling the paperwork?"

My daughter walked over and took the search warrant, but the plainclothes officer said, "I can't give you this."

My daughter asked, "If you won't give it to me, can I photograph it as evidence?"

Another plainclothes officer impatiently said, "Absolutely not!"

Seeing my daughter argue with them reminded me of an incident five years earlier. Late in the night of September 14, 2005, plainclothes police took me away on the pretext of "*hukou* inspection." My weeping daughter, 12 years old at the time, took out her camera and photographed them arresting me, saying, "I'm taking this picture, so if I can't find my mom, I'll give you this picture to get her back."

Nothing changes over time; the past keeps repeating itself. This thought weighed on my spirits.

At that moment, Skinny took out a summons and shook it in front of my face, telling me to pack a few changes of clothing and go with them. This seemed a departure from my previous experience, so I asked, "What's the crime you're calling me in for tonight? You have to give some reason, but there's nothing written on the summons."

A plainclothes officer said, "You come with us, and after we've carried out some inquiries we'll know."

"How can you detain someone before you've made inquiries?"

He insisted, "We're following the law."

My father angrily said, "Following the law? Why don't you use your law to resolve the injustice done to my family instead of always using it to browbeat us!"

Worried that Father would become too agitated, I didn't pursue what statute was involved, but prepared to go with them.

I threw together some clothes, and Skinny said, "Don't take so much! You're not moving house."

I said, "Since you've searched my home and issued a summons, I'd better take more. I don't want to trouble an old man and a girl with running around bringing things to me."

As we approached the door, they handcuffed me. Looking at my family, my heart bled. I repeatedly urged them, "Look after each other, take things one day at a time."

A 36-HOUR INTERROGATION

At around 2:00 a.m., I was brought to Fuzhou's Mawei District Kuai'an police station. The police station was ablaze with light and people bustled in and out. Two young men came to see me, after which several plainclothes officers escorted me to an interrogation room.

I sensed the oppressive atmosphere of an approaching storm.

I was pushed into what is called a "tiger seat," made of metal bands and pipes welded together with a board on top. Once I was strapped into it, I couldn't move.

In the sweltering summer heat, the windowless interrogation room was stifling. A large floor fan stood in the doorway, but it was aimed at my interrogators and gave me not the slightest relief.

Several young plainclothes officers munched on a midnight snack while joking around: "The special investigation team upstairs has brought in a lot of people; even Big Wu has put in an appearance and has brought his quilt." It seemed they meant for me to overhear them and feel intimidated.

After the plainclothes officers had eaten and drunk their fill, the interrogation began. I demanded that they produce identification, but they refused.

The interrogator asked, "What's your name?"

I said, "Go and ask the provincial PSB head, Niu Jigang. This isn't the first time I've been arrested, and he knows all about me. You people are always tapping my cell phone and home phone."

The interrogator scowled, "I'm asking you! Why are you pushing it off on Niu Jigang? Do you know about the Minqing Yan Xiaoling case? Do you know Lin Aide, Chen Yangdong, Chen Huanhui, Yang Xueyun, Guo Baofeng, You Jingyou and Fan Yanqiong?"

That's when I realized that I'd been detained because of this case.

I refused to answer any more questions until they produced the legal basis for my detention. The interrogator had no choice but to consult his superior.

Those left behind babbled, "We've looked at the material in your computer and all your online postings, and we sympathize with you. You've been petitioning on behalf of your brother for eight years, and that's no small thing. But you should mind your own business and not that of others."

The interrogator returned with several others, who set up a video camera and aimed it at me, with an empty paper cup placed in front of the video camera as a prop. He then took out some documents and shook them in front of the camera before quickly putting them away. I was too far away to see what was on them.

The interrogation started anew, repeating the previous questions, and I gave the same replies.

The interrogator said, "I'm deeply sympathetic to the injustice against your brother, but that's a different matter. Today we've detained you over the Yan Xiaoling case, not over the Fuqing bombing, so don't keep bringing up your brother's case."

The interrogation was carried out in shifts, with a man in a red T-shirt replaced by one in a white dress shirt. During the process, someone came in with a 12-hour summons for me to sign.

After an extended period under the flood lamp, I could no longer tell if it was day or night. I became dehydrated in the sultry heat. Strapped onto the tiger seat, my body went numb and ached in turn, and my intestines, deprived of food and water, began cramping. I clutched my stomach and twisted my body to relieve the pain.

The interrogators occasionally poked my head, kicked the tiger seat and yanked my shoulders back and forth, ensuring that in my extreme exhaustion I couldn't fall asleep.

After I don't know how long, someone came again with another 12-hour summons for me to sign.

After years of being toyed with, I'd learned some legal knowledge. I said to the person who'd come in, "If within 24 hours you can't find any legal basis for accusing me of a crime, you have to let me go."

He roared, "Wu Huaying, you won't cough because you think you can stall for 24 hours and then leave? Ha! I'm telling you, don't even think about it. We've already applied to upgrade your interrogation to 'residential surveillance.'"

I interrupted him, "According to law, 'residential surveillance' is supposed to be carried out in my home."

He yelled, "You still imagine it's like before, and you'll go home after a few days in detention? Do you know what this place is?"

Wasn't it the Kuai'an police station? I suddenly recalled a friend who'd signed Charter 08 mentioning the "domestic security police." Could this be where they worked their cases?

After a while, a saucer-eyed plainclothes officer who'd escorted me to the Kuai'an police station came in.

Saucer Eyes said, "Looking through your accounts, I see a lot of expenses. You haven't had a job in eight years and you've spent the whole time appealing and petitioning. How do you support yourself? What other family members do you have? Who installed your computer—did you have help?"

A plainclothes officer next to him said, "Do you know that Fan Yanqiong has written half of a book on the Fuqing Discipline Inspection Commission bombing?"[1]

Unsure of their intentions, I protested with silence.

Extended physical and mental torture had exhausted me, and I began to drift out of consciousness.

Suddenly I was shaken awake again, and the interrogator took out a photograph and asked, "Is this your daughter?"

The tiger seat was two meters away from the interrogator's table, and it was impossible for me to see who was in the photo. At that moment, I heard my daughter's voice at the main entrance, and with renewed energy I turned my head to look for her.

In the noise outside the door, I could faintly hear Fan Yanqiong's daughter Lin Jingyi crying out "Mama!" Had Fan also been brought in? I also heard someone mention You Jingyou's name; was he also detained here?

---

[1] TN: The Discipline Inspection Commission is a Communist Party organization that targets malfeasance among Party cadres. It was the office of the Fuqing branch of this organization that Wu Huaying's brother was accused of bombing.

Soon after that, several plainclothes officers came into the interrogation room. They opened the wooden bar on the front of the tiger seat and had me sign a "criminal detention notice."

It was only upon seeing the time written on the notice that I realized I'd spent 36 hours in the interrogation room. Throughout that time, I'd had nothing to eat or drink.

They took my fingerprints and my photograph. I had no strength left to resist and let them do what they wanted, just hoping for it all to end and to be allowed to sleep.

Upon leaving the interrogation room, I encountered the plainclothes officer with the southern accent and asked him, "What law have I broken? What crime are you detaining me for?"

After a moment's hesitation, he said, "For slander."

"Slandering whom?"

He was silent.

Several police officers escorted me from the Kuai'an police station. Rain poured down as if heaven were weeping for my family's suffering. Thinking of how I could no longer appeal for my brother, I felt tears spring from my eyes and flow down my face with the rain.

THROWN INTO THE NO. 2 DETENTION CENTER

At around 2:00 in the afternoon of July 1, I was escorted to a police vehicle with my bag of clothes. I didn't know where they were taking me, but I knew it would be either a jail or a detention center.

The police van pushed through the driving rain, and after winding through many curves, it brought me to the Fuzhou Municipal No. 2 Detention Center, located in Chengmen Town in Fuzhou's Cangshan District.

As we entered the detention center's foyer, a female guard surnamed Lin opened a small door and had me follow her. She took me to the detention center's clinic, where a doctor, seeing my drawn and listless expression, asked me, "Have the police been extracting confession through torture? What are these bruises on your arms?"

I answered truthfully, "The Mawei police didn't beat me, but they had me sit for 36 hours in a tiger seat and didn't allow me to eat, drink or sleep, so it was a disguised form of interrogation under torture."

After examining me, the doctor had me sign my name and press my fingerprint on a sheet of paper.

Guard Lin then took me to a small room, and without closing the door had me remove all my clothing, place my hands on my head and repeatedly squat down.

I guess my disoriented appearance after 36 hours of non-stop torture made her think I was drugged, and she worried I might be carrying narcotics on my person.

Having gone so long without food or drink, the repeated squatting and rising made me lose my balance, and I fell. The guard acted as if nothing had happened, however, and urged me to keep squatting and standing until she was satisfied. She then had me stand on an electronic scale so she could take my height and weight: 1.68 meters and 62 kilos. After taking my measurements, the guard allowed me to dress, but instructed me to place my bra and shoes in a blue plastic bucket. Just then a side door opened, and the two female police officers who had escorted me to the detention center came in and grabbed the bag of clothes I'd brought, saying, "You're not allowed to bring anything into the detention center. Have your family send clothes and money later."

I asked, "Please let me telephone my family and tell them I'm here."

After a moment's hesitation, one of the police officers dialed my daughter's number. After telling her where I was, I said, "Hire a lawyer for me, and send some clothes and money. You'll have to be strong, I'll be fine . . . ." At the policewoman's incessant urging, I hurriedly ended the call.

I walked barefoot through four large doorways until Guard Lin brought me to cell number 301 and opened the metal door. Before my eyes could accustom themselves to the darkness, I heard the door clank shut. Before me stood a 40-ish woman, hollow-cheeked and of medium height. I could see right away that she was not the easygoing type, and guessed she must be the cell boss.

After sizing me up from head to toe, she had me follow her. We passed through a barred courtyard and stepped through a second metal door into a cell. This cell was double the size of that outside, having three barred windows with clothing and other articles placed on the sills. A ten-meter corridor was lined on one side with female prisoners and on the other side with beds on which were seated more female prisoners. In front of each prisoner was placed a plastic bucket covered with a piece of cardboard, and on each piece of cardboard was piled plastic bags and bundles of red twine. The prisoners ran the twine through the plastic bags and knotted it to make shopping bags for shoes.

The cell boss pointed to two plastic buckets of water in the washroom and ordered, "Strip down and wash up."

I sized up the washroom, which was constructed of PVC. Although it was closed off at the top, a barred ventilation window exposed women to the gaze of those outside. Later I learned that the man who delivered the meals and the patrolling guards would make a point of passing by while prisoners were bathing and would peep in on them to satisfy their perverted impulses.

The cell boss ordered two prisoners to put a big stack of items on the window sill next to the washroom, and said, "Plastic buckets, towels, slippers, toothpaste, toothbrushes, soap are all loaned to you from public funds, and when your family comes, you have to pay for them. Your prison uniform is also on loan from the state, and when your family brings you clothes, you have to wash this and return it."

The cell boss and trustees kept watch on me as I bathed. Seeing the bruises all over my body, the cell boss asked, "Were you beaten?"

I shook my head: "That's just from the tiger seat."

The cell boss asked, "Where are you from? What did you do to get arrested?"

I said, "I'm from Fuqing, and I was arrested in retaliation for suing a crooked official."

The trustees had me toss my clothes out of the washroom, and using plastic bags as gloves, they inspected every seam and fold for dangerous articles or contraband.

My life is normally very regular, with three meals at set times. Being deprived of food and drink for two days and nights left me debilitated and fatigued, and the icy water poured over my body wracked me with shivers. After I finished bathing, the cell boss told me to put my clothes into an old red bucket and to wait until I'd eaten before washing them.

She then pointed to several sheets of paper taped to the "study board" and said, "As a 'newbie,' you're required to spend seven days learning production on the job, and memorizing the prison rules, the working and rest hours, rights and responsibilities and so on. After seven days, you're treated the same as the long-timers, taking turns with sanitation duties, and you have to produce 1,500 shoe bags per day, with no break if you don't finish. If you don't memorize the prison rules, the work and rest hours and the rights and responsibilities, you have to go back to memorizing them at night until you've got them down. The second week you have to memorize seven chapters of 42-line behavioral standards, and if you don't get them memorized, you get the same penalty. If anyone reports you breaking regulations, you'll be punished according to the severity of the offense."

I gasped as the cell boss rattled off all these rules.

Dinner was delivered a little after 4:00 that afternoon. Twenty-odd prisoners were assembled into three groups and squeezed into the passageway while three cell bosses and two trustees distributed the food. One woman named Juan brought over a plastic spoon on which a number had been burned with a cigarette and told me to memorize the number, saying, "You'll be using this from now on, so get it right."

After receiving our dinner, we squatted in positions assigned according to our order of arrival at the detention center. As a newbie, I was placed next to the garbage can.

After dinner, the cell boss brought a tangerine-colored prison uniform and told me to put it on, then had someone teach me the slogan "Abide by the prison rules, obey the guards." When we raised our hands to count off, we had to call out loud and clear, otherwise we'd have to keep calling out until the cell boss was satisfied.

At 6:00, the prisoners sat in two rows with their legs crossed, waiting for the patrolling guards to arrive at the window for roll call.

A plainclothes guard came gripping a list of names in one hand and a pen in the other, first pressing a switch that shut the partition doors with a clang. The cells were dead silent, and the cell boss hollered, "Count off!" The sound was like a thunderclap: "One! Two! Three!" clear and resonant, short and forceful. After taking the roll call, the guard turned to the next cell.

The cell boss then called a meeting to assign tasks and announce rewards and penalties.

During the free exercise period after dinner, newbies had to stand at the entrance to the passageway and memorize the prison regulations, their eyes closed in concentration. Everyone took the exercise very seriously for fear of being penalized with extra memorization.

At 7:00 we prepared our bedding for sleep. The prisoners vied for favored corner spots, and only I, uncertain what to do, clutched my bedding and stood next to the washroom watching their mad scramble.

The cell boss assigned me to sleep next to two long-timers, and the three of us squeezed onto a meter-wide space on the concrete floor. The day's strenuous production tasks had all the prisoners snoring the minute they dropped. Lying in my narrow space, I looked at the cell, ablaze with light, sleepless in spite of my physical and mental exhaustion. I silently prayed, "Oh Lord, please bless and protect my father and daughter outside, and give them peace. Please bless and protect my brother in his unjust imprisonment, and preserve his health until he wins redress."

At 6:00 the next morning, with the cry of "Wake up!" everyone leaped from the lower berths, folded their bedding and piled it neatly in the corner of the passageway, followed by those in the upper berths. The cell boss sat with legs crossed, watching every movement in the cell and occasionally barking orders. Rubbing bleary eyes and stretching stiff limbs, I prepared my exhausted body for a busy day.

24-HOUR INTERROGATION RECORD

Around 9:00 a.m. on July 3, the female guard who had brought me in arrived at cell number 301. I now knew that her name was Lin Meixi, that she was around 40 years old and that she was in charge of cells 301 and 302. She came in for roll call and asked how things were, and after these routine matters she had me follow her for another routine matter, my 24-hour interrogation.

While walking she advised me, "No matter why you came here, just take it as it comes. Thinking too much about it is no use. Accept your situation and watch yourself."

Lin was a cadre who had transferred from a military unit. She had cultivated the mentality of following orders as the highest duty, without asking whether it was right or wrong.

I followed her to the corrections office, and when she saw that I didn't look intimidated, she raised her eyebrows and said, "Usually when detainees come here to talk to me, they have to wear handcuffs. Today I didn't handcuff you, so place your hands behind your back." She pointed to a corner two steps away and had me push my stool back.

I was offended by her commandeering attitude, but out of courtesy I did what she said.

Guard Lin asked, "What's your name? What's your month and year of birth? Your address? What crime were you detained for? How many family members live overseas? How have you supported yourself while filing complaints over the past eight years?"

I told her, "Several years ago the head of the Fujian Province PSB, Niu Jigang, repeatedly sent police officers from the Fuzhou municipal PSB to bring me in for questioning on all of the things you're asking me about. I told them that my home life is none of their business. Niu Jigang has refused to rectify the injustice he perpetrated, and now he's taking revenge on the family of his victim and using his power to suppress the law. What crime is it to seek redress on my brother's behalf? My brother has spent eight years in prison for no reason. Think a minute—the explosion killed someone and was a provocation against the authorities, so why did it only draw a suspended death sentence? The case has been under review for eight years with three appeals, so why is it still unresolved?"

After listening to me, Guard Lin said impatiently, "Whether or not you've been treated unjustly has nothing to do with me, and it's not for you to say; the judicial organs will determine that."

Finally she produced the completed 24-hour interrogation record and asked me to sign it.

When I saw that the record stated, "suspected of involvement in Fan Yanqiong's crime of slander," I was furious: "When the police arrested me, they didn't tell me what crime I'd committed. Now they toss me into the detention center and slap this charge on me. Since today is supposed to be for questioning, I should be answering your questions and you should be writing it down. I know very well that this so-called criminal charge is because I went to Beijing several times to file complaints, and because I accused Niu Jigang by name and shamed him by exposing him on the internet."

She defended herself, saying, "This is what's in the computer, I just copied it."

FIRST COURT APPEARANCE

On November 11, 2009, the temperature plummeted in Fuzhou. That was the day of my first court appearance.

I was very calm when I awoke that morning. Around 7:00, the metal door of Cell 301 opened, and someone called out, "Wu Huaying!" I walked out of the cell, and a guard immediately hand-cuffed me.

Several court vans were parked at the gate of the detention center, and I was escorted into the last one. Before boarding, I saw Fan Yanqiong in a wheelchair being lifted into the middle van. I guessed that the first bus was for You Jingyou, but my view was blocked and I couldn't see him.

The vans left the detention center, and after winding through several villages finally connected to a smooth, broad expressway.

Less than half an hour later, the vans approached the Mawei District Court, and through the tinted window I saw a large group of people gathered at the court entrance and gazing expectantly around. Then I saw my daughter break away from the crowd and run toward the vans, shouting, "Mama! Mama!" Friends and relatives had come all the way from Fuqing to attend the trial, probably with no sleep the night before.

Bailiffs took Yan, You and me into three separate rooms. At Fan Yanqiong's protest, the police gave us breakfast. While we were eating, a bailiff pointed at me and said to his colleague seated next to me, "What's this beauty doing here? She's the one who shouted during the trial at the Fuzhou Intermediate Court a few years ago."

His words reminded me of what happened during the trial for the Fuqing bombing case in the Fuzhou Intermediate Court. In court I had exposed the wicked and inglorious role of Niu Jigang, the provincial PSB chief who had manufactured this unjust case. I never imagined that years later someone would remember this incident.

The female bailiff chimed in, "She has relatives in Japan who petitioned Wen Jiabao with banners while he was on a trip there.[2]

At 8:00 sharp, we three defendants were escorted one at a time into the courtroom. Fan Yanqiong asked to kiss her daughter, who was sitting in the public gallery, but was coldly refused by the police. I made an effort to spot friends and relatives in the public gallery, and finally saw my mother and daughter squeezed into the left-hand corner. Security was tight in court that day, and besides a professional photographer taking pictures, a video camera was set up in the aisle of the public gallery.

After reading out the court rules, the judge asked, "Is there an application for the judge to be recused?"

I answered, "Does the judge have independent judicial authority? If there is an application for recusal, will that change the outcome of the trial?"

The judge didn't respond to my question, but asked my name.

I said, "I am Wu Huaying, the elder sister of Wu Changlong, who was unjustly convicted in the Fuqing Discipline Inspection Commission bombing case, and I'm accused of 'involvement in framing another.'"(The Fujian Province Fuzhou Municipal Public Security Bureau had initially arrested me, Fan Yanqiong and You Jingyou for "suspected involvement in slander," but at the time of indictment changed it to "framing and entrapment.") "This is just a continuation of the bombing case, and is retaliation against me by those involved in my brother's unjust conviction."

---

[2] TN: Probably referring to a trip that China's premier took to Japan in April 2007. See "Special Report: Premier Wen Visits ROK, Japan," Chinaview.cn, April 13, 2007, http://news.xinhuanet.com/english/2007–04/13/content_5973888.htm (accessed January 4, 2013).

The judge read out: "Wu Huaying on June 13, 2002, was put under security detention by the Fuzhou Municipal Public Security Bureau's Gulou branch for disturbing social order."

I corrected him: "During my long and difficult petitioning process, I've been detained three times, not once. On June 13, 2002, when I blocked the sedan of the secretary of the Fujian provincial politics and law committee, I was indicted and held in administrative detention for 15 days. Because an old colleague contacted *Fujian Daily* and told a reporter about the situation, I was released the next day. The second time, I was detained for ten days for petitioning officials outside the provincial government offices. The third time, I blocked the provincial Party secretary's sedan to deliver a complaint, and was detained for 15 days."

The public prosecutor then read out the indictment.

Fan Yanqiong, seated in a wheelchair, shouted that the prosecutor was talking nonsense. She demanded that Lin Xiuying appear in court to clarify the truth, but the prosecutor ignored her and continued reading out the indictment.

At that point, the six defense lawyers strongly objected and demanded individual cross-examination, but the judge overruled them.

Faced with a kangaroo court under the collusion of the Mawei PSB, procuratorate and judge, Fan Yanqiong withdrew from the court in protest, and I announced: "Since we aren't allowed to speak at today's trial, I'm sorry, I'm not going along with your playacting; we'll put on our own show." My words drew laughter from the public gallery, and the judge pounded his gavel and shouted, "Order in the court!"

I said to You Jingyou, seated next to me, "It looks like today's trial was carefully planned and rehearsed in advance. Whether there's a trial or not, the result will be the same, and we don't have to cooperate."

As we voiced our protest, the bailiffs escorted us out of the court.

Without defendants playing supporting roles, the performance couldn't continue according to the "script." Given the lawyers' reasoned arguments, the judge could no longer insist on the original bundled cross-examination, and allowed each of us to be questioned separately.

When the bailiffs escorted us back to the courtroom, I stood in the doorway and asked loudly, "How many of our friends and relatives are in the public gallery? Please stand and show yourselves." In the packed public gallery, six family members stood up.

At that moment, Fan Yanqiong's ex-husband, Lin Hui, said to me, "A lot of friends and relatives who came to attend the trial were blocked from entering the courthouse, along with Yan Xiaoling's mother, Lin Xiuying."

Ignoring the bailiff shoving me from behind, I told the judge, "The bias in today's trial is all too clear. Your honor, are you striking your gavel at the bidding of senior officials, or for law and justice? Is PSB director Niu Jigang managing today's proceedings from some hidden gallery?" This was just what happened at the Fuzhou Intermediate Court in the Fuqing bombing case.

The judge quickly rapped his gavel and barked, "Don't refer to matters unrelated to this case."

I then questioned the prosecutor: "Who is it I've framed or entrapped? At the indictment and interrogation stage, I repeatedly asked this question, but the Mawei PSB, procuratorate and court have all either evaded or put off addressing this point, saying it would be made clear in court. Now we're in court, so shouldn't I get an answer?"

The prosecutor said, "This is the time for me to question you, not for you to question me."

I persisted, "Please answer me: Whom have I framed or entrapped?"

The prosecutor didn't reply.

Two medical personnel stood by Fan Yanqiong's wheelchair, measuring her blood pressure and monitoring her oxygen intake. Fan's appearance alarmed me. She was losing hair, and her cheeks were hollow and her complexion pallid. Her eyes, once sparkling with intelligence, were now dim and sunken. Her body had shrunk, her legs were like kindling and her voice alternated between shrill and breathy.

Just days before our arrest, we'd eaten beefsteak together. At that time, her tread had been as light and graceful as the wind. I never would have guessed that in just four months she would be sitting in a wheelchair.

During the lunch break, my mother and daughter approached, and my daughter reached for me through the iron bars, only to be pushed away by bailiffs. Seeing her tears of frustration, I quickly said, "Don't cry now, you have to be strong. You have to look after Grandma and Grandpa while I'm away."

My mother was noticeably wan and thin, her face etched with worry and sorrow.

I could understand my mother's feelings, with my brother falsely imprisoned and now me in jail. My younger sister, Wu Huayu, had petitioned Wen Jiabao while he was visiting Japan. Half a month later, she'd been involved in a "traffic accident," and the doctors said she would spend the rest of her life in a wheelchair. Thank God, she eventually made a miraculous recovery.

At this moment, I could only silently pray: May God's justice illuminate our hearts and keep my family from collapsing under hardship. Let them pass each day in hope, and let my brother be exonerated.

Throughout the trial, Fan Yanqiong and I repeatedly asked the judge to allow Lin Xiuying to attend the trial and clarify the facts.

The judge's reply was always, "Wait a moment, wait a moment."

I simply couldn't bear it anymore and indignantly burst out, "Your honor, you said to wait a moment, but the moments keep passing, and now with night approaching there's still no sign of Lin Xiuying."

The public gallery exploded with laughter, and even the bailiffs couldn't keep from tittering. The judge traded glances with the two public prosecutors, then said, "The prosecution and I feel there's no need for Lin Xiuying to appear in court."

We were being illegally detained because of Lin Xiuying's complaint over how her daughter Yan Xiaoling had died, yet "there was no need for Lin Xiuying to appear in court?" What an enormous joke!

As the sky darkened, people began gradually leaving the public gallery. Thinking of our friends and relatives standing outside in the cold, I asked the judge whether they could be allowed in to fill the vacant seats. The judge summarily refused on the pretext of legal procedure.

By the time the trial ended, it was after 9:00 at night. While signing the record of the proceedings, I saw the words "open trial" written on the top page.

As I was escorted from court to the police van, my friends and relatives were still standing outside in the icy wind and rain. I heard my daughter shout, "You're all a bunch of beasts in human clothing!" My heart ached; who had planted this rage and hatred in her young soul?

A TWO-MINUTE HEARING

On March 18, 2010, lawyer Lin Hongnan came to the detention center and told me that the Mawei Court would hold its second hearing on the "Three Fujianese Netizens" case the next day.

More than four months had passed since the first hearing, well past the legally stipulated time limit; what kind of judgment could we expect from such a court?

At 7:00 a.m. on March 19, I was escorted from the detention center, outside of which more than a dozen police officers were lined up awaiting orders. As before, we three defendants were loaded into separate vans. Police cars cleared the way for us, and behind us was a black sedan with a Fujian license plate, probably commandeered by some official from the politics and law committee. Behind the sedan were two more police cars, and at the end of the motorcade drove an ambulance with a dozen medical personnel.

The seven-vehicle convoy with its flashing lights presented an impressive spectacle. Upon passing through the detention center gates, I saw people in various uniforms lining the street: security guards, police officers and sentries posted at regular intervals to maintain water-tight security. I estimated that at least 80 people, not counting plainclothes officers, were barring pedestrians from approaching the street, apparently fearing a dramatic attempt to engineer our escape.

When the motorcade reached the expressway, police officers stopped all other traffic. I heard a bailiff grumble to his colleague, "A friend of mine was on his way to the airport when he got stopped on this stretch of the highway and almost missed his flight."

Our "VIP treatment" suggested that the nationwide concern and criticism our case had attracted on the internet had put the Fujian authorities into a blind panic.

As we neared the Mawei Court, the road was lined with police cordons and blocked to all other traffic. Our supporters were already waiting at the courthouse entrance along with groups of other concerned people from all over China, citizen journalists and media journalists. How I wished I could yell out my thanks to them as I passed!

The police vans drove through the gate of the Mawei Court, and I saw several familiar faces: Butcher, Divine Justice, Wang Lihong....

As I was escorted out of the van, I saw Wang Lihong lift a camcorder and aim it at me through the metal bars. I called out, "Thanks for your hard work, Sister Lihong!"[3]

I heard Wang Lihong say in surprise, "How did she know my name?"

Two female bailiffs rushed over and grabbed my shoulders, hurrying me toward the court's entrance hall. I tripped on the stone steps and was half-dragged inside, my prison uniform covered with dust.

Just before 9:00, we were brought outside the courtroom to wait. Standing by the door, I heard the judge read out the court rules. As we were brought in, Fan Yanqiong's daughter, Lin Jingyi, called out, "Mama!" from the public gallery. The judge immediately ordered the bailiffs to eject Lin from the courtroom. After that the three of us were escorted back outside to wait.

Around the time that the performance inside was wrapping up, we were finally brought back into the courtroom. I was astonished to see the defense lawyer I'd engaged, Lin Hongnan, was not seated at the defense table. The judge hastily read out: "Following consideration, it has been decided to send the case back for further investigation." The judge then turned to the public prosecutors and whispered something, after which he turned back to us and said, "The case has been sent back for supplementary investigation. This is the second and last time that it will be sent back."

---

[3] TN: Rights activist Wang Lihong was sentenced to nine months in prison in September 2011 for staging this protest outside of the Mawei Courthouse.

Lawyer Liu Xiaoyuan registered his protest, only to be stopped by the judge, and we were escorted from the court.

I hadn't even had time to react to the truncated hearing when the bailiffs pushed me out. From behind me came my daughter's voice: "Mama, be strong!"

In the waiting room, Fan Yanqiong shrilly cursed the unjust court, shameless government and corrupt officials, and clenched her fists in agitation while someone aimed a camcorder at her from the doorway.

At that moment, a clerk took out two "records of proceedings of open trial" for us to sign. You Jingyou worried that his daughter would be too busy running around on his behalf to study for the college entrance exam. He asked to see his family, and after being refused, even he, normally calm and collected, was infuriated. He rebuked the court for toying with us, and the judge for lacking human feeling. When the clerk brought him the record of proceedings to sign, he wadded it into a ball and hurled it to the floor as if venting all his rage and indignation on that piece of paper.

I'd spent eight years petitioning for my brother and being repeatedly subjected to illegal detention, and such experiences were all too common. Although still angry, I wasn't agitated. I quietly squatted down and picked up You Jingyou's "record of proceedings," slowly smoothed out the paper, and saw that at the end was written, "Further notice will be given of the time and place of trial."

This court session had taken just two minutes to send the case back for further investigation. Why had such enormous financial and manpower resources been expended for this hasty conclusion? I decided it must have been a tactic aimed at the Beijing lawyers who had to travel so far, and the concerned netizens who had come from all over China, in hopes that messing them about in this way would make them lose interest in the case.

The three of us were quickly loaded into our separate vans, and as the motorcade passed through the main gate of the courthouse, I could see agitated netizens raising placards and brandishing yellow ribbons before they gradually disappeared from view.

STRIPPED JUDGMENT

On the afternoon of April 9, two judges from the Mawei Court, Lin Chen and Chen Li, came to the detention center to notify me that lawyer Lin Hongnan had been suspended for a year and Beijing lawyer Jin Guanghong was recuperating from a traffic accident. They asked me, "Do you need the court to appoint a lawyer to represent you at the next hearing?" I said I wanted Lin Hongnan to notify my family to appoint a lawyer for me, and asked, "Will I be sentenced to more or less than three years?"

The judges were evasive: "That's hard to say. It will depend on the seriousness of the circumstances."

I recalled how the indictment repeatedly stated that the "circumstances were serious," so it looked like the Fujian judicial organs would take their full revenge with a long prison term.

At 7:00 a.m. on April 16, the door of Cell 301 opened again, and the detention center's vice-warden and section chief arrived. Only then did I know that this was the day of the hearing at the Mawei Court. On previous occasions I'd been summoned by corrections cadres, but now the vice-warden and section chief had come together. Previously, my lawyer had come to see me or give me notification of the hearing, but why had the lawyer my family had appointed not come this time? I carried these questions with me into the jail van. The motorcade left the detention center, the roads even more tightly secured than for the March 19 hearing. Even before the motorcade reached the Mawei Court, I could see police cordons everywhere and masses of uniformed officers.

On the right side of the courthouse gate, surrounded by a police cordon, a group of people stood holding up placards, shouting slogans and brandishing their fists. One of the bailiffs in my van said, "Even Southwest Jiaotong University has come to stand watch." Given the distance and the mass of people, I couldn't see any familiar faces before the van turned into the gate.

Inside the court, the judge recited his usual stream of high-toned language. I asked, "Why didn't my lawyer come to see me before the trial, or tell me when it was scheduled?"

Li Yingshan, whom my family had engaged as my lawyer, explained, "Due to short notice, I was still on the road yesterday and didn't have time to arrange a meeting."

Usually in the detention center, paper and pencil are controlled by the cell boss, and with no prior notice of the hearing, I had to compose my statement in my head. In court I asked the judge for paper and pen, and while Fan Yanqiong and You Jingyou were giving their statements, I quickly wrote an outline so I wouldn't lose my train of thought.

My oral "final statement" was based on this outline:

"My name is Wu Huaying. I'm the elder sister of Wu Changlong, who was unjustly imprisoned in the Fuqing Discipline Inspection Commission bombing case, and I'm also one of the 'three netizens' in the Yan Xiaoling case. I'm receiving this unjust judgment today because over the past eight years I have untiringly exposed the scandal behind the bombing case, touching a raw nerve among certain Fujian officials, and they have used the Yan Xiaoling case to retaliate against me. This is simply a continuation of the bombing case, with the perpetrators of the original injustice now persecuting the victim's family as well.

"The Mawei Court has held three sessions, but the person who can best explain the 'framing' case, Yan Xiaoling's mother, Lin Xiuying, has not been allowed to testify in court. In the absence of this witness, justice is also absent; given the claims of governing the province in accordance with law, this makes a mockery of rule of law in Fujian.

"My actions are in response to what Party General Secretary Hu Jintao has repeatedly advocated, which is that citizens have 'the right to know, to participate, to express their views and to monitor the government.' If I'm found guilty this time, it will prove that what General Secretary Hu said was wrong. Or perhaps it will show that someone in Fujian is resisting the central government and suppressing the people and creating a destabilizing factor.

"I'm the sister of a modern-day Yang Naiwu,[4] but at least Yang was ultimately exonerated, and his case was written into the history books and became known to all. My eight years of petitioning

---

[4] TN: One of the most notorious cases of injustice in the late Qing dynasty.

have been filled with humiliation and torment. The arguments I've presented to Fujian's top leaders have still not cleared my brother, but have resulted in my being repeatedly jailed as well.

"All I want to say now is that the people's courts are meant to pursue justice and punish wrongdoing, and should not be used to create injustice and take the side of wrongdoers. I hope the Mawei Court will render an independent judgment based on fact and law.

"Because of defending me, lawyer Lin Hongnan has been suspended for a year, and for that I apologize to him. This incident exposes the horrific extent to which judicial corruption has progressed in Fujian. The hidden manipulations of the avengers even extend to lawyers who dare to speak the truth. Those plotters of injustice scheming in the background will someday be nailed to history's pillar of shame. I ask the judge to uphold justice, adhere to conscience, and exonerate and free all three of us."

After I finished my statement, the judge quickly called an adjournment.

When we were taken from the waiting room back into the courtroom, the judge announced: "All rise to hear the judgment of the court."

At that moment, my calm heart became tense. They had gone so far as to suspend the license of my defense lawyer, so how could we hope for a fair judgment? Their trampling of the law was already so brazen.

I didn't hear the first part of what the judge read out, but only the last sentence: "Fan Yanqiong is sentenced to two years in prison, and You Jingyou and Wu Huaying each to one year."

After delivering the judgment, the judge asked if we intended to appeal.

I immediately answered, "Absolutely." As soon as I finished speaking, the three of us were taken from the court and escorted to the jail vans. As this happened, I heard the magisterial chords of "The Internationale" from outside the courthouse.

As the jail vans passed through the gate of the Mawei Courthouse, hundreds of netizens began chanting our names: "Fan Yanqiong! Not guilty! Wu Huaying! Not guilty! You Jingyou! Not guilty!"

Tears blurred my view of them.

Once I became calmer, I felt my one-year sentence was much better than the three years I'd anticipated. I believe this was definitely related to the concern that netizens throughout China showed to the "Three Fujianese Netizens."

In only two months, I'll be reunited with the family I think about night and day, but the thought of the chronically ill Fan Yanqiong spending another year in prison plagues me with worry and guilt.

At night in bed I toss and turn, sleep eluding me. What is most on my mind is how I will continue petitioning for my brother after my release.

ETA

UNKNOWN

Xiao Qiao

Xiao Qiao, born Li Jianhong in Bengbu, Anhui Province, in the 1960s, is a signatory of Charter 08. A professional in Shanghai's financial sector, she came to the attention of the police due to her published essays and her participation in the citizens' rights defense movement. After being repeatedly detained and placed under house arrest, she lost her employment and was obliged to become a freelance writer.

In 2008, Xiao Qiao accepted an invitation from the Culture Department of Stockholm City to visit Sweden as a "guest writer." When attempting to return to China in October 2009, she was stopped at the Shenzhen border and forced to return to Hong Kong and from there back to Sweden. Xiao Qiao is one of a number of Chinese citizens who have been denied re-entry to China without any formal procedures or any reason given. Like Xiao Qiao, many of these forced exiles have refused to take foreign citizenship and remain effectively stateless while awaiting an opportunity to return to their homeland.

THE THREE YEARS SINCE I LEFT CHINA HAVE PASSED IN A FLASH. NOW I live in Sweden, a free and benevolent country. Here, among azure seas, limpid lakes and endless forests and grasslands, people live in freedom and dignity, without worrying that if they fall ill, they won't be able to afford costly medical treatment; that their children will be deprived of schooling because they're poor; that they will be left without pensions or someone to care for them in old age. The police officers patrolling the streets are there to protect and serve the people; law-abiding citizens will not have police bursting into their homes in the middle of the night, scaring and threatening them and their families, taking away their computers and personal property or absconding with their identification documents; no one will order your boss to fire you or your landlord to evict you; no one monitors your telephone calls or e-mail, or investigates your friends and family members, nor do they hide in dark corners and videotape your private life; they don't arrest you for no reason, or secretly detain and torture you without legal warrants. Here, friends in China who are enduring all kinds of tribulations are far away from me.

Information flourishes in the internet age; even across long distances, one can contact friends and family back home through the telephone and internet. But my heart remains shrouded by a lingering homesickness for that sorely missed affection and concern and the poetic and picturesque southern landscape that haunts my dreams and leaves me dejected. When I left my country three years ago, I thought it would be a brief parting, never guessing that my date of return would fade to black.

———❖———

In autumn 2009, my stay in Sweden was approaching its end, and I began packing for my return to China. Before this, friends inside and outside of China had advised me that the situation was worsening: "If you go back it's likely you'll end up in prison and won't be able to do anything. You're better off staying in the free world; perhaps there you'll be able to do something to help your friends back in China, and at the very least you'll enjoy a free life without interference."

I felt I was doing the natural thing—going home to my mother country, where I had friends and family and dreams I had not yet abandoned. In any case, I didn't believe I was "important" enough to inspire dread in what was referred to as a "rising China," a "responsible world power" that was already strong enough to provide aid during the Western economic crisis. What reason could they have to shut out a lawful citizen and invite the censure of the international community?

Prior to my departure, however, two incidents occurred that cast a pall over my return to China: The first was in March 2009, when I applied at the Chinese Embassy to renew my passport, which was reaching its ten-year expiration. Several weeks after my routine submission of personal data, I was refused. The verbal explanation the embassy gave was: "The locality of your household registration is not willing to renew your passport." The other incident was that my friend Feng Zhenghu[1] had been repeatedly turned back at the border when trying to return to China from Japan.

When I said goodbye to my friend Zhang Yu, he told me to be prepared to return to Sweden, estimating my chance of successfully entering China at "20 percent" or less. Before then, Zhang Yu himself had attempted to fly from Hong Kong to Sweden with a connecting flight at Beijing's Capital International Airport, and even though he was carrying a Chinese passport, he was forced to return to Hong Kong. It was inexplicable! Would it endanger China for him to change planes in Beijing (he had no intention of leaving the airport)? Zhang Yu had also been refused entry to Hong Kong when he had flown there for a conference soon after my arrival in Sweden in April 2008.

In the "globalized" civilization of the twenty-first century, how many of its own citizens would China, this "besieged nation," continue to barricade inside or outside of its borders?

At the time, I thought that a feeble woman like me, neither a terrorist nor a "public enemy" and only wishing to return to her country, could not possibly be worth worrying about. At most I was prepared for them to never allow me to leave China again—a year earlier, when struggling for my right to leave the country, I'd had to engage in a difficult and humiliating two-month "negotiation."

I booked a ticket from Stockholm to Hong Kong, planning to enter China at the Shenzhen border, first, because I hoped to visit friends in Hong Kong in expectation that I wouldn't have another

---

[1] TN: A Shanghai-based scholar and rights defender, Feng was sentenced to three years in prison in 2001.

such opportunity for three to five years, and second, because I worried that Shanghai's hypersensitive "domestic security" police would be lying in wait at the airport and would toss me out as they had Feng Zhenghu. I was betting on Shanghai DomSec not putting my name on the national blacklist.

With only two weeks' validity left on my Chinese passport, I set off on my journey home.

My arrival in Hong Kong on October 11 went smoothly; the immigration officer simply reminded me that next time I passed through, I would need a passport valid for at least one month. I didn't bother to tell him that the Chinese Embassy had refused to renew my passport, and simply replied that I'd remember next time. The genial immigration officer said that regulations allowed holders of mainland passports a seven-day stopover in Hong Kong, but since my passport was close to expiring, would five days be enough? I said it was and thanked him, after which he quickly filled in the departure date and let me through.

Wu Yisan, a member of the Hong Kong chapter of the Independent Chinese PEN Center,[2] let me stay at his home for a few days. In order not to give the mainland authorities "advanced warning"—after all, I had long enjoyed the "special attention" of China's "relevant departments,"[3] and who knew if Big Brother was at this moment pressing his eye to the keyhole to watch my every move?—I didn't dare arrange any high-profile gatherings, but just contacted a few close friends from PEN. They shared my impression that the authorities would feel no need to create an "international incident" by stopping me at the border, and worried more about my safety after returning to China.

—⊰•⊱—

I planned to enter Shenzhen at the Huanggang border crossing on October 15. Judging by the map, Huanggang was closer to Wu Yisan's home than the Luowu crossing was. Later Yisan told me that the Shenzhen Bay crossing was even closer, but by then I'd

[2] TN: A Hong Kong-based branch of PEN International, focusing on freedom of expression in China.
[3] TN: An oblique allusion to the public security apparatus.

already arranged through Skype for friends in Shenzhen to meet me at Huanggang, and I didn't want to change it. My friends prepared to meet me at the border at 11:00, after which we'd have lunch together.

Worrying that my luggage would be inspected, I left my laptop computer with Yisan and then set off with two suitcases.

Yisan took me to the station where a commuter train would take me to the border, then asked me, "Can we say goodbye Western fashion?" Laughing, I hugged him. He wasn't worried that I couldn't enter Shenzhen, but expected that I would not be able to come out again for some years, and that we would not see each other again for a while. He urged me to call him right away "if by any chance" something happened, and we could go back to his home and discuss the next step.

I exited Hong Kong with no problem and arrived at the Shenzhen entry point. The frontier defense officer checked my passport against his computer screen, and a flicker of surprise lit his face. He stood up from his chair and motioned to me: "Please come this way."

I asked, "Is there a problem?"

He replied, "Your passport has a problem that I have to check." He had me bring my luggage and follow him to a small partitioned area, and he called over a colleague to watch me from the doorway. He then took my passport to "request instructions from his superior."

The "unexpected" had happened after all. I took out my cell phone and dialed the first Hong Kong number that came up, thinking it was Wu Yisan's, but the person who answered was another PEN friend, Patrick Poon. I told him I'd encountered trouble at the border, and asked him to pass the message to Yisan, Zhang Yu in Sweden and other friends. I'd said this much when the person watching me from the doorway came in and warned me, "If you use your cell phone, we'll confiscate it."

I hung up and asked, "What legal measures are being taken against me now? Is there any paperwork?"

The uniformed functionary answered, "Someone will come back in a minute and tell you. Turn off your phone, otherwise we'll temporarily take care of it."

Knowing there was no room for discussion, I turned off my phone, regretting that I hadn't notified the friends who were waiting for me at the Shenzhen checkpoint, and hoping they would figure out that the situation had changed.

After 15 minutes or so, someone escorted me to a slightly larger "Interview Room," where border inspection officers informed me that they'd been instructed to search my person and my luggage, and they requested my cooperation.

I asked, "What's the reason? Am I a criminal suspect?"

The only reply was, "Orders from above."

A female officer came over to carry out a body search, and I asked to see her superior to clarify the situation. She said, "Just cooperate first, and then someone will come and talk with you."

Because the weather was quite hot, I was wearing only a T-shirt and thin pants. She patted me down and then ordered me to take off my shoes.

I asked, "Do I look like a drug trafficker? Do you think I'm carrying heroin?"

Without replying, she checked my shoes and then told me I could put them back on.

Several others went through my luggage. One uniformed officer asked, "Do you have any other ID?"

I answered, "Your colleague took my passport. Since my ID card is no use overseas, I didn't take it with me when I left."

He seemed not to believe me and asked again, so I stated firmly that I had no other ID. Seeing his continued suspicion, I said, "Do you think I have foreign identification? I was only away for a year. I'm a genuine Chinese citizen, without even a 'green card.' I'm returning to my own country, and rather than welcome me, you haul me in like a criminal, searching my person and my luggage. What law have I broken? Did you find anything?"

He smiled without replying and continued searching my luggage. During this time, a dozen uniformed and plainclothes officers came in and out, and at least one video camera was aimed at me and the items in my luggage.

They glanced through each book they found. Someone pointed out that one of the books, *Charter 08*, published by the Laogai Research Foundation, included an essay I'd written about the imprisoned intellectual Liu Xiaobo. He asked, "Did you write this?" I replied, "Yes." He said they'd have to make a photocopy. Someone next to him commented, "So she's a writer." It looked like the people searching me didn't know why I was being detained.

Someone brought in a laptop computer to inspect the U-drive and discs they'd found in my luggage, asking, "Can we look at these? Is there any personal stuff in here?"

I asked back, "If I say there is, does that mean you won't look at it? Look as much as you want."

He said, "By inspecting it in your presence we're showing you respect. You can see we aren't deleting or changing anything."

I'd been held for more than two hours, and it was long past noon. I said I hadn't eaten lunch and asked how much longer they were going to take. After some discussion, they sent someone to buy me a pork rib rice box. By the time I finished eating, the first stage of the search was finished, and they told me I could pack everything but the books on the table. I asked, "Can I pass through now? Has a senior officer communicated with you yet?"

Most of the people and the video cameras had just left, and only two uniformed female officers remained with me in the room. They told me not to worry, in a minute someone would come and talk with me.

Having nothing better to do, I picked up one of the books on the table and leafed through it, mentally rehearsing how I'd handle the questioning that was to come.

While waiting, I asked to use the restroom. One of the female officers accompanied me and asked me not to close the stall door, which was rather disconcerting.

Around 5:00 in the afternoon, the officer who'd asked about my ID came in and informed me, "Those above have decided that you can't enter today. We're sending you back to Hong Kong." He told me that the eight books on the table were "banned" and must be confiscated, then had me take the rest of my luggage and follow them.

I asked, "What reason is there for not letting me in? Is there a legal document?"

He told me I wouldn't be given a written decision; it was his superior's order in accordance with the Regulations on Control of Exit and Entry.

I asked, "Which part of the Regulations stipulates why a Chinese citizen can be prevented from entering her own country?"

He didn't know the answer. I also asked for a list of confiscated items, and he said, "Let it go, those few books aren't worth anything, just buy some more when you get back to Hong Kong."

I said, "The books may not be worth anything, but you can't just take away a citizen's personal belongings without following procedure. These books were published openly in Hong Kong and I didn't consider them illegal. And you can see that some have inscriptions—they were gifts from friends. Their value to me is not in their price."

They continued to explain that this was their superior's decision, and said that these books might not be illegal in Hong Kong, but they were not permitted on the mainland, and they hoped I'd cooperate. Since there was no chance of crossing the border today, and friends outside must have been worried about my long delay, I finally left the books behind, thinking someone might read them and learn something.

They had me get into a car with a driver and five officers, and when we stopped in the passage between the Hong Kong and Shenzhen checkpoints, several people arrived in a car from the Hong Kong side and took me to a "Visitors' Area" while they looked into my case.

I turned on my cell phone and telephoned Yisan and Patrick to let them know I was safe. I quickly described my experience at the Shenzhen border and told them I was now awaiting a reply from the Hong Kong authorities.

Patrick told me that the Independent Chinese PEN Center had already issued a statement on my detention, and everyone's greatest worry was that I'd be locked up. Yisan said that once the Hong Kong authorities let me through, he'd hurry me back to his home and buy me dinner to help me recover.

After that, I received several phone calls from reporters. It seemed that the Hong Kong border authorities seldom encountered this kind of situation, because I had to wait more than four hours, until 10:00 that night, before a uniformed female officer who had earlier received me took me to an officer in charge. He said the mainland side wasn't accepting me back for the time being, and since my passport was about to expire, they could only allow me to stay in Hong Kong for two days, until the seventeenth, and hoped that I would leave before then. If I couldn't go back to the mainland, I should go back to Sweden first. I promised to consider this, while thinking that the two-day cushion gave me time to negotiate with officials at Hong Kong's Central People's Government Liaison Office.

Back in Hong Kong, Yisan picked me up and we went to a restaurant for a late meal. I told him I planned to go to the Liaison Office the next day to demand why a Chinese citizen should not be allowed to enter her own country. If I didn't receive a reasonable reply, I would attempt another crossing the day after. Yisan said he would accompany me to the Liaison Office.

While we were talking, a reporter telephoned and said that Hong Kong Chief Executive Donald Tsang would be attending a session of the Hong Kong Legislative Council at noon the next day. The reporter suggested that I ask Tsang for help, as well as the legislator known as "Long Hair," Leung Kwok-hung. Yisan and I then decided to attend the Legislative Council meeting before going to the Liaison Office.

—————◆—————

Around 11:00 a.m. on October 16, Yisan and I met up with Leung Kwok-hung in front of the Legislative Council offices, and Leung expressed his sympathy and support. In a short time, Chief Executive Donald Tsang entered the Legislative Council building, but I couldn't penetrate the phalanx of people surrounding him. Mr. Leung introduced me to some reporters outside the building, and I gave interviews about being turned back at the border.

Mr. Leung then accompanied me to the Central Government Liaison Office. I told the guards at the door about my situation, and that I hoped to talk with an official at the Liaison Office about my difficulty returning to China. One of the guards went inside, soon afterward returning to inform me that no one inside would receive me. I asked the guards to deliver a letter I had written, but they shook their heads in refusal, so I could only toss my letter inside the doorway. The guard said, "That won't help you, they won't read it." Although my attempt to negotiate had been fruitless, I thanked Mr. Leung for his moral support. He gave me his name card and assured me he would do his best to help if I encountered any difficulties in Hong Kong.

While Yisan and I grabbed a bite to eat, I received a telephone call saying that a Western journalist had also been refused entry by the Chinese authorities. He believed it was because he had reported on worker rights defense efforts aimed at China's sweatshops. The caller, Xiao Chen, was the Chinese interpreter and assistant of this journalist, and after reading about me in the Hong Kong newspapers, they wanted to meet me.

I arranged to meet my "fellow victim" at a nearby subway station, after which the four of us went to a teahouse to talk. The journalist, Vincent Kolo, was a Briton working for a Sweden-based leftist publication, ChinaWorker.info, and had been turned back at the Luowu border that very morning.

I told them I planned to make one more attempt to enter China through Shenzhen Bay the next day so I would at least have an opportunity to argue with them face to face. If I was turned back again, I would go back to the Liaison Office the following Monday. Anticipating my failure, Mr. Kolo and Xiao Chen arranged to go with me to the Liaison Office.

Yisan mentioned a showing that night at Baptist University of *Our Children*, a documentary about the Sichuan earthquake by Ai Xiaoming, a professor at Guangzhou's Sun Yat-sen University. The sponsors had invited Professor Ai to the showing, and as I greatly admired her, Yisan and I decided to attend in spite of being exhausted by the day's activities. As our two new friends were also interested, we proceeded to Baptist University together.

The film was wonderful, and I wept many times for the children killed in shoddy "tofu" structures, and for their unfortunate parents. It was only after the film finished and discussion began that I learned that the "relevant authorities" had prevented Professor Ai from coming to Hong Kong.

During the discussion, I expressed my gratitude toward people such as Professor Ai who shouldered the toil and risk of producing such films and leaving a testament for history. I then told the audience that I'd come hoping to see Professor Ai because I'd been turned back at the border and didn't expect to have an opportunity to visit her in Guangzhou. I found that my country had become an inconceivable place where those outside were not allowed in, and those inside were not allowed out. Was this the "Chinese characteristic" of the twenty-first century?

◆◆◆

October 17. I left half of my luggage at Yisan's home and carried one suitcase with me to the Shenzhen Bay border crossing. A reporter friend came to see me off, and took some photos of me in the main hall of the Hong Kong border inspection point before shaking my hand and wishing me luck. That was around 11:30 a.m.

As before, I crossed the Hong Kong border with no problem, but upon reaching Shenzhen I was once again taken to a separate room, and my luggage was carefully searched. In the five or six hours I was detained, I repeatedly asked to see a supervisor, voiced my wish to return to my country and protested their unreasonable refusal of entry to a citizen. I said that even if I was a "criminal" they should still let me return to China to be tried in accordance with the law. From beginning to end, however, no one engaged in any substantive exchange with me.

Around 5:00, I was informed that I would not be allowed into China and was escorted back to Hong Kong. While sorting through my luggage, I found a U-drive and several discs missing. I told the border inspection police that those things had already been searched the day before at the Huanggang border crossing, which meant they weren't problematic, and that if they weren't given back to me today, I wouldn't leave. Clearly unwilling to have me protest loudly and draw attention, they advised me to keep quiet and said they'd request instructions.

About ten minutes later, a middle-aged man in a uniform arrived with a plastic bag containing my U-drive and discs: "We're giving your things back. We hope you'll cooperate and return to Hong Kong without a fuss."

I said the fuss was caused by those denying a citizen entry to her own country. He told me this was a decision made at a higher level, and emphasized that I would not be allowed in today.

Further argument was futile, and once again I was escorted back across the border. Handing my passport to the Hong Kong border inspection official who received me, I warned her, "I'm a Chinese citizen carrying a Chinese passport. I've reached the deadline of my stay in Hong Kong, and my passport is already close to expiring. I demand to return to the mainland, and you have the complete right to refuse me entry to Hong Kong. If you cooperate with the Chinese border police and take me back, you'll only cause a lot of trouble for yourselves."

She said, "Come with us first, please." I had no choice but to go with her. After I'd waited for a while in the Visitors' Area, she came out of her office and suggested that since I couldn't go back to China, my best choice would be to "return" to Sweden that day. They could book a return ticket for me.

I said my Swedish visa was only valid for a few more days, and I couldn't return to Sweden with a visa and a passport both due to expire. I wanted to return to China; I was a Chinese citizen, my home was in Shanghai, and the Chinese authorities could not refuse me. I asked her to "repatriate" me to mainland China.

She smiled and shook her head. "It's the mainland that's refusing you entry, and we have no say in the matter." She asked me to wait again while she requested advice from her superior.

I put a call through to seek advice from lawyer Albert Ho, who told me there was no legal basis for forcing me to return to Sweden. He said to tell the border inspection officials that he was coming to Shenzhen Bay to pick me up.

When that official appeared again, I told her I was engaging Albert Ho as legal counsel and that he was coming to discuss the legal aspects with me. After hearing this, the official went back in for a moment, then came out and suggested a compromise: "You're tired now. We'll let you spend the night in Hong Kong with your friends tonight, and we'll book a flight for you to Stockholm."

(I would have to pay for it myself upon reaching the airport.) "We hope you'll return to Stockholm tomorrow."

After some consideration I agreed to this arrangement, and my passport was stamped with a new entry permit that allowed me to stay for one day, until the eighteenth.

Upon reentering Hong Kong around 7:00 p.m. I telephoned Albert Ho and told him he didn't have to come for me. He suggested that I not leave Hong Kong for the time being, and arranged to meet me at his Legislative Council office on the morning of the nineteenth to discuss the next step. After that I went back to Yisan's home.

First thing in the morning on October 19, Yisan and Patrick Poon accompanied me to Albert Ho's office. Mr. Ho gave me some legal advice, then took me on a tour of the Legislative Council building. Viewing the chamber, I imagined Hong Kong councilors engaged in heated debate. I thought of how Hong Kong residents could listen in on the debates, how they had the right to contact councilors and make appeals, and how councilors had to represent the people's interests, otherwise they might lose the next election. Comparing this to our multi-level people's congresses, with their aye-votes and applause, my feelings were bittersweet.

After parting with Mr. Ho, Yisan, Patrick and I went to the Liaison Office, where I was again told that no one would see me. I then took out placards stating, "I Want to Go Home" and "Free Liu Xiaobo and All Other Prisoners of Conscience." Vincent Kolo also arrived with a placard stating in Chinese and English, "Defending Workers' Rights and Interests Is Not a Threat to State Security."

Several reporters arrived to cover our protest, and I told them, "I came here today hoping to give the Chinese government a chance to correct its error, but the Central Government Liaison Office officials refuse to communicate."

Wu Yisan told the reporters, "The Chinese government is insane! They have millions of soldiers and hundreds of thousands of police officers, so why are they scared of a girl? Why not let her go home?"

The police arrived and asked what had happened. After we told them, the police said we could protest, but they asked to see our IDs. When they saw that my entry permit had expired the day before, they asked me to come to the police station.

I told Yisan and Patrick not to worry, because Hong Kong had rule of law, and I believed the police would treat me fairly; after reaching the police station, I would continue demanding "repatriation" to mainland China.

Upon arrival at the Western District police station, the police took me to an isolation room, on the door of which was posted the rights of a person being questioned. A policeman noticed Liu Xiaobo's name on my placard and asked if I knew him. I said Liu Xiaobo was my friend, and that he was a patriotic intellectual imprisoned by the Chinese government. Judging by the policeman's expression, he was aware of Liu Xiaobo's case. With the policeman's permission, I telephoned Patrick and told him of my situation, and Patrick said he'd contact some journalists to follow up on my story.

The policeman asked a few more questions and then took my passport away for further study. I once again asked them to "repatriate" me, and they said they'd consider my request. My situation must have been a hot potato, however, because I waited for nearly four hours before a policeman finally came in and said they had to take me to the Immigration Department.

There I waited for more than an hour before an immigration officer said they would extend my stay in Hong Kong, but hoped I would leave before my passport expired on October 24. I planned to push for mediation in Hong Kong in the meantime.

———※———

In the days afterward, friends from all over gave me two suggestions. One was that I remain in Hong Kong and continue to fight, and the second was that since I had no hope of returning to China for the time being, I should go back to Sweden and seek help from a democratic country. I consulted with lawyer Albert Ho and with

Reverend Chu Yiu-ming of the Hong Kong Alliance,[4] and they said that if I chose to stay in Hong Kong, they would do their best to help me obtain legal right of residency. However, that would set a precedent following Hong Kong's return to Chinese sovereignty in 1997, and they didn't know how long it would take. It might be faster and easier to apply to the United Nations to be recognized as a refugee and then be assigned to a Western country. I considered the fact that I would be unable to support myself in Hong Kong without legal status, and that I couldn't keep staying at Yisan's home after all the trouble I'd already caused him. After weighing all the factors, I decided to return to Sweden before my passport expired, and then work out how to continue fighting for my right of return.

After reaching my decision, I telephoned my parents in Shanghai. I hadn't told them about my plans to return home, hoping to spare them worry and to give them a happy surprise when I arrived. My father seemed shocked to hear my voice: "Where are you now?" When I said I was in Hong Kong, his voice became anxious: "Hurry back to Sweden! Whatever you do, don't come back! The police have been here and say you're being kept out for your own good, otherwise they'll arrest you and send you to prison."

I told Father I was safe in Hong Kong, but he worried that the Chinese authorities would be angry enough to cross the border and arrest me, and he told me to leave quickly.

Through Skype, I contacted Feng Zhenghu, who'd been refused entry several times and was now visiting the United States. He said he'd read in the newspaper about my situation, and he hoped Hong Kong friends would help me persevere. He said he would return to Japan and continue fighting for his right of return. He had a new plan, but didn't tell me the details. Not long after I returned to Sweden, Feng flew once more from Tokyo to Shanghai, and after being forcibly turned back, he refused to leave Tokyo's Narita Airport, staying in the airport's transit lounge for three months in protest,

---

[4] TN: The Hong Kong Alliance in Support of Patriotic Democratic Movements in China was established in Hong Kong during the protests in China in 1989. The organization continues to organize memorial activities in Hong Kong on the anniversary of the June 4th crackdown.

like in the film *The Terminal*.[5] In that way he finally regained his right to return to China. I wish all happiness to Feng Zhenghu, who remains in China, and all others engaged in resistance for their rights as citizens.

Before I left Hong Kong, "Long Hair" Leung Kwok-hung arranged a joint press conference for me and Mr. Kolo, and talked about our being refused entry to China. Then Mr. Leung and several students from Baptist University saw me off at the airport.

In December 2009, the Swedish government granted me permanent residency as a "political refugee." I've gone repeatedly to the Chinese Embassy to negotiate renewal of my Chinese passport, without success. For no reason, my own country has stripped me of my nationality and my right of return, leaving me dependent on the protection of my temporary host country. This is a huge irony for China as a member of the United Nations Human Rights Council. But the pace of world civilization cannot be long obstructed by any autocratic power; China cannot remain forever outside international trends, and the "Berlin Wall" that isolates Chinese citizens from free exchange with the rest of the world will one day tumble to the ground. I believe that day is not far off.

---

[5] *The Terminal*, a 2004 American comedy-drama, depicts a man trapped at New York's John F. Kennedy International Airport when he's denied entry to the United States but can also not return to his country, which is undergoing revolution. The film was inspired by Iranian refugee Mehran Karimi Nasseri, who lived in France's Charles de Gaulle International Airport from 1988 to 2006.

MY EXPERIENCE AS A CITIZEN

FROM DRINKING TEA TO SEARCH AND SEIZURE

Gu Chuan

Gu Chuan, born Ding Fangguan in Sichuan in the 1980s, is a signatory of Charter 08. He has served as a website editor and magazine reporter, among other jobs, and was one of the writers who contributed essays to the book The Death of Reform, *published in Hong Kong in early December 2008. The contributors, most of them young scholars in their thirties or younger, suggested that the failure of the government's economic reform policies signaled the need to establish constitutional government. Coming just before the publication of Charter 08, this book caused considerable concern in official circles.*

Gu Chuan's participation in the rights defense movement has put him under long-term police surveillance and harassment, as described in this essay. On February 19, 2011, after using Twitter to disseminate information regarding a "Jasmine stroll" (a low-key form of protest in which groups of people walk together in public places without overtly breaking regulations on public gatherings and protests), Gu Chuan was once again subjected to a house search, and he disappeared for 63 days, during which time he was tortured, an incident described by his wife, Li Xin'ai, in another essay in this collection. After a number of unsuccessful attempts, Gu Chuan and his family were allowed to leave China in July 2012 and now live in exile in the United States.

"DRINKING TEA"

The first time I was "teaed" was on April 19, 2005. At that time, I'd just started working at blogchina.com. One morning, a colleague told me that the police were asking for me downstairs at the security post. When I went down, I found two plainclothes officers from the Beijing Municipal Public Security Bureau, one surnamed Han and the other named Wang Feng. They asked me if my name was Gu Chuan, saying that Gu Chuan was very famous, like everyone on their list. They then asked if I'd once testified for Wang Yi, and I said yes.

Wang Yi had self-published four books: a collection of his commentaries entitled *Too Beautiful for the Central Government*, the first volume of Liao Yiwu's *Cases of Chinese Injustice*, Kang Zhengguo's autobiographical *My Counterrevolutionary Career* and Wang Jianhui's novel *Is There?* These books were produced for circulation between friends and were all designated with the words "For internal exchange, reproduction forbidden." He had sent me several sets. On March 21, 2005, the Sichuan Provincial Press and Publications Office confiscated 906 volumes that Wang Yi had arranged for express delivery, on the grounds of "suspected illegal publication." Wang Yi asked me to provide him with a testimony to the effect that these books were for scholarly exchange between friends. It never occurred to me that this testimony would cause Beijing Domestic Security to ask me in for "tea."

The DomSec police asked me how I knew Wang Yi and why I'd written a testimony for him. They repeatedly stressed that I shouldn't let Wang Yi use me. I replied that there was no question of being used; I'd written the truth.

They then shifted to the topic of memorializing Zhao Ziyang,[1] and that's when I understood that this was their main focus, and that the Wang Yi matter was merely a pretext. (Likewise, the incident related below when they called me in and searched my

---

[1] TN: Zhao Ziyang (1919–2005) was CCP General Secretary when he was dismissed after voicing sympathy for protesters at Tiananmen Square in May 1989. Zhao spent the rest of his life under house arrest.

house on April 9, 2010, was because of the Chinese Human Rights Defenders website, and the symposium was just a pretext.)

Zhao Ziyang died on January 17, 2005. The next day, I wrote an essay, "Our Grief," in his memory. I also participated in a signature campaign launched by Li Jian and others to offer condolences to Zhao's family. Li Jian came to Beijing to deliver the signatures, and on the morning of January 24 looked me up where I was working then, at an education research institute on the fourth floor of the National Library office building. At noon he and I went to lunch nearby with several others. As we were walking back to the office with Li ahead of the rest of us, four DomSec police appeared out of nowhere and bundled Li Jian into a parked car. All we could do was go back to the office and wait for news. After an hour or so, Li returned and said DomSec wasn't allowing him to go to Zhao's home to deliver the signed condolence letter, and wanted to send him back to Dalian, so he'd just come back for his things. He then gave the condolence letter to me and asked me to take it to Zhao's family. The Party required any members of the public wanting to express condolences to first apply over the telephone, and then on the twenty-fifth go to the Jintai Hotel to pick up an "attendance permit." I put in my application, but when I went to the Jintai Hotel, I wasn't given an "attendance permit." Even so, I passed the signed letter of condolence to Zhao's granddaughter, and she expressed her gratitude.

So when the DomSec police asked what I'd done when Zhao died, I said I'd passed on the letter of condolence for Li Jian. They said I'd been used by Li Jian, but I said that wasn't so, I'd done it as a citizen expressing condolences for Zhao Ziyang. After all, Zhao had once been general secretary of the Communist Party, so why should we not mourn him? They said the government had made a determination that Zhao couldn't be mourned, and mourning him was going against the government. They then asked me if I saw what I'd done wrong, and told me to write an acknowledgment of error. I said I'd done nothing wrong and I refused to write the acknowledgment.

They required me to e-mail them every day reporting my whereabouts, and I promised to do so. On April 19, 2005, at

5:51 p.m., I sent my first report to the e-mail address I'd been given, hansir@263.net, as follows:

Mr. Wang, Mr. Han: Greetings! Today I worked and participated in the Zhongguancun[2] Forum on protection of intellectual property rights at the Friendship Hotel. That's about all. Ding Fangguan, April 19, 2005

At 9:57 p.m. on the same day, they replied as follows:

Xiao Ding: Greetings! We received your e-mail. We hope you can keep your promise of taking a more positive attitude toward reducing the "distance" between us, and hope that your e-mail tomorrow will be more detailed. Until later.

From then on, I sent them roughly similar e-mail messages. For example, on April 22, 2005, at 6:09 p.m.:

I worked all day today, nothing further. Ding Fangguan

After several days I tired of this, and set up an e-mail to be sent to them automatically at a fixed time every day. On May 4, 2005, at 5:05 p.m., I received a response:

Xiao Ding: Greetings! We were quite gratified to see your e-mail during the May 1 holiday[3] not knowing if you were on vacation. If you're on vacation, you may not have easy access to the internet, but your persistence in spite of that is commendable, and your attitude pleases me. However, looking more carefully at your e-mails, their inadequacy is that the content and wording is always identical. I'm not insisting that you take notes of your every activity (of course, it's impossible that you've done nothing at all over the last few days, I know this very well and need say no more), but I just want you to tell me a bit about what's on your mind, because after our two previous meetings and conversations, I feel we aren't in complete agreement on some issues. You must have thought about these matters over the past few days, and must have some

---

[2] TN: Zhongguancun, a technology hub in Haidian District in northwestern Beijing, is often referred to as "China's Silicon Valley."

[3] TN: China observes Labor Day on May 1, usually as a three-day holiday.

opinions, so I propose using this channel to communicate our views. I feel this is a method you can accept and that won't greatly affect your work and daily life. If we change to a different method, looking you up every few days or telephoning you every day, that's fine for us, but from your perspective it might not be as good for your work or daily routine, and that's why we've made this arrangement, but after such a long time I'm not all that satisfied with your performance! As far as just sending an e-mail, I have no complaint, because you actually have done that regularly and without fail, but in terms of content, I'm afraid it's been unsatisfactory from start to finish. From my perspective, I think I'd be right in saying that you've been faking it. On the first day you wrote, I replied in what I think was a very sincere and clear manner. Since then I've not been satisfied with your messages, and by waiting until today to reply to you, I've been giving you plenty of time to think things over, hoping you would understand and make a good faith effort, but up to today I haven't seen that. For this reason, I'm writing today to explain this to you; it's the last time I'll say anything, and I hope you'll think it over carefully. If I still don't see good faith on your part, I think we'll have to change our method.

After that, I continued to send them the same message every day, such as this one on May 12, 2005:

Mr. Wang, Mr. Han: Greetings! Today I worked, and that's all. Ding Fangguan, May 12, 2005

That's the last e-mail I sent them.

The first time I "drank tea," they asked me my address and I told them. Several days later, a dozen policemen came to my home and tried to enter. I wasn't home, but my landlord was scared out of his wits and subsequently asked me to move.

After that they had me come in to "drink tea" twice more. One time, before May 1, I was taken to the Haidian District Dongshengyuan police station, where they asked me to acknowledge my error, and I refused. They also wanted me to write a pledge, which I likewise refused. After I was forced to move, they asked me my address again, and I said, "Last time I told you, you threatened my landlord, so this time I'm not going to tell you." The third time I "drank tea" was after May 1, and I told them I wouldn't write them any more reports.

During this third "tea," it was invariably Han playing "bad cop" and threatening me, while Wang played "good cop" to soften me up, but they still didn't have anything on me, so they finally said they'd go to my boss, Fang Xingdong, and tell him about me. Fang told me afterward, "Go have a talk with the police and get it over with."

After a while they contacted me again and said we'd go to a teahouse (the previous times there hadn't actually been tea; they'd just given me water). They drove me to the entrance of the Imperial Garden, where we just sat in the car and talked. After that, they didn't contact me again. I should mention that they told me not to associate with "sensitive persons" any more, but when I asked them to provide me with a list, they said this was a state secret.

UNEMPLOYMENT

On April 17, 2010, Zhu Di, the editor of *Southern Metropolitan Daily*'s historical commentary page, came under criticism from Guangdong's provincial Party secretary, Wang Yang, and was dismissed after publishing a commentary entitled "Love of Country Doesn't Mean Love of the Government." This incident reminded me of losing my own job as editor of blogchina.com.

On October 17, 2006, I was working the morning shift when I published in my own column an essay entitled "Patriotism Requires First Becoming a Citizen," to which I added a postscript: "This article was originally commissioned for the April 2006 issue of *China Youth* magazine, but it was considered too radical and the magazine didn't publish it. Although half a year has passed, my thinking hasn't changed. At that time, the topic of discussion was 'are Wuhan University's cherry blossoms a disgrace?', and now the discussion is on the 'September 18 incident.'[4] Both relate to Japan and patriotism, so I've pulled out this essay to publish here."

---

[4] TN: Wuhan University is famous for its annual springtime cherry blossom festival, which began during the Japanese occupation. As nationalist sentiments in China turned against Japan in 2006, some people began referring to the university's trees as "flowers of shame" and calling for their destruction. The September 18, 1931, Mukden Incident was engineered by the Japanese military as a pretext for invading what was then known as Manchuria in northeast China.

When blogchina.com's deputy editor, Guo Minghu (online name Xiaoguo Guamin),[5] read the essay, he messaged me to delete it. In a collegial tone I asked, "Must I really delete it?"

Guo Minghu thought I was challenging his authority and burst out, "Delete it or you're through!"

I fired back, "Then I'm through!"

Guo told me to process my resignation after finishing my shift, but instead I went to see editor-in-chief Wang Junxiu, who said, "You don't have to go through with it, he can't do that to you."

In fact, Guo had come to blogchina.com because of me. After becoming chief editor, I'd hired him as a columnist. In that way he came to know Fang Xingdong and Wang Junxiu, and later Chen Yongmiao recommended him as deputy editor-in-chief of blogchina.com. Before he joined the blog, Wang Junxiu had asked me what Guo was like, and I'd said he was all right. The truth was he was power-mad and fractious. He'd worked at a number of other websites such as Tianya, Bailing and Zhongsou, but had always been kicked out after clashes with staff or management.

Prior to my essay on patriotism, we'd gotten along fine, but this incident brought out his true colors. In order to ensure I'd lose my job, he contacted Chen Hua, deputy director of the Beijing Municipal News Office Internet Management Division, and said I was "registered" with StateSec[6] (I'd once mentioned in conversation that DomSec had called me in for tea). Chen then handed down three directives: 1) blogchina.com would be suspended for three days; 2) the columns of several independent writers would be terminated; 3) the blogchina.com chief editor was to be disposed of. After this, Guo telephoned Wang Junxiu and said that blogchina.com's three-day suspension had nothing to do with him, a clumsy denial that exposed his culpability. Fang Xingdong had me take a month's leave of absence until things cooled down.

After that, Guo Minghu wrote a letter to the board of directors demanding that Fang Xingdong be removed as chairman of

---

[5] TN: This phrase, literally "Small nation, small population," refers to the ancient philosopher Laozi's vision of the ideal state.

[6] I.e., State Security. Unlike Domestic Security, State Security is mainly responsible for security matters relating to foreign countries. Some individuals suspected of involvement with foreign affairs or international organizations are sometimes put under simultaneous surveillance by both StateSec and DomSec.

the board, and Fang got mad enough to kick him out. I went back to work at blogchina.com. One day, Guo Minghu went to the blogchina.com office, and seeing me there, he informed Chen Hua, who again demanded that blogchina.com deal with me. Under the circumstances, I had no choice but to leave. My unemployment was therefore indirectly related to "drinking tea" with DomSec.

MORE TEA

The next time I "drank tea" was on January 9, 2009, because of Charter 08. Just before Charter 08 was published, I heard that the charter's initiators, Liu Xiaobo and Zhang Zuhua, had been called in and had their homes searched, and the passport I'd left at Mr. Zhang's home had also been confiscated. By then I'd already signed the charter, but in hopes of getting my passport back, I decided to withdraw my signature. Even so, up to now I haven't gotten my passport back, and my new one has been confiscated as well. What a pain!

That's why the first round of signatures for Charter 08 didn't include my name. However, DomSec told me that the copy of Charter 08 in their possession had my name in the first round, and the book *Charter 08* subsequently published by Hong Kong's Open Books also included my name, even though Zhang Zuhua, the book's editor, told me that the name list he provided didn't include my name. Such being the case, I hereby formally declare: I (Gu Chuan, real name Ding Fangguan, Beijing rights defender) consent to sign Charter 08.

A month after Charter 08 was published, on the morning of January 9, 2009, I received a telephone call from Officer Zhu of the Xiangshan police station (near where I was living at the time) saying that someone wanted to talk with me. In the police station's second floor conference room, I saw the aforementioned Beijing PSB officer Wang Feng with two other DomSec cops from the Haidian Division. Wang Feng and one DomSec officer sat on the south side of a round conference table, and I sat across from them with the other cop next to me.

Wang Feng said, "It's been a while, hasn't it? Did you think we'd forgotten you?" They then asked if I knew about Charter 08, and I said I did. They asked how I knew, and I said through Boxun.[7] They asked if I'd signed, and I said I endorsed it but hadn't signed. They asked if I knew Liu Xiaobo and Zhang Zuhua. I said I knew Liu Xiaobo, but not well, and that I was a friend of Mr. Zhang and often went to his home to borrow books.

During the "tea session," my cell phone rang. It was my wife, Li Xin'ai, but they wouldn't let me answer and told me to turn off the phone and place it on the table. I did as they said. Wang Feng went out at one point, and when he came back, he passed by me, picked up my phone and took it to his table. The tea drinking ended quickly, and Wang Feng and the DomSec officer next to him went out again, at which point I thought to get my cell phone back. But when I stood up, the DomSec officer next to me (whom I'll refer to as "Tumbling DomSec") grabbed me. I broke free and moved toward my phone, and he acted as if I'd pushed him over, then grabbed me by the legs and tried to pull me down while shouting for the other DomSec officer to come and help him. The other officer came back with Wang Feng and separated us. Tumbling Dom-Sec stood up and tried again to trip me, but I dodged him. After things calmed down, Tumbling DomSec falsely accused me of hitting him and said that if I still lived in Haidian, he'd come and give me grief. I said, "How would I dare hit you? This is a police station, your turf. I just wanted my cell phone back, and you blocked me and fell down on your own." Wang Feng said, "I didn't know you'd developed such a temper since I last saw you." After the tea drinking ended, the DomSec officer with Wang Feng escorted me downstairs and soothed me, saying that he and I and Tumbling DomSec were all the same age, so he hoped I'd cut them some slack.

In April 2009, I moved to Tiantong Xiyuan in Chaoyang District. Of course this wasn't out of fear of Tumbling DomSec—we were about to have a baby, and I'd found a larger apartment there. Soon afterward, Officer Zhu of the Xiangshan police station telephoned and asked if I still lived in Xiangshan. When I said no, he asked my specific address, but I just said it wasn't in Xiangshan.

---

[7] TN: An overseas website that publishes China-related news and rumors as well as essays by Chinese dissidents.

The next time DomSec surfaced was before Liu Xiaobo's first court appearance. Two DomSec officers from the Changping Division and two cops from Dongxiaokou came to my home to "drink tea." They said they'd gotten my address wrong and had knocked on my neighbor's door, and had finally found me through my landlord. Before Liu Xiaobo's second court appearance, the two Changping DomSec cops came to my home again. Their objective both times was mainly to keep me from attending Liu Xiaobo's trial. DomSec's visits alarmed my landlord, who made us move as soon as our lease was up.

I should also mention that on January 8, 2010, when I was on my way to vacation in Thailand, a border inspection officer at Capital International Airport informed me: "The relevant department has issued a notice that in accordance with Article 8 of the Regulations on Control of Exit and Entry, you are forbidden to leave the country." On January 10, I returned to the airport and was again informed that I was prohibited from leaving.

SEARCH AND SEIZURE

On April 9, 2010, just one week after we'd moved to our new home, my wife, Li Xin'ai, looked out of our window early in the morning and saw another vehicle parked next to our car with three people inside reading newspapers, and one was a cop from the Dongxiaokou police station who had previously come to our home. Li Xin'ai said, "Are they here for us?" I said, "Don't get nervous." At 10:30, we went down to buy groceries and stopped to put a cleaning brush in our car, mainly so we could see if the people inside the other car were actually DomSec cops.

The three cops inside sat up and started the motor, and the one who'd come to our home before said, "We've been waiting for you all day! Come with us to the police station. We need to check something out."

Li Xin'ai asked, "How long will he be there?"

He answered, "It'll be quick."

After bringing me to the Dongxiaokou police station, they told me to shut off my cell phone and place it on the table, but I ignored them. Someone calling himself the deputy station chief came in and asked why I hadn't taken my phone out. I said, "That's a violation of my right to communication. You can ask me what you like, but I'm not putting my cell phone on the table."

The deputy station chief then began shouting threats at me.

I said, "I'm taking down your badge number."

He replied, "I'll tear off my badge and see what you do."

I said, "I've had enough." I stood up to leave, and he also stood up and pushed at my shoulder, but I grabbed the front of his shirt. At that moment, the other two cops came over and pushed me back into my chair. I said this wasn't the first time I'd dealt with DomSec, or with the municipal and local PSB either. When he heard this, he lowered his voice and eased back. He said that when I stood up, he thought I was attacking him. I said, "How would I dare to attack you in a police station?"

Then he started in, "If Mao Zedong hadn't taken control of China, would things be as good as they are today?"

I said, "It's because Mao took control of China that tens of millions of people starved to death. Without Mao, China would be a better place."

He went on about the Party being our mother and so on, and I said cut the crap and get to the point. But he refused to get down to specifics, insisting that I cooperate by putting my cell phone on the table. I said that was out of the question. At that moment, Li Xin'ai called, and they told me, "Don't answer it, if you do we'll take your phone away," so I didn't answer. I asked again what they'd brought me in for, and first they said that their superior was on his way, and then that the municipal PSB were on their way. Around noon they gave me something to eat.

Only later did I learn that while I was eating, Wang Na of the municipal PSB was at my home with eight or nine cops turning it upside down, and that they seized two notebook computers, two passports, a portable hard drive, a U-drive, two big folders of business cards, 32 notebooks, 62 computer printouts, 12 written agreements and receipts from the authors of *The Dead End of China's Reforms* and *The Death of Reform*, a typescript of my *The Liang Qichao Era*, a typescript of Wu Zuolai's *News Commentary Is a Form of Power*, as well as many books: *Charter 08* (collector's edition), *Charter 08 and China's Transformation*, Havel's *Essays* and Michnik's

Toward a Civil Society (translated by Cui Weiping and others), Cui Weiping's *Before Justice*, Zhang Yihe's *The Past Is Like Smoke*, *The Dead End of China's Reforms* by Chen Ziming and others, Wang Lixiong's *Inching Toward Democracy: China's Third Way*, Zhang Zuhua's *Political Reform and Systemic Innovation: Mainland China's Road to Constitutional Democracy*, *The Human Rights Yearbook (2007–2008)*, a photocopy of the Taiwan edition of Arendt's *The Origins of Totalitarianism*, and a copy each of *Gale* magazine and *Ark* magazine. They left behind two sheets of paper listing 26 confiscated items, with the case officers signing off as Jiao Shuaishuai and Li Shuo. They had also photographed a T-shirt printed with "Give back my freedom," and they had gone through our bank cards and deposit books and photographed them.

At 1:00 that afternoon, a person claiming to be from the municipal PSB took me to a different room. He and someone carrying a camcorder sat on either side of me, while a person in a police uniform sat across from me. They first showed me a summons, which made no mention of any crime. I asked them for their police identification, and the person who'd brought me in said, "According to the law, when a uniformed police officer is present, it's not necessary to produce police credentials." In fact, they were afraid their names would be made public. It's said that DomSec typically uses false names, so Wang Feng, Wang Na, Jiao Shuaishuai and Li Shuo may all have been pseudonyms.

They first asked about my relationship with the Chinese Human Rights Defenders website,[8] believing I was an employee. They said the website was backed by the American National Endowment for Democracy and the Central Intelligence Agency, as well as the US Congress, so the CHRD website was a matter of Sino-US relations. They said that working for CHRD was what was historically known as being a "traitor to China," or in modern parlance, a "running dog." I said I had no relationship with CHRD, so neither term applied to me; in fact, it was the Communist Party that was a traitor or running dog, having at one point used the Soviet ruble and having organized student demonstrations to "defend the USSR."

---

[8] TN: http://chrdnet.com/.

They asked again if I knew Zhang Zuhua, and I said he was my friend and that he was very well-connected. By this I meant that Zhang had once served on the standing committee of the Communist Youth League Central Committee with people such as Premier Li Keqiang and Vice-Premier Liu Yandong, and had been secretary of the Central State Agency Youth League under Luo Gan,[9] who had served with him on the Party Work Committee for Central State Organs. After the June 4th massacre, the Communist authorities had asked him to serve as mayor of Yingkou City so he could avoid the post–June 4th investigations, but he had refused point blank and no longer wallowed with the Communists in their mire.

They told me that when Zhang's home was searched, more than 1.6 million *yuan* was confiscated, money left over from payments CHRD had given us. I immediately stated that I didn't work for CHRD, and that the money wasn't CHRD's but belonged to Zhang's parents and in-laws. They asked who'd told me this, and I said Zhang had told me. They said, "You've become Zhang's dog and you're being used by him." I said, "I'm no one's dog and I'm not being used by anyone; this is my independent judgment."

They then asked about the next day's conference, saying it was sponsored by CHRD and they wouldn't allow me to attend. I said I didn't know who was sponsoring it, and if I wasn't participating I'd have to tell the organizer. This was a conference on environmental protection called "Environmental Disaster and Government and Citizen Responsibility." It shouldn't have caused any sensitivity, but because they were convinced it was sponsored by CHRD, Beijing's entire DomSec force had been deployed to prevent the conference from being held. I later heard that Zhang Zuhua and other participants had been called in for "tea," and several also had DomSec standing shift with them until noon the next day.[10] On the morning of the conference, local police took participant Wang Junxiu off to the southern suburb of Daxing, and he didn't return home until 6:00 that night. According to CHRD's reports,

---

[9] TN: Prior to his retirement in 2007, Luo Gan was the Communist regime's security chief and a member of the Standing Committee of the Political Bureau (Politburo) of the Communist Party Central Committee, putting him in China's innermost circle of power.

[10] When rights defenders are put under house arrest, police officers stand sentry outside their door, a practice known as "standing shift."

as many as 30 people were "teaed" because of this conference. I'd suffered the worst treatment, with my home being searched as well.

Wang Na arrived at the Dongxiaokou police station after searching my home and carried out ideological work on me, urging me to think of my parents and child. I said, "Don't give me that. I won't listen."

She said, "Whether you want to hear it or not, I'm saying it. I have to fulfill my duty to pull you back from the precipice." She went on, "Why not just tell us everything you've done? As they say, when you're in the hot seat, why not think of yourself?"

This was the devil's own logic, and as Marx was Satan's disciple,[11] her words were consistent with Communist Party logic. At the time I thought, when you say I have to think of myself, isn't that serving your own purpose? Why pretend to be thinking of my interests when all you want is to chew your way to the top?

The interview formally ended at 4:30 in the afternoon. I'd spent six hours at the police station, including three and a half hours since my formal summons, my time utterly wasted listening to their crap. When they asked me to sign off on the interview, I said, "In Liu Xiaobo's case, you arbitrarily edited your interviews with others to use as evidence against Liu, so I'm not going to sign."

They said, "Then write that you refuse to sign, and sign that."

During the interview, they asked my views on Liu Xiaobo's case, and I said, "It's criminalizing expression. The police, prosecution and courts colluded to blow it all out of proportion, and now Liu might win this year's Nobel Peace Prize."

They said, "So you're saying that imprisoning Liu Xiaobo was a good thing." They went on, "Starting with Wei Jingsheng and Xu Wenli, no one going up against the state has ended well."

I said, "That depends on what you consider a good end. Before the Communist Party took power in 1949, the Kuomintang said the Communists wouldn't have a good end, but history keeps on

---

[11] TN: Probably referring to claims in a 1986 book by Richard Wurmbrand, a pastor imprisoned under Romania's Communist regime, that Marx once belonged to a satanic cult formed by his closest comrades.

changing. Look at Mandela in South Africa, and Kim Dae-jung in Korea. Didn't they end well?"

They said, "What you're saying is that someday you'll be judging us."

I said, "You said it, not me." Of course, every Chinese citizen lives in hope for that day.

IN THE SHADOW OF A RISING CHINA

Ding Zilin and Jiang Peikun

Ding Zilin and her husband, Jiang Peikun, born in the 1930s, are both professors of philosophy at Renmin University and are signatories of Charter 08. Following the death of their son Jiang Jielian in the June 4, 1989, crackdown, Ding launched the Tiananmen Mothers Campaign to identify as many victims as possible and to rally the family members of victims to demand an official reassessment of the Tiananmen Incident, the release of all political prisoners arrested during the 1989 protests, and full disclosure and official accountability.[1] Since then, Ding and Jiang have been subjected to periodic house arrest and detention, and they and other members of the Tiananmen Mothers are put under close surveillance on the June 4th anniversary and at other politically sensitive times. Unlike most of the contributors to this volume, Ding and Jiang are the targets of State Security police rather than Domestic Security, mainly due to their overseas contacts. The Tiananmen Mothers were nominated for the Nobel Peace Prize in 2002 and 2003.

INTRODUCTION

For 74 days, beginning with the announcement of Liu Xiaobo's Nobel Peace Prize on October 8, 2010, the landlines, cell phones and internet in our Beijing apartment and our village home in

---

[1] TN: For further information on the Tiananmen Mothers Campaign, see the organization's website at www.tmc-hk.org (accessed May 29, 2013).

Wuxi, Jiangsu Province, were all cut off, and we lost contact with friends and relatives in China and abroad.

Our experience suggests that the "harmonious society" constructed by this "rising great power" is truly "advancing with the times."[2] Although the two of us have long been branded as the parents of a June 4th victim and as dissidents, and over the past two decades have experienced two periods of detention, as well as having our communications cut off and our movement restricted for 50 days, this was our longest period of confinement to date. Perhaps out of consideration for our advanced years and physical frailty, we were not moved to a different location, but were held in the Wuxi home we'd built in our son's memory. Although we were in our own home, the isolation of losing our communication, freedom of movement and regular visits from friends and relatives made those 74 days the loneliest, hardest period of our lives.

It can be imagined how much our friends and relatives worried when we were out of contact for so long. We first thought of Liu Xia, Liu Xiaobo's wife, and wondered whether she would be allowed to attend the Nobel ceremony in Stockholm. We also missed our fellow Tiananmen Mother, Xu Jue, who had fallen seriously ill in 2009. Hearing her voice every day had been a source of comfort and strength, but not knowing how she was doing left us in a state of constant worry.

For this reason, we decided that as soon as we were able to return to Beijing, the first thing we'd do was to tell all our friends and relatives of our experience and relieve their worries.

BROADBAND AND LANDLINE CUT OFF

Just after 4:00 p.m. on October 8, 2010, with the Nobel Peace Prize soon to be announced, Jiang Peikun turned on his computer, and our eyes remained glued to the screen. At 5:00 the announcement was made that the prize had gone to Liu Xiaobo. A reporter from Radio France immediately telephoned, but Ding Zilin had barely spoken when the line broke up and then went dead. The

---

[2] TN: All recent political slogans.

phone rang again, and this time the call was from a reporter for *HRIC Biweekly*.[3] Ding Zilin quickly said, "This is the first good news we've had in 21 years," and then the line went dead again. The phone kept ringing after that, but there was no sound when we picked up.

At 5:13, we used our cell phone to call Liu Xia in Beijing, but the operator said Liu's line was busy. When we tried again later, the operator said the line was disconnected. At 5:30, the landline at our Wuxi apartment was completely disconnected, and when Jiang Peikun tried to access the internet, he found that we'd lost our broadband.

That night and the next morning, we used our cell phone to contact several other Tiananmen parents and tell them of Liu Xiaobo's Nobel Prize. Everyone was excited and eager to spread the word, and it was suggested that we should draft a statement.

At noon on October 9, considering Jiang Peikun's health, we used our cell phone to contact State Security in Beijing and told them that Wuxi StateSec had cut off our internet and landline. Beijing promised to send someone to "sort things out." The next morning, around 10:00, Beijing StateSec officers arrived at our home and explained that Wuxi StateSec was worried that we'd accept interviews from foreign media, issue a statement or even go to the Shanghai World Expo to meet up with foreign reporters. After some discussion, we reluctantly promised not to publish a statement or accept interviews, on the condition that our home phone and broadband would be immediately restored.

On the morning of October 11, cut off from everything happening outside, we brought Freegate[4] to the home of a relative in a neighboring village and accessed foreign websites from there. We saw a report that when Liu Xia visited Liu Xiaobo in prison and told him he'd won the Nobel Prize, he'd said his heart was troubled, and that this prize was for the souls of the Tiananmen victims, then broke down in tears. At that, we could no longer control our own emotions, and Ding Zilin's face streamed with tears. Under

---

[3] TN: An online periodical published by the New York–based NGO Human Rights in China.

[4] A software application developed by Dynamic Internet Technology (DIT) that enables internet users from mainland China and other countries to access websites blocked by their governments.

the circumstances, we decided to ignore personal safety and do all in our power to release a statement.

That night, we brought a draft statement to the home of another nearby relative, whose daughter helped us e-mail it to another Tiananmen parent in Beijing. We asked him to incorporate the views of other Tiananmen parents and then have it posted on an overseas website. We were relieved to soon receive a text message saying the statement had been issued.

CONFLICT WITH WUXI STATE SECURITY

While we were engrossed in sending e-mail from our relative's home, four strangers suddenly burst in the door and made a grab for the computer and U-drive. Stunned for a moment, our relatives sprang forward to protect their computer.

Ding Zilin demanded, "Who are you? Show us your ID!"

One of them flashed his ID and said, "Wuxi Municipal State Security Bureau." Then they tried again to grab the computer and U-drive, nearly shoving our relatives to the floor.

"You bandits! Get lost! You burst in here with no reason—what heinous crime did we commit? If you want to search this house, come back with a warrant!" Ding Zilin shouted at them while pushing the four men out the door.

The shock of the incident and Wuxi StateSec's belligerence upset Ding Zilin so much that she fell into a swoon. Our relatives tried to revive her, one girl weeping in distress. Jiang Peikun slipped a nitroglycerin tablet between Ding Zilin's lips. A car was parked nearby, and the driver took Ding Zilin to Zhangjing Hospital, where she finally regained consciousness after an hour of emergency treatment. Pulling the IV tube from her arm, she borrowed a relative's cell phone and telephoned the two Beijing StateSec officers, telling them to come right away. She then made her way home, supported by her relatives. Fearing that the computer would cause her relatives further trouble, she stopped at their home and brought it back with us.

The Beijing StateSec officers arrived just then. They told us to hand over the computer and made Wuxi StateSec withdraw quickly and leave us in peace.

DING ZILIN BECOMES LISTLESS AND FORGETFUL

After returning home, Ding Zilin became listless and kept mumbling, "I want to go back to Beijing." Going to our relative's house to send e-mail, fighting with Wuxi StateSec, going to the hospital, telephoning the Beijing StateSec police—all of the events of October 11 had vanished from Ding Zilin's memory.

While Ding Zilin was being rushed to the hospital, local police officers, the secretary of the local politics and law committee, the head of the neighborhood committee and other officials all arrived at our relative's home, and even the landlord was notified. The police used the pretext of checking our relative's *hukou* to ask all sorts of questions.

Jiang Peikun burst out, "What are you doing here? What's this to do with you? Get out of here! Out!" He then asked Wuxi StateSec, "What are the police doing here?"

StateSec answered, "We told them to come and help out."

That day we found that our cell phone had also been cut off— the screen stated "Emergency calls only." Jiang Peikun asked Beijing StateSec, "We're both sick people. Now that our communications have been cut off, what are we supposed to do if there's an accident?" Beijing StateSec said they'd intervene with their Wuxi colleagues.

Wuxi StateSec was unwilling to leave our relative's home, and at 11:00 that night they forced our relative's daughter to come to our house, take back the computer and hand it over to them. Mindful of the personal information in the computer, Jiang Peikun tried to put them off by agreeing to print out the statement, but they said they'd already "intercepted and seized" it from the internet, and what they wanted was other data in the computer.

Finally Beijing StateSec took the computer from Jiang Peikun, promising that after Wuxi StateSec finished inspecting it, they'd return it to its owner. Wuxi StateSec left our relative's home at 1:00 a.m.

On the morning of October 13, at our request, the Wuxi and Beijing StateSec officers came to our home to discuss returning the computer. Wuxi StateSec said, "The computer will be returned quickly," but refused to give a specific date.

When Ding Zilin insisted on the computer's immediate return, Beijing and Wuxi StateSec went outside to consult their respective superiors, and Wuxi StateSec finally promised that the computer would be returned the next day.

RELATIVES FORCED TO SIGN A "STATEMENT OF UNDERTAKING"

On October 14, the Beijing StateSec officers returned to Beijing. Wuxi StateSec, however, aided by the politics and law committee secretaries of Xishan District and Xibei Township, forced our five relatives to sign a "Statement of Undertaking" to "not provide Ding Zilin or Jiang Peikun with telephone, cell phone, computer or other communications access; purchase a telephone calling card for Ding Zilin or Jiang Peikun; or reveal any information about Ding Zilin or Jiang Peikun to the outside world. This undertaking remains in effect until Ding Zilin and Jiang Peikun leave Wuxi, and violation will incur legal penalty." Our relatives had no choice but to sign it, and when they asked for a photocopy, the StateSec officers refused.

On October 16, Wuxi StateSec came to our home, and Ding Zilin made a formal protest: "Cutting off our broadband and telephone, fighting with us over sending e-mail and forcing our relatives to sign a Statement of Undertaking are not consistent with the Constitution and law and are a blatant violation of our legitimate rights. It's as bad as the Cultural Revolution." Wuxi StateSec just ignored her.

From then on, we were completely cut off from the outside world, and even some family members didn't dare contact us. When we pointed out our age and health and the need for access to emergency measures, the police agreed to give us three more telephones through which we could contact three relatives with the police listening in.

A HEALTH EXAM AT WUXI HOSPITAL

In the half month after Ding Zilin fainted and lost her memory on the evening of October 11, her health returned, but she remained lightheaded and unsteady, with severe back pain. On the morning of October 26, Wuxi StateSec officers Li and Yu came to our home, and we proposed returning to Beijing so Ding Zilin could have a physical examination.

As soon as we mentioned returning to Beijing, the officers smilingly advised us, "Professor Ding, you're too weak for such a long trip. It would be better for you to have your physical here. The treatment will be provided free of charge, the same as in Beijing."

They went on, "We'll line up the best hospital and doctor in Wuxi. Or you could go to the Taihu Convalescent Hospital, where you can get a check-up and also convalesce if necessary." It seemed they'd prepared these two options in advance, the implication being that they didn't want us returning to Beijing.

At that point we were uncertain what had gone wrong in Ding Zilin's brain and how serious it might be. The consequences of neglecting treatment were dreadful to contemplate. Jiang Peikun had also suffered from coronary heart disease and cerebral infarction since a surprise attack by local police two years ago. Since we couldn't go to Beijing and didn't want to go to Taihu, the best we could do was agree to a physical exam and treatment at a local hospital.

On the afternoon of October 28, StateSec officers Li and Yu informed us that they'd made an appointment for Ding Zilin the following Tuesday at People's Hospital with Vice-Director Wang, a neurologist. They told Ding Zilin to fast in preparation, to bring her medical records and to write up a statement to submit for the medical expenses.

Ding Zilin arrived at People's Hospital at the appointed time on the morning of November 2, the two StateSec officers accompanying her throughout the examination process.

Ding Zilin explained to Dr. Wang that the medical record from Zhangjing Hospital stating that "the patient fainted due to a dispute among family members" was not correct, and that her illness had resulted from a clash with StateSec. The Zhangjing Hospital record had been written up while she was unconscious and with no family members present. Ding then gave Vice-Director Wang her previous medical history, explaining that her first fainting episode had occurred on June 4, 1989, upon learning that our son had been shot. She had subsequently fainted five times, this last spell being the longest and most severe. The fainting spells had come at closer intervals in the last two years.

The doctor immediately scheduled a full examination of her heart, blood pressure, joints, blood work, brain, back and so on, as well as an MRI. That day's examination established that Ding Zilin had elevated blood pressure.

MEMORY LOSS DUE TO "CEREBRAL CONCUSSION"

Ding Zilin asked the doctor the question that troubled us most: Why did this fainting spell last nearly an hour, and why did she forget everything that had happened in the previous 12 hours?

The doctor unequivocally replied, "It's due to 'cerebral concussion.'"

Ding Zilin asked, "Will I get my memory back?"

The doctor replied, "No."

After leaving the hospital, Ding Zilin gave the Wuxi StateSec officers the letter they'd requested she write explaining the consultation fee: "Undergoing a spell of illness after a clash with Wuxi 'StateSec' officers on the evening of October 11, and prevented from traveling to Bejiing, it was necessary to seek treatment in Wuxi, with medical costs borne by Wuxi 'StateSec,' although not at my request."

At noon on November 5, Ding Zilin kept her appointment at People's Hospital for a brain and lumbar MRI. As soon as she reached the hospital, she saw StateSec officers Li and Yu waiting for her. Ding Zilin was puzzled, having been told that only Officer Yu would be accompanying her. At the hospital entrance, after the MRI was completed, officer Li said, "Professor Ding, can you rewrite what you wrote for us last time?"

"Why? Was it inaccurate?"

"On the contrary, it's just that you didn't need so much detail. You don't need the first part." (He was referring to the "clash with Wuxi 'StateSec' officers.") "This is just for the accounting department—they don't need to know so much."

"Your financial affairs officers are also StateSec personnel, so why shouldn't they know?"

"Professor Ding, please rewrite it. Don't cause problems for me and Xiao Yu."

Hearing Officer Li put it that way, Ding Zilin grudgingly agreed, while raising another point: "Regardless of the results of the exam, the weather is getting cold, and Jiang Peikun has a heart condition. When we left Beijing, the doctors at Beijing No. 3 Hospital repeatedly reminded us not to spend the winter down south, and said we should return to Beijing by the end of this month at the latest."

At 3:00 in the afternoon on November 9, the Wuxi StateSec officers again accompanied Ding Zilin to People's Hospital to get the results of her physical. After a week's rest, Ding Zilin's blood pressure had stabilized, but she was found to have suffered a lacunar stroke.

Ding Zilin said she wanted to return to Beijing for treatment, so the doctor just wrote a prescription for some over-the-counter medication. He reminded her, "You need to keep yourself from becoming too agitated in order to prevent a recurrence." In the presence of the StateSec officers, he added, "What happened is long past. Let it go." Ding Zilin understood the meaning behind his words.

WAS WUXI STATESEC "LET OFF"?

On leaving the clinic, StateSec officer Li could barely conceal his glee, and said to Ding Zilin, "Professor Ding, you can relax knowing there are no great problems with your health, and we're also very gratified!" They were clearly pleased at being "let off" from the responsibility they'd have otherwise borne. But there was no way of knowing whether this most recent spell would have lasting repercussions.

Ding Zilin took out the medical exam statement she'd rewritten at their request and gave it to Officer Li. She'd changed "a clash with Wuxi 'StateSec' officers" into "fainting for some reason." Flicking his finger at the phrase "although not at my request," Officer Li said, "This sentence is superfluous."

Ding Zilin responded, "That's as I intended." He then grudgingly accepted it.

At the main entrance to the hospital, StateSec officer Li told Ding Zilin, "Regarding your request to return to Beijing at the end of the month, I consulted my superior, and I can now unequivocally inform you that my superior does not agree." He went on: "At this point I'm responsible for you here in Wuxi. If anything comes up, contact me directly. There's no need to call Beijing. We're under the direction of the province."

Ding Zilin again pointed out that we had not prepared to winter in the south, and Jiang Peikun's health would suffer for it. The policeman replied, "You can stay for a while at the Taihu Convalescent Hospital. It's nice and warm there, and meals are included."

FORGED E-MAIL

On the afternoon of November 14, we received an unexpected visit from Jiang Peikun's old high school classmate and his family. We were delighted but also astonished; it had been more than a month since we'd received any visitors, and we wondered what this signified. And indeed, this old friend, who never used a computer, pulled out a printout of an e-mail sent by another old high school classmate in Canada:

2010.11.12 4:37

XX: We've been out of touch for a long time. How are things with you? Because of Xiaobo getting the award, we haven't been able to leave our home, but this gives us time to attend to some matters we've previously had no time for. Up to now we're still unable to make phone calls, but fortunately we have a SIM card at home for wireless internet access. All is well here, except that the weather is rather cold, and we're making use of the oil radiator we bought. I've attached for your enjoyment photos of Liu Yi's series of paintings: "1989," "Tiananmen," "Great Land" and "Sacred Lhasa."[5]

Wishing you the best!
Ding Zilin and Jiang Peikun

---

[5] TN: Works by the artist Liu Yi have been posted on the internet. For example, "Tiananmen": http://map.woeser.com/?action=show&id=178; "Great Land": http://woeser.middle-way.net/2010/06/blog-post.html; "Sacred Lhasa": http://auction.socang.com/AuctionSpecShowProduct/1532173.html (accessed November 14, 2012).

This was the e-mail "we" had sent to this old classmate on November 12. Below that was his reply:

I'm familiar with your situation in Wuxi. It is truly unfortunate. You must cheer up and get through this difficult time together....

Reading this shocked us. Since issuing the Tiananmen Mothers statement from our relative's computer on the evening of November 11, we hadn't sent e-mail to anyone, and this message was clearly a forgery. Our further inquiries found that many friends and relatives who had previously contacted us through the jielian. jiang@gmail.com address had received similar e-mails, even though we had long ago abandoned that address after our password had been stolen. It was only Wuxi StateSec who knew our present circumstance, our e-mail addresses and the fact that we kept an oil radiator by our bathroom door. In addition, on October 11, Wuxi StateSec claimed to have "intercepted and seized" the statement we'd sent to Beijing. This showed that they were easily able to compromise the confidentiality of our communications.

WHAT CONSTITUTES "BREAKING A PROMISE"?

On the afternoon of November 23, StateSec officers Li and Yu came again to our home. Ding Zilin immediately brought up the forged e-mail, and once again protested their actions since October 8, pointing out that they had violated Article 35 of the Constitution[6] as well as our civil rights: "You're law enforcement officers. Is it residential surveillance we're under right now, or surveillance under some other legal or constitutional provision?"

Somewhat nonplussed by Ding Zilin's question, Li replied, "According to my personal understanding, we've just cut off your communications, but you still have freedom of movement. Haven't you been allowed to see your old classmate?"

---

[6] TN: Article 35 of the PRC Constitution (as amended in 2004) reads: "Citizens of the People's Republic of China enjoy freedom of speech, of the press, of assembly, of association, of procession and of demonstration." See the official English translation of the Constitution at http://www.npc.gov.cn/englishnpc/Constitution/node_2825.htm (accessed May 29, 2013).

Ding Zilin asked, "Why do I have three strange men following me whenever I go shopping?"

Li said it wasn't their people.

Ding Zilin went on, "So you're saying we're free to visit friends in Shanghai and Suzhou?"

"If you go to Shanghai or Suzhou, you need to give us a heads-up."

"How can giving you a heads-up be called freedom of movement?"

This seemed to exasperate Li, who suddenly became stern: "It's because you keep breaking your promises. You promised not to issue a statement, then you did. You promised not to make telephone calls, then you did—and according to our accurate information, you even telephoned Beijing." The phrase "according to our accurate information" was ample proof that they were employing unlawful means to monitor whatever we said.

These words irked Ding Zilin, and she interrupted him, saying, "Everything we've done has been open and aboveboard. There's something we need to make clear today: Everything you've stipulated and all the measures you've taken against us have been unlawful. When you cut off our broadband and telephone on October 8, we asked Beijing StateSec to act as intermediaries in restoring our communications as quickly as possible to avoid escalating the matter. On the request of Beijing StateSec, we agreed three times not to issue a statement for the time being, a compromise we felt we had no choice but to make. We've all along understood that issuing a statement or making telephone calls are a citizen's legitimate rights. You can't use some kind of 'promise' of your own devising to replace the Constitution and laws. Making such a promise is a compromise within the scope of the Constitution and laws, and keeping it is just a matter of whether or not we're in a position to withdraw it."

Ding Zilin then brought up the forged November 12 e-mail: "You've blamed us for telephoning Beijing, and this needs to be clarified today. On November 14, when we saw the fake e-mail sent to our old classmate, we immediately used his cell phone to telephone some other families of June 4th victims, fearing that others might have also been deceived. As expected, we immediately found two others who had received the e-mail and never suspected it was fake. That's why we telephoned Beijing. At any rate, we didn't use our relative's telephone, as in the Statement of Undertaking we signed. Does using someone else's telephone constitute breaking our 'promise'?"

Li backed off and said, "Can you let me see the e-mail someone sent in your name?"

Jiang Peikun immediately went upstairs and fetched it.

After reading it, Li remarked, "The tone is really similar to yours."

Jiang Peikun said decisively, "This was obviously done by you StateSec people; only you would have access to the e-mail address of our old classmate in Canada, and only you would have noticed our oil radiator when you were using our bathroom."

Ding Zilin put in: "You need to get to the bottom of this and give us an explanation, otherwise you'll use it as a pretext to frame us."

Li put the forged e-mail in his portfolio and promised to look into it.

As they were leaving, Ding Zilin asked, "When can we buy tickets to Beijing? Please give us a definite answer. The prescription for Jiang Peikun's daily medication runs out at the end of the month."

Li quickly said, "We'll be in touch. When the weather gets cold, we'll find a warm place for you." They took several of Jiang Peikun's empty medicine bottles and promised to promptly deal with the matter.

This conversation lasted nearly two hours, and the intensity of the exchange left us feeling drained and exhausted.

"IF FOREIGN JOURNALISTS COME KNOCKING ON YOUR DOOR, THEN WHAT?"

On the afternoon of December 1, a relative from a neighboring village brought us the medicine Jiang Peikun needed. Wuxi StateSec had told their Beijing counterparts to buy the medicine and send it to this relative to pass along to us.

Just as our relative was giving us the medicine, Wuxi StateSec arrived. They had a "new assignment": "If by some chance a foreign reporter comes knocking at your door after the prize is presented [referring to Liu Xiaobo's Nobel], how will you handle it?"

Ding Zilin replied: "How would anyone find us in this village?"

They persisted, "But what if?"

Jiang Peikun said, "If by some chance someone knocks on our door, we'll invite them in for a cup of tea. We won't leave a visitor standing outside—that's basic courtesy. How you deal with foreign journalists is your business. You have your ways."

They left unsatisfied.

In the days that followed, we began counting on our fingers the days before we could return to Beijing. Ten days, nine days, a week....We paid close attention to weather forecasts on the Beijing, Jiangsu and Wuxi television stations. Several times the Wuxi station reported an approaching cold front, and we dug out our thickest quilted jackets and blankets. Fortunately, the cold front skirted our area, and the temperatures remained mild. We felt that Heaven was looking after us.

On December 6, however, fierce winds and cold descended. Jiang Peikun immediately fell ill with influenza, chills and throat pain. Thank Heaven, a week's worth of the Azithromycin from Beijing got him through the worst of it.

WAITING TO RETURN TO BEIJING

StateSec agreed to let us return to Beijing at 10:00 p.m. on December 14. After buying our train tickets, we were able to relax for the first time in more than two months. We passed each day carefully warding off any illness that might delay our departure. Never in more than 20 years had we been so anxious to return.

The refreshing aroma of wintersweet brought in from the cold consoled our suffering spirits.

It had been 16 years since we had started building our village home, and it was full of memories, both sweet and sad. In 1994, unable to bear the continued harassment of Beijing StateSec, we had accepted a relative's invitation and invested all our resources in designing and constructing this 110-square-meter house, intending it as a vacation home where we could rest, write and meet up with friends every spring and autumn, and it had ably served that purpose. Since the 1990s, three books and many essays and letters related to June 4th had been written here, as well as the script for the documentary film *The Road of the Tiananmen Mothers*. Many other parents of June 4th victims, as well as schoolmates, students and friends old and new had left their footprints here. The first idea for Charter 08 had germinated here.

This lovely refuge had nevertheless also been the scene of many distressing incidents: In August 1995, the Wuxi procurator-ate (actually StateSec) had taken us from here to a secret location, where we were held for 43 days. In April 2004, when Ding Zilin was in Wuxi and Suzhou tending graves for the Qing Ming festival, our home had been searched and Ding Zilin had been detained for seven days. In October 2008, a surprise attack by local Wuxi police had caused Jiang Peikun to suffer a stroke, and he'd spent three days and nights in intensive care before being plucked from the grip of death. And now Ding Zilin had fainted and suffered a cere-bral concussion in a conflict with Wuxi StateSec. How many more traumas awaited our declining years? For more than 20 years, we had felt that freedom was the most precious thing for us and for China. Without freedom, even with access to all that the internet could bring us, we would feel like someone blind and deaf groping his way in the darkness—like we felt now.

Liu Xiaobo was our true friend, and his winning the Nobel Peace Prize should have been an honor for the Chinese people, yet the rulers of this so-called "rising great power" could not face it with equanimity. Even more inconceivable was that this mat-ter had vanished without a trace, and we, his friends, had likewise receded from the public gaze.

BACK IN BEIJING, BUT NOT HOME

December 14 finally arrived. Early that morning, Jiang Peikun went to the market and bought a kilo of fresh river shrimp, which we planned, as in other years, to cook and bring back to Beijing to share with Xiaobo and Liu Xia. Although Xiaobo was in prison, we could still give some to Liu Xia once the award ceremony had passed.

The weather was very cold that day, and Ding Zilin kept a muf-fler around her neck as she carefully cleaned the shrimp. When someone knocked on the door, we thought it must be relatives coming to say goodbye, but instead we found two officers from Beijing StateSec.

Ding Zilin demanded: "What's this? Are you going back on your word and not letting us return to Beijing?"

"Not at all!" our visitors hurriedly assured us. "You're going back tonight, but the situation has changed somewhat, and our superior has ordered that you not return home until the end of the month. Out of consideration for your health, we pushed for the current plan, which is to let you return to Beijing and stay somewhere else for a while first. It won't be for long, at most until the end of the month or perhaps until Christmas. Fearing that you wouldn't be prepared for this, our leader sent us to escort you back. We hope you'll understand."

We had no choice in the matter, and in any case, we had to leave this frigid place.

Our visitors suggested escorting us to the train station, but we refused, saying our relatives were taking us.

At 9:00 that night, we left for the train station with our relatives. Our car had just emerged from the lane when we spotted a taxi parked there, and the two Beijing StateSec officers came forward and told us to change cars.

So it was that we made the journey to Beijing sharing a compartment with the Beijing StateSec officers, arriving at the South Station soon after midnight. A StateSec car awaited us.

Our arrival coincided with Beijing's coldest day so far. At our request, we first went home to collect some warm clothing and blankets, as well as money for medical needs, and then we were driven to an outer suburb. In the days that followed, we eagerly looked forward to returning home. On December 18, Ding Zilin could no longer hold back: "December 20 is my birthday, and the twenty-first is Jiang Peikun's birthday. Ever since Lian's death, our elder son has spent our birthdays with us in Beijing. Having lost Lian, are we also to be deprived of contact with our remaining son? Doesn't your superior have any humanity? Doesn't this show the hypocrisy of the official slogans of 'people first' and 'harmonious society'? We're already so old, why don't you just arrest us and send us to prison for ten years and be done with it?"

The people "accompanying" us did not venture to advise us.

The next morning, one of our "companions" said with a smile, "Professor Ding, I have good news."

"What good news, that we can go home?"

"Yes! We'll take you home on the twentieth so you can spend your birthdays with your son."

Ding Zilin hardly slept on the night of December 19, recalling how on her fiftieth birthday her two sons had moved her favorite chair into the middle of the house, and after seating her in it, they had solemnly kowtowed three times before her. That joy had been too brief, and now she had only one son left. Thinking back on more than 20 years in a black pit of despair, it was hard to imagine how she had survived that nightmarish time.

We finally returned home on December 20. Our home telephone, cell phone and internet were all suspended, however, and it took repeated negotiations to have our communications restored on the twenty-first.

Suddenly relieved of more than two months of tension, Ding Zilin fell ill with chills, vomiting and chronic coughing, and was confined to bed for three days.

Reading birthday wishes from overseas friends on the internet, Ding Zilin was encouraged by their warmth in the midst of her illness. She is filled with gratitude toward those in China and abroad who were so concerned for her during those 74 days.

EIGHT DAYS

Wang Lihong

Wang Lihong, born in the 1950s in the coastal city of Qingdao, Shan-dong Province, is a signatory of Charter 08. After working in a Bei-jing municipal bureau in the 1980s, she moved into the business sector in 1991.

Wang joined the frontlines of the rights defense movement in 2008, and her engagement in several iconic cases raised her to the status of "Big Sister" in the movement. In the "Three Fujianese Netizens" case, she organized more than 1,000 netizens for a "popular surveillance" around the courthouse. The relatively light sentences handed down to the Fujianese Netizens in April 2010 have been credited to what is now considered an emblematic campaign of the rights defense movement.

The essay below describes Wang's detention after she took part in a celebration of Liu Xiaobo's Nobel Peace Prize on October 8, 2010. She refused police demands to sign a pledge of silence following her release, saying, "As a person of conscience, I cannot remain silent in the face of suffering."

On March 21, 2011, the authorities detained Wang Lihong in connection with the Three Fujianese Netizens popular surveillance, and she was sentenced to nine months in prison on the charge of "rabble-rousing."

ON OCTOBER 7, 2010, I ARRANGED TO MEET SOME FRIENDS THE NEXT DAY AT the Fenghuangzhu Restaurant on Jiugulou Road to see who would win the bets on whether Liu Xiaobo would win the Nobel Peace Prize.

Upon reaching the restaurant, we found a piece of paper taped to the door: "Business suspended due to electrical outage,"[1] so we decided to shift to Ditan Park.

We sent a youngster to reserve a table for us at another restaurant while we waited at the entrance to the park. As we were about to set off for the restaurant, someone said, "It's just two minutes before 5:00 [the time when the Nobel Peace Prize was to be announced], so let's just wait."

Rewarded with the news that Liu Xiaobo had in fact won, we joyfully embraced and cheered. A reporter at the scene interviewed us, and I said that what made us happiest was that people in the international community cared about China's human rights situation.

Everyone then started singing "The Internationale," and we had our pictures taken holding posters proclaiming "Celebrating Liu Xiaobo's Nobel Prize" and "Speech is not a crime, long live freedom!"

The police began to arrive, so we left Ditan Park for the Xinwei Hotpot restaurant. As we sat down, a couple of cops followed us in, and we applauded.

The lead cop said, "What's all the racket?"

I said, "What racket? Aren't you glad we're welcoming you? Let's all celebrate together."

Just then dozens of cops swarmed in and began forcing us out of the restaurant. I moved very slowly, with Tiantian helping me pack up the computer, so we were the last ones out. A'er was already inside the police van when we climbed in. The van took us to the Heping Lane police station, after which Tiantian and I were separated from the others for transfer elsewhere. As we were being escorted to another police van, we asked, "Why are you taking us away, and where are you taking us?"

"To the Jingshan police station."

At that moment, a cop in a yellow T-shirt who was standing in the compound suddenly shouted, "Stupid bitches!"

I turned on him: "What did you say?"

---

[1] It is common for the police to disrupt gatherings of Chinese dissidents by demanding that a restaurant turn down a reservation on the grounds of "electrical outage," "water supply disruption," etc.

He fired back, "What did you say?" He looked ready to fight, and others nearby pulled him away.

Just then I heard Tiantian angrily demand, "Why are you hitting me?" I turned and saw her skirt lifted up, exposing her black stockings. Tiantian shouted, "Why are you looking at my legs, you thug?" I was also shoved violently as I shouldered my backpack.

Tiantian has a heart condition, but never thinks of herself while fighting for the rights of others. I once asked her, "Why bring trouble on yourself?" and she replied with a smile, "Without human rights and dignity, why bother living?" Seeing her shoved and kicked angered me, and I shielded her as we entered the van.

Inside the police van, I received a call from the beat cop Xiao Liu,[2] who asked, "Where are you?"

I said, "On the way from the Heping police station to the Jingshan police station."

He said, "I'll meet you there."

At the Jingshan police station, Tiantian and I were initially held in the same room. A big cop sneered, "What a disgrace, at your age!"

I said, "What about my age? I haven't done anything wrong! And you? You think those threads make you a tough guy?"

He said, "That's right, I'm a tough guy, what about it?"

Angered by our rough handling, I told the lead cop, "I vigorously protest! I'm not talking with you!" I maintained my silence right up until they declared that I would be detained for eight days and told me to sign the detention order. I said, "I protest! I don't accept it, and I'm not signing it."

A cop who said he was the assistant station chief told me to get into the police van to be taken for a physical. I asked, "What about my backpack?"

He said, "We'll give it to your son. After the physical you'll come back to the police station." I got into the van, which ended up taking me all the way to the Changping Detention Center.

---

[2] Beat patrolmen, charged with monitoring household registration and public order, are often required to assist Domestic Security police in monitoring dissidents.

In the van, the deputy station chief said complacently, "You guys are just messing around. You should try reading more. I read all the time, especially *The Classic Anthology*."[3]

Less than impressed and in no mood to laugh (I doubted he'd actually read *The Classic Anthology*, or even if he had, that he'd understood it), I just said, "Your knowledge structure is too antiquated. As a law enforcement officer, you should be reading *Sociology* and *Political Science*. You should go online and look up the phrase 'banality of evil.' Why do you have to be so rough? I have friends who are cops, and I've gone to lots of police stations, and I feel that the atmosphere of a police station is closely related to its leadership. If the station chief is humane, the cops there won't treat citizens so brutally—quite the contrary. I would have thought that the cops around the Imperial City would be a little more civilized, but you've set me straight on that. Maybe you don't know how civilized law enforcement is done."

The deputy station head (I later learned his name was Wang Bing) said, "I believe there are only three types of people: police, civilians and criminals."

I said, "That's too simplistic. Do you think anyone who doesn't display sheeplike obedience is a criminal? And that once someone is designated a criminal, that you can treat him as you like?"

Wang said, "It's who the civilians say are criminals. For example, when civilians are getting on with their lives, and a bunch of tattooed thugs are hanging out on the streets, doesn't that scare the civilians? And shouldn't we deal with them?"

"So it's up to you to decide who's a criminal?"

"Are you saying it should be up to you?"

"It should be up to the courts, after prosecution and trial. Your regarding someone as a criminal doesn't make him one."

"I'm not wasting my breath on an extremist like you. Someday you'll be sorry, that's all I'm going to say."

The police van drove full speed on the Badaling Expressway until we reached the detention center. Although far from home, I

---

[3] TN: *The Classic Anthology* (*Guwen Guanzhi*) is a Qing dynasty collection of more than 200 essays dating from the Warring States Period (476 BCE) to the Ming dynasty (1644). Parts of the anthology are still used for teaching literary Chinese in the secondary schools of mainland China, Hong Kong, Macao and Taiwan.

had the strange sensation of homecoming. Perhaps it was my fate. I'm sure the deputy station chief would have been surprised by my equanimity.

The person at the detention center's reception desk was pleasant and scowl-free. As I was waiting to register, I heard Butcher's voice outside the door: "Sister!"

So Butcher had been brought in too! He originally hadn't planned to attend our gathering, and after arriving had remained low key. If even he had been brought in, it was unlikely that others had escaped. I was overcome with guilt and called out, "I'm so sorry!"

After registration came the physical exam, which found me in good health except for my arthritic neck, for which I was being medicated, and a herniated lumbar disc, for which I wore a back brace.

I then changed into prison garb. Because of the cold, I was allowed to wear insulated underclothes, but my quilted jacket had a zipper so I had to take it off, along with my back brace and glasses, which left me half blind. I groped my way to the second floor and waited while the duty guard put her key in a door and called, "Open Cell 14!" The door opened with a clank, and I dimly perceived two rows of beds and several people coming forward.

The guard (surnamed Sun, as I later learned) said to those inside, "This new inmate, Wang Lihong, is severely nearsighted, so please look after her."

Several voices said, "Sure, no problem."

Two people led me inside, where I was told to place my things in a cubicle and sit down on a bed as the guard closed the door.

I thought, so here I am at last. The previous year I'd written an article entitled "I'm Prepared." Now my prison life had begun.

With the help of my cellmates, I spread out my quilt and squeezed into my sleeping bag as I was asked, "What are you in for?"

I said, "For singing and chanting slogans at the park entrance."

A babble ensued:

"So you're a political prisoner!"

"Good for you!"

"How can you be detained for singing at a park entrance?"

Just then the cell door opened, and the guard Sun called out, "Wang Lihong, come out for interrogation."

After putting on my clothes, I followed the guard downstairs, gripping the banister. In the reception area Butcher was still registering, and he called out, "Sister!"

Squinting at him, I raised my clasped hands and said, "Sorry, so sorry!"

Butcher asked, "How many days for you?"

"Eight days. How about you?"

"Also eight days."

"I'm really sorry."

"No more talking, move along," the prison guard said.

The interrogation room was frigid. Seated by an open window, I shrank against the cold.

The interrogator said, "Are you cold? I'm only wearing two layers and I'm not cold."

I said, "I'm a lot older than you! Of course you kids don't feel the cold. I haven't eaten or slept all day and night, and right away you call me in for interrogation, so how would I not feel cold?"

The interrogator said, "If you cooperate you can go back sooner."

In fact, since seeing Butcher come in, I'd already decided to "cooperate" and say everything that had happened. This is what I recall of my interrogations:

INTERROGATION 1

"Name?"

    "Wang Lihong."

"How many of you were at the Fenghuangzhu Restaurant on the seventh?"

    "Four or five."

    "Tell the truth."

    "That's the truth."

    "Who else was there?"

    "I'm not willing to talk about others."

    "We know anyway."

"So why ask?"

"We want you to say it."

"Let me make it clear that I have one principle: I'll talk about myself, but not about others. So don't bother asking."

"Whose idea was it to go to Ditan?"

"Mine."

"Taking all the credit does you no good."

"It's the truth. A few days ago I was at a bookstore near there and saw it was spacious, so that's why we went there."

"What time did you go?"

"A little after 4:00."

"You started once you got there?"

"No, at first we planned to go in."

"Why didn't you?"

"We were about to go in when someone said it was almost 5:00, so we waited for the announcement, and we were all so happy that we just celebrated on the spot."

"How did you celebrate?"

"We took out our posters and sang."

"What did you sing?"

"'The Internationale.'"

"What slogans did you shout?"

"What was on the posters—celebrating Liu Xiaobo winning the Nobel, no crime in speech, long live freedom, free Xiaobo."

"What did you mean by it?"

"We were happy."

"What do you mean that there's no crime in speech?"

"It's wrong for a peaceful man like Liu Xiaobo to be imprisoned for 11 years. This is the twenty-first century. It's unacceptable to convict someone for what he says."

"Who made the posters?"

"I did."

"Where did you have them made?"

"I don't want to say."

"Why not? It only involves you."

"It also involves someone else who was just doing business and didn't know what was going on, and I don't want to drag them into it."

"Were the posters and photos done at the same place?"

"No."

"Where did the photos come from?"

"They were downloaded from the internet."

"Those were on the internet?"

"All over—do a search and you'll see."

"How much did it cost to make the posters?"

"Three or four hundred."

"Where did the money come from?"

"I can put together that much."

"So it was your own money?"

"Yes."

"And the yellow ribbons?"

"I prepared those. I bought a spool of yellow ribbon and cut it into pieces."

"Who did the badges?"

"I did."

"What was on them?"

"Liu Xiaobo's photo."

"What else?"

"The words 'We're with you.'"

"What else?"

"'Sharing the light of justice.'"

"There was a date, too, wasn't there?"

"Yes, October 8, 2010."

"What were you planning to do with them?"

"Originally I planned to take them to lunch, and if Liu Xiaobo won, I'd take them out and hang them on the wall, and we'd take pictures and celebrate. If he didn't win, I wouldn't take them out, and we'd just have lunch."

"How did you learn that Liu Xiaobo won the prize?"

"Through Twitter."

"What's Twitter?"

"It's a kind of microblog."[4]

"That news was on Twitter?"

---

[4] TN: Microblogs (*weibo*) are the Chinese version of Twitter, and are hosted by a number of web service companies.

"It had been discussed on Twitter for a month already. There were two views: One was that he would win, and the other was that he wouldn't. There were also some overseas democracy activists who wrote to the Nobel Committee opposing Liu Xiaobo getting the prize."

"How did you know about October 8?"

"It was on Twitter. Some people were betting dinner if they won or if they lost—I'm not sure which, because I didn't place a bet."

INTERROGATION 2

Dongcheng District DomSec (hereafter Gestapo): "Wang Lihong, you've been busy running all over the country! Fujian, Sichuan...."

"Sichuan? I haven't been there!" (Afterward I remembered Sichuan was for Liu Xianbin.)[5]

Gestapo: "You were also at Huangchenggen." (He was referring to the rally for Ni Yulan on June 16 that year.)[6]

"Huangchenggen? I wasn't there. Don't you have a video? Look and you'll see."

Gestapo: "What was your 'Three Fujianese Netizens' case all about?"

"I'd like to clarify whether you're criminal police or DomSec."

"Seems you know a lot about the internal organization of the Public Security Bureau. Who's your friend in the police?"

"You think I'd tell you?"

"So tell us about the Fujian matter—we'd like to know more."

"It's all on the internet—do a search and you'll know everything."

"We'd like to hear it from you."

"To begin with, there was a 26-year-old girl in Minqing, Fujian Province..." I went on to tell him about Yan Xiaoling and the Three Fujianese Netizens.

---

[5] A Sichuan-based democracy activist and independent writer jailed for "incitement to subvert state power" on the basis of his writings.

[6] On the day of the Dragon Boat Festival in June 2010, netizens held a gathering in support of Ni Yulan, a lawyer and activist against forced removals for urban development. Disabled as a result of torture in custody, Ni became homeless upon her release and was living on the streets.

"So you went there?"

"We went for a popular surveillance to express our concern. Have you ever been on the crime squad? In your experience, isn't there something suspicious about this case? So many scholars, professors, even retired prosecutors and judges have said the judgment was wrong, so why shouldn't we express our concern?"

"What professors and scholars have written articles?"

"Yu Jianrong from the Chinese Academy of Social Sciences, Wang Yong from China University of Political Science and Law.... You can find lots of them on the internet."

"How many people did you organize to go?"

"We didn't organize anything, we just said on the internet that we were going, and others went too."

"It must have cost a lot for so many people to go there. Where did the money come from?"

"Lots of people paid their own way and there were donations for those without money."

"Who donated? How much?"

I said nothing.

"There must have been accounts kept for so much money. Who was your accountant?"

"Why would we need an accountant for so little money?"

"Someone must have kept the accounts."

"I did it myself."

"You must have had some kind of organization, otherwise why would people trust you?"

"There was no organization."

"So, no organization, and Wang Lihong says she needs donations and people just sent in their money? You must have a lot of face, Sister Wang!"

"There were more than 5,000 people in our 'Three Fujianese Netizens Concern Group.' Some contributed effort, others contributed money. If someone posted on the internet that they needed money, someone else would donate the funds."

"So how does anyone know that you didn't take that money to buy groceries?"

"Anyone who doesn't believe me can send me his remittance form and I'll refund his money."

"You must have had someone managing the funds. You couldn't publish everything on the internet. What are you hiding?"

"There's nothing to hide. Why are you asking about Fujian, anyway? What's that to do with you? Even the municipal DomSec told me, don't talk about Fujian, we don't even care about Tianjin. So why is Dongcheng District DomSec so interested?"

"Hua Ze is from Dongcheng, so isn't that related? I saw your video, Hua Ze went there to film it."

"I told Hua Ze to go, because she used to work for CCTV and knows how to take videos."

"How do you know her?"

"Through the internet."

"I guess you girls get along pretty well."

"Well enough."

"You tell her to go and she goes?"

"I told her about it and asked her to help by filming it, so she went. She didn't know what it was all about."

"So I'll write down that you told Hua Ze to go to Fujian."

"Why do you want to write that? Leave her out of it. You're asking about the Ditan Park case, and Hua Ze didn't go there. She has nothing to do with this matter, so why are you writing about her?"

"So I'll just write that you know Hua Ze."

"Don't write that, either. Why do you want to write things that have nothing to do with what you're asking about? If you write it, I won't sign. Your interview sheets have written on them: 'You may refuse to answer questions unrelated to the case.' Do you feel eight days aren't enough, and you want to frame me for something else?"

"Of course we have to ask. For instance, if we catch a petty thief who just stole a pen, we're definitely going to ask what else he's done. Who knows—he could be a murderer!"

"Huh! And you say you're not laying a trap."

"We're just asking."

"A few days ago I told the interrogator that I'll talk about myself but not about others."

Gestapo stared.

"And I told the interrogator that on anything involving others you should just write 'won't comment.'"

"So you're trying to be Sister Jiang."

"It's nothing to do with 'Sister Jiang.' As long as you don't put me in a tiger seat or force me to drink chili water, I'm not talking."

"So if we put you in a tiger seat, you'll cough like Fu Zhigao?"[7]

"I'll bear up as well as I can."

"I don't think a tiger seat will be necessary."

"Then just write, 'won't comment.'" (When I signed the record later, I saw he'd written, "Unwilling to talk about others.")

"What were you doing at Ditan that day?"

"Taking pictures."

"Why were you taking pictures? Did you plan to post them on the internet?"

"Maybe."

"What do you mean, 'maybe'? Was that the plan or not?"

"Just write what I said. 'Maybe' will do."

"It won't do. It's either yes or no."

"Then...no!"

"So all of you were standing there shouting slogans and taking pictures so you could go home and stick them in your photo albums?"

"Most of us use electronic photo albums."

"Don't get agitated, we're just chatting."

"I wasn't getting agitated. Why should I?" (I later saw that he wrote in the record: "We just wanted to take pictures for our own enjoyment.")

"What's your sense of this matter? Do you think what you did was right?"

"I feel we didn't break the law. We didn't disturb public order, we didn't disrupt traffic. You're making a mountain out of a molehill and abusing police power. I want a lawyer. I want my case reviewed."

"If you want a lawyer, tell the detention center."

"The detention center said I had to tell you."

"That's enough for today. We'll talk again."

---

[7] TN: In the revolutionary novel *Red Crag*, Fu Zhigao betrays Sister Jiang by buckling under interrogation, symbolizing weakness and cowardice.

"Again? Maybe after I get out."

"Once you're out you won't talk to us."

"I won't now, either."

INTERROGATION 3

Interrogator: "Do you know Liu Xiaobo?"

Wang Lihong: "No."

"Have you ever met him?"

"No."

"So why all the fuss?"

"We were happy."

"What's to be happy about?"

"It was the first Nobel Peace Prize for mainland China, so of course we were happy."

"Didn't you know there was another Chinese who got a Nobel?"

"I don't think there was."

"I'm talking about a Chinese called Dalai. Have you heard of him?"

"Seems like the Dalai Lama has an Indian passport."

"Do you know that the Dalai Lama is a separatist who's pushing for Tibetan independence? That's the kind of person who gets a Peace Prize."

"I heard CCTV say that the Dalai Lama wants independence, but someone found a recording of a speech by the Dalai Lama, and he didn't say a word about Tibetan independence."

"So you're saying that when they [Norway's Nobel Committee] give a prize to a criminal that the government has sentenced to 11 years in prison, there's no ulterior motive?"

"I think your thinking is that anyone who has a different opinion must have an ulterior motive. I think that when you give an 11-year sentence to a peaceful person like Liu Xiaobo, who wants nothing but the best for China and hopes there will be no bloodshed during this period of transformation, that's just beyond the pale."

"You said transformation. What kind of transformation, in which direction?"

"I mean political reform. Recently Premier Wen raised political reform six times within a month. You can read about it on the internet."[8]

"That's not the same thing."

"Of course it is. Don't they both wish the best for the motherland?"

"So, Deng Xiaoping raises political reform and so-and-so raises political reform...and that's all the same thing?"

"I'd like to ask you, aren't you supposed to be a criminal cop? Aren't you supposed to be asking about public security? So why do you keep asking about Liu Xiaobo?"

"Sign here, please."

INTERROGATION 4

Interrogator: "Tell me your sense of these last few days."

Wang Lihong: "What do you mean?"

"Your sense of the government sentencing you to eight days."

"It makes no sense."

"You're still dissatisfied?"

"Of course I'm dissatisfied. I'm really angry. The longer I'm here, the more steamed I am about it."

"So your eight days here have been wasted."

"Not at all. Once I get out I'm going to apply to have my case reviewed."

"You still think you've been treated unjustly?"

"Of course!"

"If you've been treated unjustly, how about Wu Gan?"[9]

"There you are! That shows you know Butcher has been treated unjustly! I can't understand why you arrested him. He wasn't even planning to come, and he never did anything. He's not in any of the photos, he didn't sing or yell slogans, he just stood off to the side. You can look at the video. I really can't understand why you arrested him. It's bizarre!"

---

[8] TN: See, for example, Malcolm Moore, "Wen Jiabao Promises Political Reform for China," *The Telegraph* (UK), October 4, 2010, http://www.telegraph.co.uk/news/worldnews/asia/china/8040534/Wen-Jiabao-promises-political-reform-for-China.html (accessed November 14, 2012).

[9] Referring to the aforementioned "Butcher," a rights defender who uses the online name of "Super-vulgar Butcher."

"So you think there was nothing wrong with shouting slogans and singing at Ditan?"

"I don't see anything wrong with it. We were in an open area singing and shouting slogans, without affecting public order or traffic."

"No effect? Do you know how many people were heading over there?"

"That's just what you were anticipating. How can you make a 'fact of the crime' out of something that didn't happen? How can you convict someone on the basis of projecting what will happen?"

"That was the first day back to work after the National Day holidays, and a lot of people were getting out of work then."

"You keep saying what might have happened, but nothing happened."

"What did you want to happen?"

"Nothing happened. It was a fart in the whirlwind and you've made such a big deal out of it based on 'what might happen.' It's an outrage! It's an abuse of police authority."

CELLMATES

I was held in Cell 14, on the east side of the second floor of the Dongcheng Detention Center. It was about 40 square meters in size, and to the right of the iron door a row of eight beds (each about 90 centimeters wide and about 1.8 to 2 meters long) formed one large bed referred to as the "big board." To the left of the door, behind a glass partition, was a washroom seven or eight square meters with a squat toilet and a water faucet. Beyond the washroom was about a meter of empty space, and beyond that a row of four beds known as the "small board." The aisle between them was about a meter wide. On the wall above each bed space was posted a number. Generally speaking, the person who slept in the first space should be the head prisoner, who was usually the most experienced and could help the guards oversee the prisoners. In Cell 14, however, the first space was under a window and subject to drafts, so in our cell the head prisoner slept in the eighth space, at the inner end of the row.

The head prisoner in Cell 14 was named Chunyan, of old Beijing stock and looking like a proper Manchu. At 50, she was fair-skinned and retained her youthful form. She'd been brought in for taking drugs, but I never saw or heard of her going through withdrawal. She strutted her 1.65 meters down the aisle as if it were a fashion runway, or as if strolling through the Wangfujing shopping district. She said she'd been on the streets since the age of 14 and had seen everything. Possibly due to menopause, she was always hot and bothered, the Velcro straps on her prison uniform constantly popping open and exposing her cleavage. Sometimes she'd make an effort to restick them, saying that as long as no handsome guards were on duty, she'd keep her bounty to herself.

Chunyan loved to sing. Even in normal speech her voice was lovely, but her singing voice was truly outstanding—sultry, bluesy and alluring. She would sing, "I want to go home, I want to go home, I want to go home to Mama. I'm my mama's baby, if I don't visit her, who will? Mama, how can you know / how I suffer here? Cold steamed buns, Cabbage soup, Weeping and crying / for my mom and dad, Drop by drop my bitter tears / Rain down on my heart...." She was always crooning to herself, and others would sing along. The guards, overhearing, didn't interfere. In the quiet prison cell, tears flowed silently without interruption.

Chunyan treated me with respect and told the others to look after me, making sure I got the first helping at meal time. After the evening meal, hot water was delivered, but usually only enough for three people, at most. Seeing me always using cold water to wash up for bed, Chunyan used her own basin to fetch hot water for me, leaving me both grateful and humbled.

Chunyan was in the detention center "awaiting trial," and rather than jeopardize her case, I'll say no more about her until a better opportunity arises.

There was one prisoner older than me in Cell 14, a woman named Wang Shaorong. Born in 1953, she was a resident of Xicheng District who had been "sent down" to Xingkaihu, Heilongjiang Province, in 1969.[10]

---

[10] TN: From 1955 to 1969, Xingkaihu, located in a harsh and desolate border region, was the site of a labor camp for the "ideological remolding" of political and social undesirables

Wang Shaorong had exquisite features with traces of her youthful beauty. At 57 she had not grown stout, and only a slight stoop betrayed her age. Her voice was warm and gentle until she spoke of "their unlawful treatment of me," at which time it became steely. During our afternoon rest, draped in the rays of the setting sun, she would smile contentedly and say, "What a blessing the sun is!"

In the six long hours from 4:00 until bedtime at 10:00, she would shred a steamed bun and place it in her bowl, then sprinkle some instant noodle seasoning on top and call it a "sautéed bun," which she would then savor in nibbles, bringing some small pleasure to the day. It was only at meal times that the guards allowed the prisoners to sit about as they pleased, and Shaorong turned her steamed bun into a delicacy as a means of whiling away the time.

Wang Shaorong was a practitioner of Falun Gong, and at home she was constantly spied upon and harassed by her neighbors. On August 4 that year, police intercepting her near her home had found a Falun Gong pamphlet in her handbag, and a search of her home uncovered more such literature. Ultimately Shaorong was sentenced to two years' re-education through labor (RTL)[11] for "using religion to disturb public order." On the day of her arrest, she fell ill and was taken to the hospital, where a doctor wanted her admitted for blood abnormalities. After a conversation with the doctor, the police took several packets of medicine and escorted her to the detention center, where she was now waiting to be "sent down" to the RTL camp.

I asked, "Can you take two years of RTL?"

"Even if I can't, I'll have to."

"Would you like me to contact your family and have them send you some money when I get out?"

"Don't trouble them. I still have almost a thousand *yuan* with me."

---

during various political campaigns. Wang Shaorong would not have been a prisoner there, but would have been one of the urban youth sent to work in the hinterlands during the Cultural Revolution.

[11] TN: Re-education through labor (*laojiao*) is a form of administrative detention for periods of up to four years, imposed for "minor crimes" without recourse to the courts.

"I've heard other inmates say that life is expensive in the camps. If you don't have enough, your health will break down in no time."

"It's true, if you want to take a physical at the RTL camp, you have to pay for it yourself—they say it costs nearly two thousand *yuan*. You also have to buy all your own personal items."

I told Wang Shaorong that people were campaigning for the barbarous RTL system to be scrapped. She politely said, "That's really good." It was clear she saw little hope of that.

Qin'er was a Hubei native who'd married a Beijing man. At 31 she was an attractive professional woman with a curtain of hair, large, pretty eyes, and a bee-stung upper lip. Once after returning from an interrogation, she said she'd bumped into Butcher, who'd smiled at her. (I'd described my "co-defendant" to her and told her of Butcher's role in the Deng Yuqiao case.)[12] I laughed and said, "Butcher likes pretty women!"—but who doesn't?

Qin'er worked for a well-known real estate chain. Talking about work made her perk up immediately—it was clear that she was very dedicated, and she'd earned good money. She'd been arrested for taking "meth." According to her, she'd been under a lot of pressure and was feeling depressed, and she'd been arrested the first time she tried the drug. She learned at the detention center that someone had "fingered" her. Although she had no past record, she'd been sentenced to two years' "forced withdrawal." She felt this was too harsh and requested a review of her case, hoping to go to a neighborhood rehab center instead, even if it meant daily urine tests. But at her inquest she was told, "So you want to sue us to review your case? Forget it, it's not going to happen."

Wu Mei was a Wenzhou businesswoman, plump and red-cheeked with a cascade of dyed and permed hair that made her look around 30 when she was actually 50. She had the light, deliberate stride of a cat. She and her husband ran a printing factory in Beijing. One day her uncle had come to Beijing and asked her

---

[12] TN: Deng Yuqiao, a 21-year-old pedicurist in Badong County, Hubei Province, was charged with stabbing to death a local official who tried to force her to perform sexual services. Reports of her case drew millions of internet postings supporting Deng. The police reduced her charge from murder to "intentional assault," and although found guilty, she was freed without sentencing on grounds of "mental state."

to go gambling with him. They'd barely settled into their chairs when the police raided the establishment and arrested them. She said she'd just arrived and hadn't placed any bets, but the police said that if she didn't confess, she'd be sent to RTL, while if she confessed she'd be home before she knew it. She then said she'd bet a hundred *yuan*, thinking that would get her home sooner, but she'd ended up in detention for ten days, and the 5,000 *yuan* she'd brought for gambling stakes had been confiscated.

Ling, a native of Heilongjiang, was pretty and vivacious, with a straight nose, delicate pink lips and a youthful glow. At 22, she'd studied interior design and was planning to get married within the year, but then out of curiosity she tried out prostitution. (Yes, there are many reasons for prostitution, and this girl didn't do it for the money, but out of sexual curiosity!) She'd been caught in the act and transported stark naked from the hotel room to the Heping Lane police station with only a blanket covering her. During the interview, her picture had been taken, supposedly for her file. Then a dozen or so plainclothes cops had burst in with cameras and camcorders. Humiliated and angry, she asked, "Are you really all cops?" The only response was the clicking of camera shutters.

During the two days and nights from the time that she was arrested until she was sentenced to half a year of RTL, Ling was given nothing to eat or drink and wasn't allowed to put on clothes. Those few days were very cold, especially at night, and in her drafty cell in the police station she shivered herself senseless. It was only upon arrival at the detention center that she was finally given a prison uniform. "I've already confessed and the interview is done, so why don't you let me get dressed?" she'd asked, but no one had paid any attention.

Among all the inmates of Cell 14, Ling was under the greatest mental pressure, and she spent much of her time with her head buried between her knees.

Wang Guan'er, in her thirties, earned her living at a sauna. Short and jolly, she was good for a laugh. She said that on the day of her arrest, she'd been taking a break with some of her co-workers at the front of the sauna when the police suddenly burst in and took them to the police station. There they had been kicked and beaten and accused of prostitution. They'd also been forced to wear three layers of surgical masks doused with mustard oil that convulsed them with gagging. Seeing her younger co-workers so badly beaten, Wang Guan'er had confessed to giving "massages." The others, toughing it out, had finally been "rolled," but she'd been sentenced to a year of RTL for "vice by manual method"—such a creative name for a crime!

Xiao Gan, also in her thirties, was petite and busty. During exercise I invited her to jog with me, but she said it was too hard on her without a bra to wear. A Guizhou native, she'd married a man from Jiangxi, and after giving birth to a daughter she'd been surprised by the birth of twin sons. This happiness was soon tempered by the expense of raising so many children, especially the prospect of school fees. As a result, she'd gone into prostitution and had been arrested. Poor to start with, she now faced the expense of RTL. (The saying went, "Even a rich family can't support a prisoner.") Even so, she hoped to be sent down as soon as possible so she would have a chance to telephone home.

On the twelfth, a woman named Sun Erniang burst in like a whirlwind. In her forties, she was reed thin and coppertoned. She looked like she'd just set down her hoe, but in fact she'd been scalping tickets at the Beijing train station for ten years. How had such a street-smart person been arrested, we wondered? She casually replied, "If you walk along the river, your shoes are going to get wet now and then." Although speaking with a Shandong accent, she was actually from just across the border of the neighboring province, Jiangsu. She'd been inside three times already and was old pals with the guards. This time she was in for five days.

Around 4:00 a.m. on the thirteenth, four more girls arrived. They'd been arrested together while distributing leaflets for vice dens. They all looked around 20. Newcomers to Beijing and unable to find work, they'd answered a want ad they'd seen on the internet for handing out promotional cards at a hotel. They hadn't even started when they were arrested and sentenced to five days in detention. Everyone in the cell said they'd been trapped: The ad had been a trap, the agreement with hotel security had been a trap, and their betrayal to the police by an insider had also been a trap. I couldn't help but wonder what lasting scars these girls would bear from their first experience in the city: hunger, being deceived and arrested. . . . And how would they make a living in the future with criminal records?

On the fourteenth, two more "meth heads" came in. One was a successful businesswoman who owned a chain of eateries. Beautiful, stylish and on the rise, she was so out of sync with her new surroundings that she seemed to have dropped in from another dimension. Both of the women were in for five days.

The cell's "meth heads" said there were different types of drug users. They looked down most on heroin users, because once people became addicted to heroin, they lost all their human quality and were capable of anything. Methamphetamine, on the other hand, was a synthetic drug, and according to these women, it wasn't addictive; professionals and people in the artistic field, feeling under pressure, would sometimes take it while on multi-day mahjong sprees. However, when I was later put under house arrest in a guesthouse, one of the female cops "looking after" me was a former narc, and she said meth was just as hard to quit as any other drug and that the damage it caused to the central nervous system might be even greater. She did agree, however, that heroin addicts were the worst.

On the fifteenth they dragged in two women who looked like farmers, ignorant, cowering and mute, their faces etched with hardship. Because they'd been frying crullers at the wrong time and place, and had encountered the wrong person, their lives had been thrown onto a whole new trajectory, and now they were being twisted into crullers themselves, with five days in detention.

According to my cellmates, just before my arrival, an older woman of 68 had departed after being arrested for selling maps at Tiananmen Square. Cellmates had seen that her "big ticket" (detention order) had written on it: "Disturbing public order . . . evidence: 1 RMB." That meant that some high and mighty "vice cop" had arrested an old lady who had just sold a map for 1 *yuan*. The old woman hadn't understood that Tiananmen Square is one of China's most sensitive spots, and that no one is allowed there but the denizens of Zhongnanhai. Although she and I were ships passing in the night, it seemed I could see Kafka's words in the ravines of China's landscape etched on that bewildered old face.

The Dongcheng District cops seemed very industrious—nearly every day brought new arrivals. My cellmates said the cops had arrest quotas to maintain. I'd heard this before, but this was the first time I'd seen people actually being brought in to fill quotas. It made me think of the many other quotas that had been filled in our great nation in the last 61 years—the Anti-Rightist Campaign, the purges against counterrevolutionaries—it was strange to be caught up in such a quota myself (although there were other possibilities, of course).

All kinds of messages had been scrawled on the walls of Cell 14 with ink extracted from salted duck eggs: "I'm stuffing myself for ten days after I get out!" "I'm going to party when I get out!" "Where is hope?" "Sisters of Cell 14, let's set up a QQ group!"

I left a few lines of my own:

All human lives are equal.

Every life has value.

Never, ever, give up hope.

These lines seemed a bit sour compared with the others, but I hoped they'd help someone who read them.

In the long river of life, eight days don't count for anything. But those eight days from October 9 to 16 left me with a feeling of deep gratitude.

In those eight days I met these cellmates, with whom I'd never expected to cross paths. These women of all different backgrounds had been brought by fate, desire, quotas, whatever, to Cell 14 of the Dongcheng Detention Center. In a difficult time, these ordinary people carefully protected the remnants of their self-respect, while not forgetting to help others. Going out for exercise, they took me by the hand; some let me go before them at meals, some gave me warm water to wash my feet before bed. Because I couldn't take my shift patrolling the halls at night, others had to take it for me, but no one ever complained. Some even said that after leaving detention, they'd like to take part, through action or contributions, in the "Wang Lihong Compassionate Volunteers Workshop" and engage in public interest work to make their lives more meaningful.

Now that I'm out and have returned to the Big Prison that is China, I wonder where they've all been scattered. I wish the best of luck to these cellmates, the dust and ants of China. I will forever treasure the love and friendship they gave me during those eight days.

This essay is an attempt to repay their kindness.

MY FEBRUARY 19

Li Xin'ai

Li Xin'ai, a signatory of Charter 08 born in the 1980s, was educated as a journalist and has edited discussion forums for several blogs and media websites. In 2007, she sued telecom monopoly China Mobile for "violating the right to free communication," but after a year of delays the court left the case unresolved. Married to the journalist Gu Chuan, who relates an earlier detention episode elsewhere in this volume, Li here describes a subsequent detention from the family's point of view.

In this instance, Gu Chuan was detained during the tense period of the Jasmine Revolution in Tunisia and other countries of North Africa and the Middle East in late 2010 and early 2011. As in those countries, appeals went up over the internet to organize protests in China demanding political reform. The first such protest was planned for February 19, 2011, the day that starts Li Xin'ai's account below. Gu Chuan was part of a mass roundup of activists throughout China at that time.

Li Xin'ai's essay highlights the common practice among Chinese authorities of persecuting the families of activists along with the activists themselves. Spouses and children are frequently put under house arrest or close surveillance and prevented from working or attending school. The families of lawyer Gao Zhisheng, activist Hu Jia and blind legal activist Chen Guangcheng are well-known examples of the phenomenon. While public attention focuses on the activists, their family members often suffer in obscurity.

ON THE MORNING OF FEBRUARY 19, 2011, THREE UNINVITED GUESTS CAME
to visit. They were three officers from the Beijing Public Security
Bureau's Changping District subdivision: Chen Shijie, Wang Dong
and Chen Zhi.

Since moving to Changping District in April 2009, we'd normally dealt with two middle-aged DomSec officers, Zhao Shuquan
and Chen Wanjun. Their attitude was reasonable, and Gu Chuan
had never clashed with them.

The three officers at our door today looked younger, perhaps
only in their thirties, and Chen Shijie was only a junior officer in
the DomSec subdistrict. Gu Chuan hated the way he beat around
the bush, and asked him to come straight out with why he'd come.
In fact, we guessed they were here because the "Jasmine Revolution," the recent popular uprisings against tyranny in Tunisia, was
making them restless.

Gu Chuan didn't feel like wasting time with them, and his
brusque tone must have irritated Chen Shijie. They finally threatened, "Don't use Twitter to organize 'Jasmine strolls' in the cities,
and don't discuss Jasmine matters on the internet, or you'll bear
the consequences."

Our unpleasant discussion ended on this note, and it seemed
no different from normal. It turned out, however, that they had a
plot brewing and were using the Jasmine Revolution as a pretext
for mass arrests throughout China.

A little after noon, Chen Shijie telephoned, and claiming to
have "dropped his keys," he asked me to look for them. Suspecting
nothing, I looked around and finally told him, "I can't find your
keys. You must have left them somewhere else."

He asked, "Is Gu Chuan there?"

"Yes."

Gu Chuan had been planning to go out that afternoon to buy
toner for our printer, but not wishing for me to deal with our two
children alone, he first rocked baby Enen to sleep. As Gu Chuan
was putting on his jacket to go out around 4:00, there was urgent
knocking at our door. Looking out the peephole, I saw Chen Shijie
and Chen Zhi standing in the doorway. I turned to Gu Chuan and
said, "They're back. I told him we didn't have his keys, so why are
they here?"

Completely unsuspecting, Gu Chuan opened the door, and a couple dozen people charged in. They'd been hiding out of range of the peephole.

Chen Shijie marched over to our laptop computer, and sensing his ill intent, I rushed over and grabbed it. He tried to snatch it from me, and two uniformed police officers, one male and one female, came over and twisted my arms back. I shouted, "Let me go! You're hurting me!" (I later learned that they were People's Police officers from Changping's Dongxiaokou police station, the woman named Wang Yahui, and the man with badge number 056376.) These bandits then roughly pushed me onto a stool, and Gu Chuan, who had not yet put on his shoes or jacket, was bundled out the door by four or five others.

Our older boy, Luoluo, was weeping with terror, and I demanded that they release me so I could comfort him. They refused and said, "We'll see to him." I indignantly cursed them as beasts and henchmen of evil.

A man in plainclothes aimed a camcorder at me and started filming, and two others went through the books on our shelves, while a woman and a man comforted my son and several others stood around like zombies watching the proceedings.

After shouting at them for a while, I calmed down and noticed that a button on my nursing blouse had been torn off during the struggle. I asked to go to the bedroom to change clothes, and policewoman Wang Yahui accompanied me. While changing, I found large bruises and abrasions where my arms had been twisted. I burned with resentment, hoping that one day they'd pay for their wickedness.

Chen Shijie started squawking, "This morning I told you not to send out Twitter messages, but you did anyway. This is the result of your disobedience."

I demanded that he produce the relevant warrants, and he shook a search warrant in front of my face. They hung around after they finished searching to prevent me from contacting others for as long as possible.

They seized our laptop (the third one they'd taken), a desktop computer (left in our care by a friend), two Nokia cameras and several books containing Gu Chuan's essays. I refused to sign their confiscation receipt and demanded that they immediately return my cell phone.

Our evening meal had been delayed, depriving three-month-old Enen of water and milk and Luoluo, less than two years old, of anything to eat. I asked to go out to buy food, but Chen Shijie refused and proceeded to telephone for pizza, spaghetti and mushroom soup. It was only when Chen and the others left after 10:00 that night that the children and I were able to eat. Although the DomSec cops withdrew, three auxiliaries were posted outside our door.

After I put the kids to bed around midnight, I lay tossing and turning in bed. Without a computer or cell phone and with police posted outside my door around the clock, how could I regain contact with the outside world?

I suffered a bout of diarrhea, and upon returning to bed after taking some medicine, I found Enen's little hand unusually warm. Children are so sensitive; were they being affected by my emotions? I fidgeted until dawn, then wrote a note with a plea for help and a friend's phone number and dropped it out the window, but none of the people walking by took any notice of it.

———◆———

The kids woke after daybreak on February 20. Luoluo didn't want breakfast and threw a tantrum, demanding to go out to play. I had no choice but to try to force my way out with the children. The auxiliary cops said, "Don't give us a hard time!" As I continued to insist, a female DomSec officer surnamed Dong turned up.

I told her, "The kids want to go out to play, and I need some help from my church friends. I can't deal with two children on my own." She wouldn't let me out, but she let me use her phone to call a friend from church, while warning me not to reveal my situation.

With my cell phone confiscated, I couldn't remember the phone numbers of any of my friends, but luckily I had the business card of a friend named Sun Hao, and I had the policewoman call that number.

As soon as Sun Hao answered, I told him, "Changping DomSec took Gu Chuan away yesterday, and now I'm being held under house arrest with the kids. I can't contact anyone, so please get word out for me."

The DomSec cop quickly hung up the phone and scolded me: "I told you not to go running off your mouth!"

After we went back inside, I was alarmed to see a bloodstain in Enen's diaper. He'd had loose stools that morning as well—what was the matter with him?

I went sobbing to the female DomSec cop: "Hurry and let me take my child to the hospital! He has blood in his urine!" After examining the diaper, the policewoman telephoned her superior for instructions. Then Wang Dong from the Changping substation and cops from the Dongxiaokou police station drove us to the Aviation General Hospital near Beiyuan. After an emergency pediatric examination, Enen was diagnosed with a urinary tract infection, and the doctor ordered him admitted for observation and treatment.

Admission to the hospital required a deposit of 4,000 *yuan*, and I asked the DomSec cops for help processing the paperwork. They requested instructions, after which a middle-aged DomSec cop surnamed Li arrived at the hospital. The Changping cops referred to him as their leader. Li had come to our home after Gu Chuan was abducted on the nineteenth, and when I'd asked him to identify himself, he'd only said, "My surname is Li. You'll be seeing a lot of me."

After a discussion with Li, the doctor agreed to a deposit of 2,000 *yuan*. After that, a fat policeman from the Dongxiaokou station, Xu Zheng (the plainclothes cop who'd taken a video of me while our house was being searched on the nineteenth), had me sign an IOU, saying untruthfully, "I just took this money out. It's a personal loan, and you have to repay it." At his request, I signed a paper stating, "Today I borrowed 2,000 *yuan* from Liu Tao." At that time I didn't know Xu Zheng's true identity; the Liu Tao on the receipt was in fact another DomSec cop from the Beijing Municipal PSB.

With Enen in the hospital, I was even less able to look after Luoluo, and I again requested finding a church friend to help. This time a female DomSec cop surnamed Cao agreed to let me use her cell phone.

I dialed Sun Hao's telephone number, but as soon as I said, "This is Li Xin'ai," the line went dead, and when I dialed again, all I got was a busy signal. I then realized that my message about Gu Chuan's situation hadn't been passed on, either because Sun was under pressure, or because his phone had been cut off.

I had no choice then but to call Pastor Joseph at Agape Church. Since the DomSec cop was listening in and I didn't want her to take the phone away, I could only refer vaguely to my situation, and I asked Pastor Joseph to pass the message to my friend Wang Jinglong.

On the evening of the twentieth, Auntie Hou from church came to the hospital with three other church friends to lend a hand.

Looking at pitiful little Enen broke my heart. Luoluo, running around the hospital ward, seemed to have forgotten yesterday's terror. I felt conscience-stricken that my two small children had to go through this hardship at their age.

When the doctor prepared to give Enen an antibiotic IV, Auntie Hou and I objected that he should be thoroughly examined first. The doctor explained, "The hospital lab is closed for the day, and we can't carry out further tests until tomorrow. If we don't give him an IV, there's no need for him to stay in the hospital, and he'd probably be more comfortable at home."

After thinking it over, I decided to take Enen home, and the doctor gave me a prescription for Amoxicillin. Sixty-year-old Auntie Hou stayed with us to look after Luoluo. I'd expected Gu Chuan to return home quickly after being called in for questioning, as had happened the year before, but now I was kept waiting with no word from him.

Auntie Hou came to our home for more than 20 days, until she fell ill with bronchitis. I'm deeply indebted to Auntie Hou and some college friends who helped me with the children during those lonely, anxious days.

On the morning of the twenty-first, Brother Ji from church helped me take Enen to the hospital for a checkup. He was no longer feverish, and his urine and other indicators had returned to normal. For the next two months, however, he suffered from chronic diarrhea, a misery to all of us.

After taking a stool sample at the hospital, the doctor said the problem wasn't serious, but no Western or Chinese medicine seemed to have any effect. The doctor suggested giving Enen some allergy tests and switching him to formula. I said, "The first time he got diarrhea was after I ate pizza and also got diarrhea. Could this be related to the cheese on the pizza?"

The doctor believed it was.

It was the villainous DomSec cops who injured my baby's health and forced him to be weaned at less than six months. I'm still furious every time I think of it.

Enen's formula cost more than 300 *yuan* per can. Making the switch stopped his diarrhea, but if I gave him anything else, it started up again. He went through at least one can of formula every week, a significant increase to our household burden courtesy of DomSec. Now, at ten months, Enen needs supplementary foods, and satisfying his hunger means dealing with his ceaseless defecation. I can only pray that Enen will soon be cured of this ailment.

———✦———

After I made contact with my church on February 20, word of Gu Chuan's abduction got out. While we were at the hospital, Sister Li Jinfang called the cell phone of Cao, the female DomSec cop, and asked for me. Cao lied, "I'm a church friend of Gu Chuan and Li Xin'ai. They're standing in line for their child to see the doctor, and their cell phone battery is dead, that's all." Cao pulled the wool over Li Jinfang's eyes, but Wang Jinglong saw through her, because Cao referred to herself as a church friend rather than as a brother or sister in the normal way. Wang Jinglong then contacted me through Auntie Hou's cell phone and learned the truth.

Later, while away on a business trip, Wang Jinglong had Brother Ji find a cell phone for me to use, and after returning to Beijing, Wang visited us several times, bringing 2,600 *yuan* worth of milk powder and earning my eternal gratitude.

Sister Li Jinfang often telephoned to comfort me, and also passed on Professor Zhang Zuhua's best wishes. If not for the caring they showed while Gu Chuan was in custody, my suffering would have been all the greater.

Every day, Dongxiaokou police officers and our housing development's security guards were posted downstairs. When I went out shopping, they were on my heels, as if afraid I'd try to escape.

Enen's diarrhea made him fussy, and I had to hold and comfort him constantly. Unable to look after Luoluo properly, I took him down to the church every morning and then picked him up in the evening. My child, less than two years old, became a little vagrant, and even with my church friends looking after him, I knew he must be missing his mom and dad. Every time I took him to the church, he gave me a heartbreaking look, afraid his mom would disappear as his dad had done, and wanting me to stay and play with him. I could only steel myself and slip away.

One day at church, Luoluo scalded his hand, raising a big blister. It pained me to try to explain these hardships to a child too young to understand or even experience them. Why has this hateful government continued to persecute people for more than 60 years? Is China truly God-forsaken? Is it right to ask, "Who gave you the misfortune to be born in China"?[1] I don't want my children to repeat the fate of previous generations; I want them to grow up healthy and happy, and to live decent lives free of fear, deception, lies or the stench of blood, in a clean world full of love and freedom.

One evening, Luoluo came home from church in low spirits, and no matter what I said to him, he shouted, "No!" and violently shook his head. I knew he resented the loss of his parents' company and being stuck in a room instead of playing outside in the sunshine. Unable to control my rage any further, I telephoned the DomSec cop Wang Dong and demanded, "When is Gu Chuan coming home?" But his only reply was, "I don't know."

---

[1] TN: The prominent physicist He Zuoxiu, during an interview in December 2005, expressed the opinion that loss of life is the price that must be paid at China's current stage of development, and that anyone who is dissatisfied should just curse his fate at being born in China. See "Coal Mine Deaths and the Price of Development," EastSouthWestNorth blog, December 16, 2005, http://www.zonaeuropa.com/20051216_1.htm (accessed December 2, 2012).

Wang Dong, the policeman assigned to me, was originally from the criminal division, and he was always courteous, but I detested the female DomSec cop Cao who accompanied him. During the time Gu Chuan was in secret detention, Wang and Cao came seven or eight times to carry out ideological work on me.

On March 18, the municipal-level DomSec cop Li also came over, hoping to bring me around: "Gu Chuan has already acknowledged his errors, and whether he comes back or not depends on your attitude." I didn't believe a word of his nonsense.

Friends told me that a DomSec cop from the municipal PSB, Zhu Xu, had complained about Gu Chuan and me putting out daily Twitter messages demanding that the police return our computer, passports and other belongings confiscated on April 9, 2010. Zhu Xu said, "Gu Chuan isn't old, but he's as stubborn as an old democracy activist."

Our dear teacher Zhang Zuhua and good friend Wang Junxiu[2] arranged for legal counsel for Gu Chuan. Wang first sought out Xia Lin at Beijing's Huayi Law Firm, but Xia was already engaged in another case, so Wang went to Zhu Jiuhu,[3] who agreed to the appointment. However, the Chinese government's unlawful tactics of abduction and disappearance prevented Gu Chuan from receiving effective legal counsel.

Every day passed like a year as I waited for Gu Chuan's return. I concealed the truth in telephone conversations with my parents, not wishing to cause them unnecessary worry; in any case, they were too busy farming their cotton field to look after the children.

During this time, the Agape Church gave me great care and help I was also very moved by an old colleague of Gu Chuan's, Mai Tian, who telephoned to offer his support. He said, "I'm too tied up to help you in any other way, but if you tell me your bank account number, I'll wire you some money." Although I declined, I greatly appreciated the concern of this man whom I'd never met.

---

[2] TN: Zhang Zuhua is a political theorist and activist. Wang Junxiu, an internet commentator and investor, co-founded China's most popular blog-hosting website, Bokee.com.

[3] TN: Lawyers Xia Lin and Zhu Jiuhu are both known for taking on controversial cases.

I likewise declined offers of financial assistance from Su Yutong in Germany and Guo Baosheng in the United States.[4] Guo asked, "Are you afraid that accepting money from me will get you into trouble?" I assured him, "No, I still have enough to get by." Thankful as I was, I felt there were others in greater need.

I did accept humanitarian aid from Amnesty International and Chinese Human Rights Defenders after others applied on my behalf and passed the funds to me. I would like to express my gratitude to them here.

⟹•⟸

The time of Gu Chuan's secret detention was the most difficult period in my life. Every day I took advantage of Enen's naps to cook. Sometimes he awoke just as I finished, and I'd have to soothe him back to sleep before I could eat my food, now cold. I often washed clothes and diapers late into the night. One day I began spotting and thought my period had resumed, but it was just a symptom of exhaustion. The mental pressure and physical burden drove me to tears.

Gu Chuan and I had always maintained a low profile so as not to attract criticism, but the authorities were not prepared to let off any advocate of social transformation.

On the afternoon of April 4, I dialed the emergency police hotline reporting the disappearance of my husband Gu Chuan, and with Enen accompanied the responders to the Dongxiaokou police station, leaving Luoluo at the church. The police said Gu Chuan had not disappeared and that his precise location was known. I asked what that precise location was, but they just looked mysterious and said they couldn't reveal it, while adding, "This matter isn't being handled by our police station. You've come to the wrong place." They then ignored me, but I was determined to stay until I got a result, and I declared a hunger strike.

Around 10:00 that night, Wang Dong and the municipal PSB DomSec cop Li came to the police station and advised me to go

---

[4] TN: Su Yutong is a blogger and activist, and Guo Baosheng is a labor activist who was imprisoned for subversion.

home, but I refused to leave and they couldn't force me. That night, some unknown netizens sent text messages voicing their support and concern, which moved me very much.

The next day, kindhearted Sister Wang came to the police station to keep me company and help me look after the children. In the afternoon, Liu Tao from the municipal PSB and the DomSec cop Zhang came and advised me to go home. I made my demand: "Either let Gu Chuan return home right away, or help me look after my children."

Liu Tao replied, "Gu Chuan can't go home yet," and continued with his lies about how Gu Chuan was "performing well" inside.

I said, "I don't believe it. If Gu Chuan is 'performing well,' you've tortured him into it."

Liu Tao said defensively, "He has absolutely not been tortured."

I said, "In any case, I won't believe anything you say until you let me see him with my own eyes and he confirms it."

I demanded to know what crime Gu Chuan had committed, and what they meant by holding him for so long. They refused to suggest any crime or to state exactly why they'd arrested him. All I had was Wang Dong's single reference to Gu Chuan being suspected of "inciting subversion of state power."

Finally Liu Tao promised to find a nanny to help me with the kids and to arrange an appropriate time for me to speak to or even possibly see Gu Chuan. The condition was that I couldn't tell anyone about what we'd discussed today, and I couldn't mention the police officers' names on the internet.

During Gu Chuan's secret incarceration, I telephoned Sun Di in the municipal PSB's DomSec branch on several occasions, but he always put me off by saying, "I know nothing about this. I'm not clear." Eventually he stopped taking my calls.

The lease on our apartment in Tiantong Xiyuan was supposed to run out on April 2, 2011, but DomSec bullied our landlord into extending it by a month. This made me believe that Gu Chuan would return home by May 2.

On the afternoon of April 21, the municipal DomSec cop Li came to our home again and said, "I have news. Gu Chuan will come home soon, so just be patient."

After that they allowed me a telephone call with Gu Chuan. Wang Dong used his cell phone to call Chen Shijie's cell phone, and at long last I heard that familiar voice: "Is everything all right with you and the kids? I've acknowledged my errors and have made a clear debriefing of my personal issues, seeking lenient handling by the government." After these nonsensical comments, the line was cut. Gu Chuan later told me that Liu Tao had drafted this statement for him to read out as a condition for letting him talk.

At 4:00 in the afternoon on April 22, there was a knock at my door, and when I opened the door, Gu Chuan was standing before me, wearing a sweater and dark glasses and a smile on his thin, sickly face. Those 63 days had seemed like a lifetime.

Gu Chuan had been abducted in winter's frigid bleakness, and his return came with the gaudy blooms of spring. The children and I had long put away our jackets, but Gu Chuan was still wearing the black sweater he'd left in, as if suddenly appearing from another dimension.

Throughout his secret incarceration, Gu Chuan had been forced to wear a black hood, had been deprived of sleep, nourishment and exercise, and had been subjected to constant verbal and physical abuse, stripped of his clothes and forced to kneel for extended periods, among other torments. When his interrogator, Chen Shijie, found Gu Chuan intransigent, he threatened our children, distressing Gu Chuan and plaguing his conscience. Gu Chuan continued to suffer from chronic leg pain for days after returning home.

After more than two months' absence, Luoluo hardly knew the father he'd always loved to play with. I knew Gu Chuan's physical pain would soon heal, but his mental regret and vexation would recede only slowly as he reestablished his warm connection with his children.

The night before his release, Gu Chuan had been forced to sign both our names to a pledge forbidding us to tell anyone of his secret incarceration, or to write "reactionary" articles, send Twitter messages, accept media interviews, get together with friends in our circle or go to church. It was particularly emphasized that he was not to contact Li Jinfang or Zhu Jiuhu. He had to submit an ideological report every day. DomSec made Gu Chuan responsible for any "unharmonious language" I might use, and threatened to re-arrest and imprison him at their discretion.

We discovered that Chen Shijie had removed his phone number from our cell phones when he returned them to us, indicating the guilty conscience behind DomSec's formidable power.

⚊◈⚊

When our lease in Tiantong Xiyuan ran out in May, we planned to leave our luggage at the church and return to our native place to rest for a few months before looking for a new apartment in Beijing. DomSec disagreed, however, saying Gu Chuan was not free to leave Beijing at this point. Since we had to continue renting in Beijing, we decided to move to Yanjiao, on the eastern edge of Beijing, where rents were cheaper, but DomSec vetoed this plan as well, insisting that we remain in our current neighborhood.

While looking for a new apartment, we discovered that someone had parked a van outside our building. One day I walked over to the man sitting in the driver's seat and asked, "Want to help us move?" Seeing his identity exposed, he quickly made a telephone call: "Hello? Chen Shijie? I'm from the Dongxiaokou police station. They want us to help them move. So, we should withdraw?" After hanging up, he drove off with his half-dozen colleagues. I later asked Chen Shijie why he had us under surveillance, but he flatly denied it.

In a steadily inflating housing market, we finally found an apartment costing 2,000 *yuan* per month. DomSec frequently asked us how much money we had left and told Gu Chuan to apply for a living allowance, but we refused. I regret it now, because it's only right that Enen's milk powder and our expensive rent should be added to their stability maintenance budget.[5] In any case, these

---

[5] TN: Maintaining social stability (*weihu wending*, shortened to *weiwen*) became a priority under the Hu Jintao-Wen Jiabao administration. The government has devoted massive funding to a labyrinthine stability preservation apparatus that employs both legal and extralegal measures to quell popular discontent.

are taxpayer funds that should be available to members of the public. But we objected to them always trying to wash away their crimes with money.

After moving, we tried to leave town in secret, but we were intercepted and forced to return. Chen Shijie yelled at Gu Chuan, "Don't you know what's good for you? If you don't go home now, I'll be seeing you in the detention center."

We don't want our children to grow up in a horrible country like this, with tainted milk powder, contaminated vaccines and toxic ham. In this befouled China, living in health and peace is a luxury.

We're grateful to so many who remembered us in our time of trouble, not only friends but also complete strangers. Popular surveillance is truly powerful, because a dictatorial government fears nothing more than people standing together and protecting each other in love and solidarity. I believe that regardless of what terroristic tactics it employs, the Chinese Communist Party will someday die a natural death. I would like to quote a poem written by a netizen, "The Age of Deletion," to express my scorn for the Communist dictatorial regime:

> You can delete my text,
> But not my speech.
> You can delete my photographs,
> But not my shouts.
> You can delete my video,
> But not my howls.
> You can delete my truth,
> But not my justice.
> You can delete my voice,
> But not my conscience.
> You can delete my vision,
> But not my truth.
> You can delete my name,
> But not my integrity.
> You can delete my rights,
> But not my ardor.

You can delete my life,
But I'll exchange it for imperishable freedom.[6]

There is a faith that surpasses all earthly power, which is in Lord Jesus. There is a persistence that triumphs over all the world's horrors and threats, which is the pursuit of justice and truth. Injustice cannot prevail, and evil must be expunged.

---

[6] TN: This poem is attributed to an author with the pen name "Brandy on the Rocks."

THE ABDUCTION OF A DRIFTING SPIRIT

Hua Ze

Hua Ze (online name Linghun Piaoxiang, or Drifting Spirit), born in Beijing in the 1960s, is a signatory of Charter 08. Formerly a director of documentary films for CCTV, she began participating in the civil rights movement in 2010 by filming ongoing rights cases such as the Three Fujianese Netizens and disseminating them over the internet. On October 8, 2010, she was detained for her involvement in an online statement welcoming Liu Xiaobo's Nobel Peace Prize, and was held for 55 days. She is currently a visiting scholar at Columbia University in New York City.

THE ABDUCTION

I'd been on a work assignment in the northeast for half a month, and going online after a day's filming I became aware of tensions in Beijing following the announcement of Xiaobo's Nobel Prize. After discussions with Teng Biao, I decided that upon returning to Beijing, I'd stay at his office in Wangjing District until the situation cooled off enough for me to go home.

Wary of being traced, as soon as we boarded our flight on October 27, 2010, I shut off my cell phone and removed its battery and SIM card, cutting off my communication with the outside world.

After arriving in Beijing around 3:00, I said goodbye to Teng Biao and the others and joined Teng's assistant Huanhuan on the airport bus to Wangjing. While on the airport expressway, I realized to my great annoyance that I'd left my laptop at the airport.

After dropping my things at Teng Biao's office, I called the airport's lost-and-found office and learned that my laptop was in their records. I immediately set off for the nearby Civil Aviation Management Institute, where I could catch a bus back to the airport.

Just as I reached the institute's entrance, I was grabbed from behind and a black hood was pulled over my head. My first thought was, so the black hoods are this thick—and they smell like dirty feet!

I heard myself scream "Help!" and struggled desperately in hopes that someone would witness my abduction and call the police. During the struggle, I managed to pull off the black hood long enough to see seven or eight big men stuff me head-first into a van. I remember a last shot of my feet kicking futilely at the van's door. One of my captors snarled, "Keep that up and we'll throttle you!" After that I blacked out.

Groggily regaining consciousness, I felt the van stop and thought it had reached its destination. But then it went on, starting and stopping several times before resuming full speed. I realized it had been passing through stoplights and now was on the expressway to the suburbs.

After I don't know how long, cold water dashed against my face, and I found myself in a dark room with a single light aimed directly at me. Faces hovered around me and a hand reached out and grabbed my collar, yanking me from the ground and shoving me onto a stool. My head slammed against a wall. I tasted blood and my chest ached. I thought of Zhazidong Prison, where the Kuomintang tortured Communists in the novel *Red Crag*.

I passed out several more times before regaining consciousness on a bed. I felt as if I'd been washed ashore by a huge wave, and although I was terribly weak, clarity gradually returned: So it had happened at last, and so suddenly! I wondered what time it was and whether my friends knew I was missing. By tomorrow at the very latest, Huanhuan would go to the office and see that I'd left without returning, and she would certainly tell Teng Biao.

Looking around, I gathered that this was a small suburban guesthouse. The room was about 12 square meters, with a door and toilet on the north side and a window on the south. A desk and chair had been moved from the east wall and stacked under the window, and a stool had been put in their place. This was where I'd bumped my head, and my bed was on the west wall opposite. Five or six men milled around whispering to each other, and one of them noticed I was awake.

Before the interrogation began, I prepared for the worst and set two principles for myself: I'd accept death before dishonor, and I'd talk about myself but not a word about others.

THE CONTEST

Struggling to sit up against the headboard, I felt a sharp pain in my back.

The interrogation began. The others withdrew, leaving only No. 1 (I'll refer to my interrogators in the order of their appearance). He looked about 30 years old, his heavily moussed hair swept back in a pompadour. He wore a fitted jacket, and his open collar revealed a heavy silver necklace. I wanted to tell him: That's ugly, it looks like a dog's choke chain.

After exercising his wrists in an exaggerated manner, he lit a cigarette and slipped it into a transparent cigarette holder, then holding it with thumb and forefinger in a feminine fashion, he strolled over and plopped next to me on the bed. I lowered my head and refused to look at him. After a while, he pressed his finger against my brow to lift my face and pushed a drooping lock of hair behind my ear. Then he inhaled deeply from his cigarette and blew the smoke slowly into my face. It was clear he wanted to infuriate me, so I closed my eyes and refused to play along. After another interval (which seemed to last a century), he laid his arm lightly on my leg, leaned toward me and whispered in my ear, "Look at me. Eh? Come on, look at me."

I raised my eyes and coldly met his teasing gaze less than a foot away. One of his eyebrows shot up as he winked at me.

"Back off, please," I said with as much strength as I could muster.

"How far?"

"The farther the better."

"Why?"

"I hate smoke."

He stood and strolled to the desk, stubbed out his cigarette, then returned.

"See, no more cigarette. Can we talk now? What's your name? Eh?"

"I have nothing to say to you. Bring in your superior." Then I shut my eyes and refused to acknowledge him.

That little thug was patient, however, and kept talking to himself for about an hour until someone came in, whispered in his ear and then went out again. Soon after that, four or five others came in. I thought I recognized one of them as Zhou, the head of Beijing's Dongcheng District Domestic Security Division, who'd called me in for a talk several months earlier. On that occasion we'd sat with a table between us, and although his words seemed threatening, he'd had a smile on his face the whole time. Now he was somber and wore dark glasses, and he seemed much shorter than I remembered. He seemed to be playing a supporting role in this abduction, so I couldn't be sure it was him.

"Get up and come with us," someone said.

I moved to the edge of the bed to put on my shoes, but as soon as my feet hit the floor, a shooting pain threw me into a cold sweat. My ankle was injured. Before I could do anything, the black hood was on my head again, and two people began pulling me staggering through the door and down a long corridor, then out the front door, where I was loaded like cargo into the van.

This time the van didn't go far before stopping, and I was taken into a large room, then ten steps farther I turned into another room, where I was pushed onto a square stool. The clamor of human voices then withdrew, leaving just one man who began pacing around me. In the silence of the room there was only the sound of his footsteps, round and round; then he stopped and pulled off my hood. Accustomed to darkness, I closed my eyes instinctively against the room's glaring light.

"What's your name?"

I saw a pair of hiking boots, and my eyes traveled gradually upward to hiking pants and a blue knit sweatshirt covered by a casual jacket. I saw a fair-skinned, doe-eyed youth, "No. 2." He seemed to like the great outdoors.

"What's your name?" he asked again.

"You kidnapped me without knowing who I am?"

"Answer my question."

"Hua Ze."

My eyes having adjusted to the environment, I looked around. I was sitting in the middle of a 20-odd-square-meter room. About three meters in front of me were two chairs and a table, and on the table was a box-type briefcase—recording equipment! It was the classic interrogation setup I'd seen in so many films.

"You got off the plane this afternoon."

"Yes."

"From where?"

"Dandong."

"What were you doing there?"

"Filming."

"How long were you there?"

"Three days."

"What were you filming?"

"A lawyer at work."

"Doing what?"

"Meeting the client and his family, going to the court and the procuratorate to make copies of the case file."

"That took three days?"

"Our schedule was very tight."

"Which lawyer?"

"I don't want to say."

"Why not?"

"I won't name others."

He paced a little more and then said, "You look pretty weak."

"I'm too sore and tired for this stool."

He brought a chair over. "Sit on this. Is that better?"

"Yes. Thanks."

"Shall we continue?"

"Go on."

"Why were you filming that lawyer?"

"I wanted to."

"Why?"

"Does there have to be a reason?"

"Doesn't there?"

"I don't need a reason for wanting anything."

I heard him control his breathing, pause for a moment, then resume.

"Where will it be broadcast when you're done?"

"Wherever anyone will pay for it. I'll show it on CCTV if they want it."

"What if no one buys it?"

"Then I'll just give it away to whomever I like."

"Are you filming only this lawyer, or a series?"

"I haven't decided. I may film more if I feel like it."

"What do you mean by feel like it?"

"You wouldn't understand if I told you."

"How did you come to know this lawyer?"

"It's been a long time, I don't remember."

We went over the filming of the lawyer for a long time, but he learned nothing.

The door crashed open and a tall man with a posse of four or five others burst on the scene.

"No. 3" was around 40 years old with small eyes, wearing a Western suit and shoes so shiny that a fly would have slid off of them. He slapped his cigarette box and cell phone on the table, then sat down with his legs crossed and jiggled them constantly while saying in a hectoring tone, "Don't give my brothers here a hard time. You wanted to see the boss, right? So here I am. Let me tell you, I'm too busy to bullshit with you. Will you talk or not?"

"Haven't I been talking with your brothers all along?"

"It always gets stuck at your not remembering something or not wanting to say something. Is that talking? You think you can call the shots here? Forget it! Let me tell you, once you're here it's not that easy to leave. I ask and you answer. That's what's called talking. Get it?"

"Please show me your ID. What department are you with?"

"If I told you, it would scare you to death!" (I'd been dealing with DomSec for a couple of days now without being scared. Was he State Security?)

"Try me."

"I can't say now. That's for later."

I laughed and No. 3 gnashed his teeth in anger. "I can make you disappear from the face of the earth. Do you know that?"

I kept laughing and stared at him as if watching a play. Just then I heard a dog barking outside.

"I'll bring the German shepherd in to play with you. Believe it?"

"Sure!" By then I was weak with laughter.

No. 2, off to the side, spoke up: "How can you be so arrogant? What's so funny? Any sane person would be terrified."

"Why should I be scared? You abduct a feeble woman like me by force and don't even dare identify yourselves, which means you're even more terrified than I am. As long as you're so scared, I don't have to be."

No. 3 was clearly enraged. He slammed his fist on the table: "I'll ask you one last time: will you talk?"

"I have nothing to say."

"Okay, if you want to be Sister Jiang, I'll help you! I'm always polite before resorting to force, but no more Mr. Nice Guy! Wait here!" He practically ran to the door, the others swarming after him.

I tossed one more sentence after him: "I don't expect to leave here alive!"

The door slammed shut, then opened again, and "No. 4" came in. He yelled at me: "Stand up! You've been sitting comfortably, haven't you?"

I stood up shakily, and he kicked the chair out from under me.

"You're in business, eh?"

I looked uncomprehendingly at him.

"No husband and no proper way to make a living, eh?"

I understood. "So you're saying that what you're doing is a proper way to make a living?"

"Shut up! When our leader talks to you, you should feel lucky. Who asked you to answer? You're better off keeping your mouth shut."

There was in fact no point talking to that skinny runt.

"Why can't you get a man? Why can't you get a decent job? What are you?"

What was his logic? Had he even gone to school?

He rambled on with those same two questions, apparently obsessed with my lack of a husband or a proper job.

I just looked at him without speaking.

"Okay, so you won't talk. You're not talking, right?"

Hadn't he just said it was better for me not to talk?

He circled me fiercely and stopped behind me. Now that "Mr. Nice Guy" was gone, what was I in for? All the torture methods people talked about swirled through my mind. I recalled what one person always said: "The most despicable are those who cower while inside and act tough when they come out." I wouldn't give anyone a reason to criticize me for this. Besides, given my constitution, I would die before I could suffer too much, so I was ready.

Why was he still not doing anything after such a long time? My right foot hurt so much that I had to shift all my weight to my left foot. I was beginning to sink into a trance. Don't fall down, whatever you do, don't fall! Don't let them think you're scared.

I heard someone talking to me, and my mind gradually cleared. No. 2 was holding the chair and telling me to sit, playing Good Cop.

"Why are you trembling?"

"I'm cold."

He went out and came back with a white bed sheet: "There aren't any clothes. Take this."

I wrapped the sheet around me. No. 2 pulled up a chair next to me, and started in gravely and earnestly:

"Why are you so stubborn? All we want from you is the right attitude."

"After illegally abducting a law-abiding citizen in broad daylight, what right do you have to talk about attitude?"

"There's no point going on about how you got here—it won't change anything."

"I can't change anything, but I can refuse to cooperate with you hooligans."

"Hooligan? Who's a hooligan?"

"Whoever harasses me and tries to make me disappear from the face of the earth. I can tolerate a proper gangster, but not a hooligan."

"What's the difference?"

"A gangster does his best to cover up his indecency because he knows how ugly it is. A hooligan parades his low-life character as if he's proud of it."

"Oh, that makes sense. But aren't you a bit arrogant? You know, you act like you're picking a fight."

I corrected him: "I'm not picking a fight; you're not worth it. Make me disappear? Don't give me that!" I became increasingly angry. "Doesn't that mean death? Well, as a taxpayer, I'm sick to death of paying your salaries and watching and hearing about your villainy day after day."

He only became more patient: "Have you ever considered that we won't kill you, but will just let you linger?"

"Fine. When the oil runs out, the lamp is extinguished!"

"Why can't you just play along? If you haven't done anything wrong, what's the harm in talking about it?"

"I've told you, I'll talk about myself, but not about others."

"Why think about others when you don't even know if you'll ever leave here?"

"Inner peace and a free conscience are much more important to me than physical freedom. You wouldn't understand that."

He paused for a while. "I'll think about that, and you should, too. It's late now. Get some rest."

I said I needed to use the washroom, and he had a female guard accompany me. After I came out, I found a mattress and bedding laid out on the floor. The guard said, "You can make do with this, can't you?"

What? No torture or wearing me down? In any case, the first thing was to stretch my weak, shivering body under the warm covers.

A man and a woman sat in chairs on each side of the mattress. For the first time in my life, I closed my eyes under a 200-watt bulb and the gaze of two guards.

Exhausted as I was, I had trouble sleeping through the night, feeling as if my heart were pounding out of my chest. My body ached from the strain on my shoulders, belly and limbs during the abduction. I was conscious of the footsteps of the guards changing shifts, their murmurs, the squeaking of their chairs, even their breathing.

As the light of dawn began filtering through the room's heavy curtains, a compact, burly man entered (he was one of those involved in my abduction the day before), then walked over with his hands in his pockets, glaring maliciously at me, and kicked my mattress twice: "Get up! You think this is a convalescent home?"

I got up, tidied the bedding, and silently sat down on the mattress.

No. 2 came in and pulled up a chair next to me.

"Let's continue where we left off."

I repeated: "I'll talk about myself, but not others."

"That's your principle?"

"Yes."

. . .

"What does the name Hua Ze stand for?"

"It means an ocean of flowers in literary Chinese."

He began to ask about things he seemed to think were important, but which I considered boring and trivial: my family background, my childhood environment, my education.... Our conversation proceeded in this piecemeal, rambling fashion.

"You have at least a couple dozen people dealing with me. Do you think that's a good use of taxpayer funds?" I asked.

"What makes you think we're using taxpayer funds?" he asked, looking at me with interest.

"So you're with An Yuan Ding?"[1]

"Could be."

"Must be a tough job. Hard on the conscience."

"What makes you think that?"

"You seem educated—a university graduate, at least. Will you tell your family that you kidnapped me?"

---

[1] TN: A private company engaged by the government as a "stability maintenance contractor" to intercept petitioners and other undesirables in Beijing and detain them or send them home. See Global Voices, "China: Glory to the Stability Maintenance Contractors," September 27, 2010, http://globalvoicesonline.org/2010/09/27/china-glory-to-the-stability-maintenance-contractors/ (accessed November 26, 2012).

"You can't call this kidnapping."

"Then what is it?"

"We call it 'bringing them in.'"

"You know it's against the law, right?"

"There are many levels of law, some you don't know about."

I looked at him curiously: "So tell me, what department are you with, really?"

"You wouldn't understand. Even if we someday encounter each other under different circumstances, you won't understand."

"At least tell me your name. Although you're a member of a mafia-style organized crime ring, when you're brought to trial someday, I can testify that you didn't torture me during my abduction."

He laughed. "And when do you think that will happen?"

"Man proposes, Heaven disposes. Maybe ten years, maybe overnight. I believe it will happen in our lifetime."

"What are you going to do in the meantime?"

"Record this era's changes with my pen, my effort and my video camera."

He nodded and changed the subject. "You should eat. What would you like?"

"I want to brush my teeth first, otherwise I can't eat."

He used a quarter of an hour trying to persuade me that rinsing my mouth with water was enough, but I insisted on a toothbrush and toothpaste.

Finally he said, "It's not that hard to get a toothbrush, but last night you seemed emotionally unstable, and I'm afraid you'll hurt yourself."

So that's why I had people watching me while I slept and went to the washroom: "You're afraid I'll commit suicide?"

"Yesterday when you talked about dying without blinking an eye, you scared me."

Now it was my turn to laugh: "Don't worry, I won't kill myself. If I die, it'll be on your account."

"If you die here, no one will know."

"Not necessarily. You think there's no one with a conscience among you? Maybe no one will talk about it today, but can you be sure they won't ten or twenty years from now? Don't be so confident."

"You're really not afraid to die?"

"Every life ends sooner or later, whether it's boring or interesting. What's there to fear?"

"You'd better eat something and get some strength if you want an interesting life."

"I need to brush my teeth first."

"You're so stubborn. You know, a lot of your friends are smarter than you."

"I know."

The negotiation ended with me being given toothpaste and rubbing it on my teeth with my finger. After that I ate some vegetables, a few slices of mushroom and some instant noodles.

No. 2 went out and was immediately replaced by two guards. It looked like I was being allowed to rest some more.

That was the end of that day's "conversation." What were they up to? Were they going to keep on like this after ceremoniously kidnapping me? It seemed we could never understand each other. We were as different as dogs from wolves.

Everything was deathly still apart from a dog's barking. Off in the distance I heard the rumble of an aircraft, and I guessed we were positioned east of the airport. Was this one of their secret locations for detaining dissidents? How many of these places did they have, and how many people had they detained? Had anyone been tortured here? Were people able to live normal lives after leaving here? A year ago, I never would have guessed I'd end up in this situation. I imagined all kinds of things as evening fell, followed by another dawn.

The thug returned and kicked my mattress. I turned my back to him. He yanked off my covers, but I remained prone, ignoring him. He circled my mattress angrily and began yelling, "You bitch, who the f— do you think you are?" He kept on in this offensive manner.

Finally I sat bolt upright and shouted, "What are you? Get lost!"

He pushed up to me: "Say that again and I'll kill you!"

No. 2 barged in and I called out to him, "Get this thug away from me and don't let him back until you decide to kill me!"

No. 2 restrained the thug, who as he left pointed at me and said, "Just wait, I'll drag you out and bury you!"

Quaking with anger, I said, "I'm waiting for you to bury me. I know you're capable of it, but just remember, someday you'll go on trial for this!"

It was the third day of my abduction; how could I let my friends know what happened to me?

There were at least five teams watching me, with a man and a woman on each two-hour shift. Whenever No. 2 came in, the guards left, and whenever No. 2 went out, the guards returned. From what I could pick up from their brief conversations, the guards had been deployed from different departments, and it was possible they knew nothing about me. If I talked out loud about who I was and how I'd been brought here, would one of them leak the information? I couldn't believe that everyone I'd encountered these few days was coldhearted. I was thinking with my head buried in my knees when, bang! In burst another group of people, one of whom sat next to me on the mattress. It was No. 1, the little hooligan. He jabbed my ribs with his elbow: "Raise your head! Look at me!"

I remained motionless and silent as he poked me again and again. He lit a cigarette, inhaled, and found a spot where he could blow the smoke through my arms. I moved away but kept my head in my arms. He shifted to the center of the mattress. "Hey, how do you keep your cool? Were you trained in Taiwan?" There was laughter all around.

From this remark I determined that they were StateSec rather than DomSec. They'd been told that I was a spy or secret agent, a threat to state security, an enemy of the people. Otherwise how could such an educated young man be so ruthless and devoid of conscience? How else could they feel that they were engaged in respectable work? This time they weren't here to interrogate me, but were clearly just bored and wanted to toy with me. I kept my head in my arms and said nothing. Eventually they lost interest and left.

No. 2 came in now and then to chat with me, and I realized he was sifting through the items in my backpack.

"Is your backpack for carrying a camera or a video camera?"

"Both."

"Where are they?"

"I left them with a friend."

He wanted to know what the SD card was for. Since it was professional equipment, he couldn't view the data with an ordinary camera.

"You shot the *April 16* documentary?"[2]

"Yes."

"Not much to it. Anyone who can tell a story could do it. There's no technique."

"Glad you like it! The best documentaries don't show off technique."

"Why do you care about those people?"

"I love them."

"Aren't you something! You love so many people but you don't get married."

"We're talking about different kinds of love."

I wondered if the scenes in *April 16* that had stirred so many people would move him at all. I wanted to tell him that was love.

"How many cell phones do you have?"

"Several."

"Why did you take them apart?"

"To clean them."

"Why switch them off?"

"To save on cellular fees."

He was examining my cell phones. I had two cell phones, and the one I used for Twitter was new. He'd defiled it.

"You've lived well, visited lots of places."

"Yes, my ideal is to see the world."

Was he looking at my photos? They weren't on my U-drive. Was he reading my blog?

"You've earned a lot of money."

"Every cent I've earned is clean."

"Wouldn't you like to go back to that life?"

"All the time, but there's no going back."

---

[2] Referring to April 16, 2010, when the Three Fujianese Netizens went on trial at Fuzhou's Mawei Court, and hundreds of netizens from all over China gathered to protest outside the courthouse.

"I could help you."

"How could you help me? Can you cure the babies of their kidney stones or release Zhao Lianhai?[3] Can you resurrect the children who were crushed in shoddy schools during the Sichuan earthquake?"

"So there's nothing you like about this country?"

"Let me ask you something: Why did you kidnap me? Have I broken any laws? Would the government of any civilized country do such a thing?"

"Sure! The American CIA kidnaps people."

"You've watched too many American movies, kid. The CIA only targets foreigners. It doesn't abduct American citizens."

"Don't you know how to compromise?"

"It's possible to compromise over different interests. But how can you compromise with a thug, or with someone who rapes you? If he wants to rape you ten times, and you say two times, is that a compromise? If he wants to rape you for an hour, and you say 20 minutes, is that a compromise?"

No. 2 shook his head and left.

Another sleepless night. I awoke in the morning feeling unusually weak. My denim overalls hung loosely on me. I put on my shoes and rose unsteadily, treading on my pant leg. I bent down to roll up the cuffs, and when I stood upright, everything went black.

I heard a clamor that seemed far away. Someone was pinching me beneath the nose, fingernails almost piercing to the bone. The pain forced my eyes open, and I saw the thug's gloating face. I lay on my back, helpless. Five or six people were standing around, including No. 3 and Zhou, the head of the Dongcheng District DomSec team—yes, now I was sure it was him, even though he was still wearing dark glasses and said nothing.

"Let's go. Put on your coat and come with us."

I was lifted up, and for a third time the black hood was pulled over my head as I was stuffed into the back seat of a sedan with a

---

[3] TN: Zhao Lianhai is the father of a baby who contracted kidney stones after consuming tainted milk powder in 2008. He was sentenced to two and a half years in prison in 2010 after organizing protests by the parents of other victims.

man on each side of me. I had no idea where we were going as the car wound through the streets. A telephone rang, and I heard it answered by Zhou in the front passenger seat. He gave a long sigh, and I sensed that this assignment hadn't gone as planned.

After we'd driven for about two hours, I heard a train station announcement: "Attention all passengers…" I was being sent home!

"Where are you sending me? I don't even have a change of clothes. You have to notify my family." I pulled off my hood. The two men yelled and restrained me, and pulled the black hood on again. The man on my right pushed on my head until my chin pressed into my chest. Searing pain shot through my back, still injured from my abduction.

I yelled, "Let me go!" and struggled. The DomSec cop Zhou turned around and told me to quiet down.

The man on my right grabbed my hand and kneaded the skin harshly: "Go ahead! Keep struggling," he said in a voice so soft that only I could hear. It was the thug, getting his revenge. "Go ahead, yell! Aren't you tough? I'll throttle you, you bitch!"

I shouted back, "You scum, you're not fit to carry my shoes! Kill me if you dare!"

He twisted my arm back at a 30 degree angle. My limbs convulsed and then went numb, and I lost consciousness.

"Get out!"

"I can't move my legs."

"Enough of your damn faking!"

The thug kicked me and pulled me out of the car, my hood falling off in the process.

I was on a train platform, at the entrance to a train car. The bright autumn sunlight bathed my face. In broad daylight I was being kidnapped and dragged along by two men. Tears sprang to my eyes.

I sobbed, "Let me go! Let me go!"

Someone grabbed me from behind: "Don't do this to her! Let her go!"

I raised my head: "Who are you?"

"I'm Chen Ming.[4] I'm here to take you back to Xinyu."

---

[4] A pseudonym.

Chen Ming was the head of the Jiangxi Xinyu Film and Television Bureau, and the husband of a close friend. After years apart, we were reunited under these conditions.

Chen Ming carried me half-paralyzed onto the train. Other passengers hadn't been let in yet, and our sleeping compartment contained only me, Chen Ming and two plainclothes police officers claiming to be cadres from the neighborhood committee.

Forty minutes later, the train left Beijing West Station. After 68 hours I'd slipped from the gangsters' clutches and had begun my house arrest.

HOUSE ARREST

Xinyu is a prefecture-level city in Jiangxi Province. Twenty-one years earlier, I'd been a reporter there for *Xinyu Daily*. After resigning in 1989, I'd spent a period of time roaming around, but had been obliged to return to Xinyu to apply for a passport, because I was still formally registered in the newspaper's collective quarters. My good friend Jianjian, Chen Ming's wife, agreed to let me switch my household registration to their home address so she could handle such trivial matters for me in the future. That's how Chen Ming became my "head of household."

About a month before my abduction, DomSec had called on Chen Ming to inquire after me, telling him I'd been involved in some major rights defense campaigns. Chen Ming went home and told Jianjian, "Could this really be Hua Ze? Would she get involved in such things?" Jianjian replied, "That's her, all right. I know her."

On the evening of October 28, Chen Ming was notified by his superior that he was to accompany municipal DomSec officers to Beijing to bring me back, and that his travel expenses would be covered by his work unit. I wondered if Chen Ming regretted this "incautious association" that led him and his work unit to be implicated along with me.

On the train, I asked to examine my backpack, and as I unzipped it my cell phone dropped out. A female plainclothes officer grabbed it and said, "I'll hold your cell phone for you." She didn't know I had another cell phone that I used for Twitter. I'd never made a phone call with it; it was as clean as a newborn baby. I'd taken the precaution of entering the phone numbers of two friends into the Twitter phone, and this attention to detail saved me.

I slipped the Twitter phone into my trouser pocket, and after the train left the station, I went to the restroom and telephoned my two friends. The first call I made was to Pu Zhiqiang,[5] but he didn't answer. The second was to Teng Biao, and when I got through, the line was very bad. I told him that I'd been abducted, that one of my abductors was from Dongcheng District DomSec, and that I was now being escorted back to Xinyu. I said my laptop was still at the airport, and I urged him to find a way to get it back for me. When I'd said that much, the line was cut off. Then Pu Zhiqiang called back and told me he'd also been under house arrest since returning to Beijing on the twenty-seventh, but he was still allowed contact with the outside world. I told him what I'd told Teng Biao. He paused and then said, "This is the life you've chosen, and it was going to happen sooner or later. You have to learn to deal with it on your own." I said, "Yes, I understand."

Later, living in solitude for 50 days, I had a chance to repeatedly ponder these words, and I treated them as the sincere advice of a veteran to a new initiate; this was indeed our life.

After making these two phone calls, I decided to save the phone battery in case I needed to call for help—even though I didn't know who could save me, or how. In any case, I wanted my friends to know what was happening to me.

On the train, the two plainclothes officers asked me with great interest about Liu Xiaobo, the first mention of his name since I'd lost my freedom. Their questions indicated that I'd been abducted because I'd signed a statement welcoming Liu Xiaobo's Nobel Peace Prize. I was also able to confirm that it had been StateSec that abducted me.

This is a barbarous country and a thuggish regime, preferable to the late Qing regime a century ago only in that dissidents are abducted and "disappeared" instead of beheaded or banished. This has to change!

---

[5] TN: A veteran of the 1989 Democracy Movement, Pu is now a prominent rights defense lawyer.

I began to tell them about the June 4th incident, and about Charter 08 and the Nobel Peace Prize...and at this point I began to enjoy myself. Since the government was using abduction and imprisonment to let me share the honor of Xiaobo's Nobel Peace Prize, I would prove myself worthy by sowing the seeds of fire.

As the train drew toward our destination, the two plain-clothes officers and Chen Ming told me, "We're only responsible for bringing you back. We won't be seeing you again here in Xinyu. We hope you'll cut your losses by admitting your error and moving on."

I smiled and thanked them for their good intentions, but said that my dictionary didn't contain the term "admitting error."

I was met at the train station by a Xinyu DomSec officer, Chen Jianjun. He was around 40 years old and looked like a career soldier with little education. As soon as we got in the car, he started lecturing me: Don't wash your dirty linen in public; if you expose things internationally, it affects China's image. Don't look for legal loopholes; the law isn't everything. You might have started out with good intentions, but you were used by overseas anti-China forces.

I don't claim to be good at dealing with official boilerplate, but seeing him brainwashed to such a degree compelled me to patiently reply: It's for the sake of China's image that we're calling for the release of Liu Xiaobo; how can a Nobel Laureate be held in prison after we've dreamed of the Nobel for a hundred years? Laws are formulated by the ruling party, and how can protecting the dignity of the law be considered looking for loopholes? If we don't use the law as a weapon, are we supposed to use tanks instead? As for the overseas anti-China forces, I wanted to know exactly how they were using me.

He said, "I don't understand you. We'll talk more later."

I sternly told him, "If you don't understand, then don't go labeling people. Spend some time understanding the situation and then come talk to me."

I can't stand unprofessional people, and I wondered why everyone I'd encountered this time was so amateurish. Why couldn't they spend some time understanding me, and learning that I responded much better to persuasion than to force? Even shameless occupations such as DomSec and StateSec should take their work more seriously.

In Xinyu, I was taken to the Xiaofang Guesthouse on the northern edge of town. Six stories tall, it was probably once furnished to three-star standards, but now looked obsolete. At least the bedding was soft and clean, and the bathroom was spacious. I was in room 9207 on the second floor, apparently the only three-person suite in the guesthouse. Two female police officers stayed with me, and two male police officers stayed next door. Four police officers in each of two shifts gave me a total of eight personal "bodyguards."

DomSec officer Ouyang informed me of several rules: "No contact with the outside world, no visits with friends, and no leaving the building."

The DomSec officers all said they were from the criminal branch, economic crimes branch or public order branch. None admitted to being DomSec, suggesting the secretive nature of the division. Even so, after numerous encounters I could spot DomSec cops at a glance. Three of the eight were from the municipal level, and the others were deployed from various sub-branches. My security clearance was higher than they'd dealt with before, and the officers from the sub-branches had been deployed without their superiors being informed of the nature of their assignment.

Municipal DomSec Division Chief Hu arrived—he was simply called the leader, but I worked out his identity over time. He politely explained that this action was coordinated under the Public Security Ministry, and that how long I stayed here depended on orders from above. Xinyu didn't want to hold me a minute longer than that, and they hoped I'd cooperate. He advised me to treat this as a time to relax and recuperate.

I asked Officer Hu if I could contact my 70-year-old mother so she wouldn't worry. He said he'd seek advice from his superiors.

No one came to talk with me, nor did anyone tell me the reason for restricting my freedom. I'd embarked on an indefinite term of house arrest.

I went into the bathroom and sent a message to Teng Biao telling him where I was and that I was being treated well. With little battery power left, I switched off my phone rather than wait for his reply.

Then I took a shower. I'd spent five days in my clothes, even while sleeping, and I couldn't bear them a moment longer. After removing my clothes, I examined the injuries from my four-day abduction, in particular a deep, crescent-shaped wound above my upper lip that still stung. The base of my spine still ached so much that I couldn't turn over in bed, and I had bruises all over my arms and legs, as well as a sprained right ankle. I couldn't remember getting some of the injuries, and wondered what had happened while I was unconscious.

Exhausted after my shower, I stretched out on the bed nearest the window and peered through the bars at the sky over Xinyu. I was a stranger to this city and didn't even know where the guesthouse was situated.

I had to accustom myself to the constant presence of two "bodyguards" in my room and could only hope that they didn't snore, grind their teeth or talk in their sleep. A chronic insomniac, I required the utmost quiet and cleanliness in my sleeping environment.

I reckoned that my November trip to Europe was now out of the question; I would probably be restricted from leaving China in the future. Had Teng Biao retrieved my laptop yet? I would lose my perfect credit rating if I was unable to pay off my credit card charges for the airfare to Europe, and there was sure to be a hefty penalty plus interest. Would my health suffer without my daily medication?

But the more I thought about these things, the more they paled in comparison to my loss of freedom. Maybe I couldn't travel the world, but some people had never even left Beijing. It didn't matter if my credit was bad, since I had no intention of taking out a loan. Teng Biao would do his best to get my laptop, and if he failed, well, that's just the way it was. What did it matter if I couldn't take my medicine? During my abduction I'd been prepared to die anyway. My only lingering worry was my mother, who suffered from a heart condition. Many friends had been arrested while celebrating on the day the Nobel Peace Prize was announced. When my mother left Beijing for Jiangxi the next day, I had promised her that nothing would happen to me. Now I just wanted to tell her, Sorry, Mom, I broke my promise!

I could only take things as they came; anger and frustration would only affect my judgment. I told myself to use this time as training in inner calm.

Early the next morning, the DomSec officer who'd met me at the train station, Chen Jianjun, came into the room, talking on the phone while pointing at me and saying, "Did you make a call to Beijing? Do you still have a communication device?" He turned and signaled to the two female bodyguards: "Search her, her bag and her bed!" They found my cell phone, and I lost all hope of further contact with the outside world.

Every day followed a similar schedule:

Out of bed at 7:30 in the morning, a shower and then breakfast downstairs; in the morning, reading, writing in my journal and yoga; downstairs for lunch at 11:30; in the afternoon, reading and Pilates, then a shower; dinner and television, then sleep.

At first I had a hard time getting used to the constant din of my "bodyguards" watching television from morning to night, but I soon learned to read, write and exercise with the noise in the background.

One evening after dinner, I wanted to go out for a walk. Chen Jianjun telephoned for instructions, and the answer he received was that I could go, but not beyond the guesthouse courtyard. This gave me one more activity to look forward to

Every evening, I put on my red sweater, overalls and black windbreaker (the sum total of the clothes I had with me since my kidnapping), and then went down with my four "bodyguards" to walk 20 laps around the courtyard (it must have looked ridiculous).

The courtyard was rectangular, about 80 paces from east to west and 35 paces from north to south. On my first day out, I found a small osmanthus tree in the courtyard's southeast corner. Its green leaves and fragrant white blossoms brought life to my long and lonely captivity.

After a week, I still hadn't received a reply to my request to phone my mother, so I raised it again at breakfast on November 9.

Chen Jianjun said, "Originally it would have been possible, but your contacting someone with a concealed telephone has had negative repercussions, so we can't let you call your mother."

"What kind of negative repercussions?"

"I can't tell you."

I flared up: "If I were in prison, you'd contact my family, but toward a law-abiding citizen you won't show even this basic humanity. The Beijing police should have told you I had another phone—that's not my fault. I have a right to get word to a friend. Now you're punishing me for that? Fine. I'm declaring a hunger strike, as of now. When I collapse you'll have to take me to the hospital, where I'll scream for help and tell everyone you've kidnapped me." I pushed away from the table and stalked off, hearing the scramble of their footsteps behind me.

"Xiao Chen is immature. Don't be angry with him!"

"Immaturity is one thing, but he should have some humanity. Everyone has parents."

"We can't make the decision—we need permission from higher up."

"I've given you nine days. Even the United Nations would have replied by now."

Upon returning to my room, I began my first hunger strike, fighting for the right to call my mother.

That morning, Division Chief Hu arrived: "I'll request instructions from our leader, and it shouldn't be a big problem, but it takes time. Have something to eat first."

"Go request instructions. I won't eat until I've called my mother."

The next morning, Chen Jianjun came in beaming: "Upstairs says you can call your mother, under two conditions: First, you can't say you're abducted or under house arrest, and you can't say you're in Xinyu; second, I have to hold the phone and keep it on speaker. Will that do?"

In any case I only wanted my mother to know I was safe. They dialed her number and placed the telephone by my ear. I heard my mother's worried voice: "Where are you? Why has your cell phone been switched off? We all thought something happened to you."

I calmly lied to my mother: "I'm on a trip to Europe and my cell phone isn't working. International roaming is so expensive, I haven't been able to call you regularly. Don't worry, I'm safer abroad than at home!"

Whenever I'd traveled before, I'd always called my mother before boarding the plane and upon arrival, and I'd always sent an e-mail to my brother with my itinerary, the phone numbers of my friends overseas, the addresses of the hotels where I was stay-ing, and information on my insurance policies. Having failed to do any of these things this time, I wondered if my mother would believe me.

From then on I was allowed to call my mother once a week, as long as I didn't give any indication of my current situation.

I filled long, sleepless nights with thoughts both warm and painful:

Christmas Eve ten years ago, at a bar in Sanlitun, I became acquainted with a Peking University doctoral student named Xu Zhiyong. During a quiet conversation amidst the clamorous par-tying of our friends and acquaintances, Zhiyong told me about his ideal of constitutional government and his field research on grassroots elections in the villages. His words moved me deeply, because I shared his ideals. Ten years later he'd represented my case fighting for free expression, and had given me invaluable assistance.

I'd become acquainted with Teng Biao at a legal aid seminar. When Zhiyong told him about my lawsuit, he said without hesi-tation, "Great! I'll support you!" The next time we met was at the Daxing Court, supporting Zhao Lianhai. Facing plainclothes police officers who were filming us, he said loudly: "My name is Teng Biao. Do you dare state your names?" All the women present swooned.

I'd spent more than a year filming citizen movements and legal cases launched, assisted or followed by the Open Constitution Ini-tiative: forced demolitions, equal access to education, the July 4 "Twitter Day,"[6] Zhao Lianhai, the Three Fujianese Netizens...our

---

[6] Netizens organized a Twitter campaign on July 4, 2010, to mark the release of You Jingyou, one of the Three Fujianese Netizens, from prison.

shared ideals and activities had forged a deep bond among us. I regarded Zhiyong and Teng Biao as more than comrades-in-arms; they were my brothers.

Early the year before, after publishing my article "Seeking China's Path," I'd been harassed by DomSec and a friend had urged me to seek legal advice from Pu Zhiqiang. Half an hour after calling him, I was a babbling supplicant in Zhiqiang's chaotic office. He interrupted me: "It's nothing. You'll be fine."

"But if I do have problems, will you be my lawyer?"

"Yes."

From then on, whenever trouble arose, I'd tell him about it in my rambling fashion until he assured me that I was blowing the situation out of proportion—until October 24, when I parted with him at Yichun to meet up with Teng Biao at Dandong. In the next few days, all of his phone calls and text messages ended with the words: "Take care!" and I sensed he was warning me. It struck me painfully that in this country, a warning was the best my lawyer could do for me.

The first I'd heard of Cui Weiping was when I read a series of her essays while preparing a biographical film on the poet Haizi. Her words moved me, and from then on I read all of her writings that I could find. The first time I met her was at a dinner sending off Butcher to Fuzhou to prepare the groundwork for supporting the Three Fujianese Netizens. Publicly joining the support group, Professor Cui said, "Today we're not focusing on the world, but on Butcher." A few days later, she wrote a long poem entitled "The Righteous Ones," with one stanza devoted to me.

I also recalled Big Sister Wang Lihong, Butcher, Tiantian, Wang Yi, Zhang Hui, A'er, Qiangben.... Thinking of them brought a warm flush to my cheeks, a feeling that poured from my heart and silently merged with the dark night to welcome the dawn.

After dinner on November 14, not long after returning to my room, I was sitting on my bed reading when there was a knock at the door. I thought it was the "bodyguard" from next door, but when Ouyang opened the door, I heard someone outside saying they were looking for Hua Ze. Ouyang slammed the door shut, and I heard someone outside shouting, "Hua Ze, Hua Ze, answer me, let us know you're inside!" I quickly sat up as my bodyguards stared at me.

The voice outside became louder, "Hua Ze, we love you!" Tears poured from my eyes, and I rushed to the door. With Ouyang standing next to me, I could only open the door a crack. I saw a woman and two men, all strangers.

"I'm Hua Ze, who are you?"

"We're netizens, here to see you."

"Where did you come from?"

"They're from Xinyu and I'm Chen Maosen from Fengxin. Do you remember me?"

"Of course!"

We'd had some exchanges on Twitter, and I remembered a headshot of a good-looking young fellow; he turned out to be even more handsome in real life. I reached out the door and shook hands with all of them. The warmth was indescribable, and the woman gave me a bouquet before Ouyang pushed the door shut.

The room was deathly still. Then Ouyang said, "Those two are from the Xinyu steelworks. They're so-called rights defenders, very bad sorts who provoke people to oppose the government." I stopped listening, my only thought being that if Ouyang recognized those two netizens, they must have recognized her as well, and they would report my situation that night on Twitter. I would not simply disappear from the face of the earth.

Ouyang changed her clothes and rushed out, leaving the other "bodyguard" with me. Once she'd reported the big news that I'd been located, everyone would be in a frenzy.

First thing the next morning, Division Chief Hu arrived and told me to pack up for relocation.

My new home, the Xinlantian Business Hotel, was not far from the Xiaofang Guesthouse. It abutted the street, and if I wanted a walk, I'd have to leave the grounds. In fact, they'd already started allowing me occasional walks outside the guesthouse's main entrance.

This hotel didn't have its own dining room, so we had to eat at the restaurant next door, where a decent meal inevitably exceeded the police expense budget. There was no climate control and the room was frigid. While I offered no opinion, my "bodyguards" found it intolerable. After ten days, when they saw that the coast was clear and that no more netizens were visiting or planning to kidnap me, my bodyguards insisted on moving back to the Xiao-fang Guesthouse.

Around the end of November, I learned that I might be kept under house arrest until after the 2011 Spring Festival, or even longer. I set a mental deadline to be released after Xiaobo's Nobel was presented on December 10, otherwise I'd go on hunger strike. I needed to find a way to get this information out.

One evening in the bathroom, I wrote on a slip of paper: I'm under house arrest and can't contact my family. Please pass this message to 186...and 139...(Teng Biao and Pu Zhiqiang's phone numbers, which I'd committed to memory on the train). Then followed the content of my message to Teng and Pu: 1) My cell phone had been confiscated, and this message was being sent with the help of a stranger, so it should not be published. 2) If I wasn't released after the Nobel presentation, I would go on hunger strike, and I needed their help. 3) If their freedom was not also restricted, I appointed them my lawyers. I had a power of attorney written out to Pu Zhiqiang at home (I provided information on where it could be found, and how to get the key to my home). 4) Xinyu DomSec was holding me under house arrest at the Xinyu Xiaofang Guest-house, room 9207. I placed that note and 50 *yuan* in an internal pocket.

When I went out for a walk on the evening of December 1, I slipped the note and money to a stranger I'd identified as a good prospect. (Regrettably, I can't provide further details here.) I didn't know if this stranger would be able to send the message, but it was the best I could do, and I'd have to leave the rest to fate.

When I went out for a walk two days later, the stranger was waiting for me and gave me an OK signal.

As the day for the Nobel presentation approached, I felt I'd entered a long, dark tunnel with a light at the end that I couldn't yet see. My nights were tormented by heart palpitations that attacked me just as I fell asleep. I went limp with indescribable anxiety, wanting to yell and fighting to keep from going mad. All I could do was keep telling myself, don't fall apart!

Even if they released me the day after the Nobel, being cut off from the world for 45 days was too great a price for someone who valued freedom more than life. Sometimes I wondered if I'd been more cooperative at the outset and told them everything they wanted to know, they might have released me or simply restricted my movement. Even so, I felt no regret. Their violence ruled out the possibility of negotiation or surrender. No one could coerce me, whether through violence, profit or even affection. Frailty is not a lack of power, significance or dignity. The difference between the weak and the strong is not one of physical strength, but of steadfast conviction.

Ultimately I held out until the day of the Nobel presentation. My situation suggested that anyone hoping to go to Stockholm for the presentation was under restriction. I hoped that the podium would have an empty chair, and that the cameras would also zoom in on the empty seats of the absent guests. There would be no better illustration of China's human rights situation and the immense significance of Xiaobo's Nobel Prize. Thinking of that scene, I wept. (After my release, I saw shots of exactly what I'd imagined—an empty chair!)

On the morning of December 11, I announced that I was going on hunger strike.

That afternoon, Director Zhang of the Xinyu Municipal PSB arrived. He said he'd personally requested instructions from the Jiangxi Provincial PSB the day before, and he expected a reply in the next few days. He hoped I'd be patient, and he asked me what I wanted. I said, "First, tell me why I'm still under house arrest, and two, tell me when it will end."

Resigned to my fate, I lay on my bed and let my consciousness drift, my body floating and weightless. It seemed that my soul was rising from my body and looking down at me:

How long can you keep this up?

I smiled: I'll fight to the bitter end.

Are you trying to destroy yourself?

No. This is my purification. They want to destroy me with coarseness, ugliness and emptiness, but I resist with delicacy, purity and fullness. They can destroy my body, but not my inner being; that they can never destroy.

On December 15, Division Chief Hu came with replies to my demands: First, there was a concert a few days after the presentation, and besides that, many rights defenders from all over China had converged on Beijing, and the Beijing police were too over-whelmed to let me back yet. Second, I would definitely be released by the twentieth, but only on the condition that I started eating.

I ended my hunger strike that day.

On the evening of December 17, Division Chief Hu once again honored me with his presence: "I have good news for you. You'll be freed on the twentieth. Where do you want to go?"

"I want to go back to Beijing."

"How?"

"Either by air or train is fine."

"Have Chen Ming buy a ticket for you."

"I didn't come here on vacation or to visit friends and relatives. You brought me here, so you take me back. I have no money, so if you don't send me back, I'll wait here until friends from Beijing can come for me."

I received my answer the next day: They would buy a sleeping berth ticket for me for the twentieth, and they'd see me onto the train.

FREEDOM! FREEDOM?

On the morning of December 19, Division Chief Hu instructed me to pack my bags. They'd been unable to buy a berth ticket in Xinyu, so they'd asked the Fenyi PSB to handle the arrangements. I'd go to Fenyi today, and I'd be taken to the Fenyi train station tomorrow afternoon.

The illogicality disturbed me. Xinyu was a prefecture-level city, and Fenyi was a county under its jurisdiction. If the Xinyu PSB couldn't buy a train ticket, how could the county bureau arrange for one?

Fenyi was only 30-odd kilometers from Xinyu, and the county seat was just over half an hour's drive away. Our two cars passed through Fenyi's bustling downtown and continued to the out-skirts, the landscape around us growing increasingly rugged, until we reached a resort at the foot of a mountain where Fenyi PSB officers awaited us. Our group comprised the village's only outsid-ers. Perhaps because we were in the mountains, it was much colder than in the city. That night I huddled in my blankets, immersed in wild imaginings: Were they taking me to a labor camp? Would I be arrested? A friend had been arrested for "inciting subversion" this past May, and after being released on bail, he'd told me that the Jiangxi police had asked about me.

My "bodyguard" was playing a computer game next to me, and I asked her to check when the train for Beijing left Fenyi the next afternoon. She went on Baidu, then looked at me in surprise and said, "That train doesn't stop in Fenyi."

I began to lose my temper. "Ask your leader where it is they're taking me."

This "bodyguard" was a young, artless girl. She said, "We've received orders that our duties end tomorrow afternoon. You'll be released tomorrow for sure. Don't worry, the leader will arrange things."

A little later, Director Zhang of the Xinyu Municipal PSB telephoned and said he needed to see me, and someone from the Fenyi bureau went to pick him up. After a long time, another "bodyguard" came in and said he'd been unable to pick up the leader, but he'd definitely come the next day, as he wanted to see me off. I was becoming increasingly uncomfortable with the situation.

After a sleepless night, I rose the next morning, and went out to sun myself in the courtyard. I was in a state of confusion: If they were going to release me, why bring me here? The "bodyguards" rushed out and comforted me: "Everything will be fine. The leader will arrange things, and if they don't release you today, we'll go on hunger strike with you."

We finally set out around noon for a high-class restaurant in Fenyi, where a table awaited us. Director Zhang, Division Chief Hu and four others from the provincial PSB were there. One older man (who looked like a leader) said, "We're taking you to Nanchang for a flight to Beijing."

"When can I have my cell phone back? I want to telephone a friend to pick me up at the airport."

"Don't worry, you'll get it back."

I had no appetite, suspicious of the detour. One of the officers from the provincial bureau was a woman surnamed Xiong, who seemed too polite for DomSec. "Ms. Hua, hasn't Jiangxi changed a lot? Perhaps you could give us some good publicity."

"I don't do publicity, only criticism."

"But Ms. Hua, don't you make historical documentaries? Jiangxi has a very rich history."

"Actually, I once did some research on Jiangxi's ancient academies of learning, but the department I was with at the time felt this topic lacked audience appeal, so they didn't approve it."

"Well, if you suggest a program, we'll make the arrangements so there are no problems with expenses and access."

"Hahahaha...that sounds great."

Interestingly, her demeanor suggested an amnesty rather than a labor camp.

After lunch, I joined the four provincial bureau officials and one Xinyu "bodyguard" in a Ford minivan, while Xinyu's Chen Jianjun followed in a sedan, and we set off for Nanchang.

As we approached Nanchang, the older man from the provincial bureau said, "We still have a few hours. Let's take Ms. Hua to the Tengwang Pavilion."[7]

In the pavilion tea shop a carefully scripted "friendly chat" ensued:

"Ms. Hua, you've been in Jiangxi for nearly two months now. I trust our Xinyu colleagues have properly attended to your needs?"

"Very well, thank you."

"You've studied law and so have I, but we won't talk about legal questions. Some things can be left for history to decide, would you agree?"

I just smiled.

"I'm not talking to you in an official capacity today, but I wonder if I might offer you some advice, strictly as your elder."

"Please do."

"Don't get involved in Liu Xiaobo's matters from now on."

"Which Liu Xiaobo matters?"

"For example, signature campaigns."

"They don't often happen."

"That's good. And there's no need to talk about the Jiangxi police."

---

[7] TN: One of the Four Great Towers of China, first built in 653 CE and located northwest of Nanchang.

"I have nothing bad to say about the Jiangxi police; they've been very civilized."

"From now on we're friends, and if anything comes up in Jiangxi, you need only say the word and we'll do our best to assist. You can exchange phone numbers with our Xiao Xiong and stay in contact." Was she now assigned to me? "We welcome you to visit often, but preferably not in this way."

"I'll be back. But whether I return in this way is probably not up to me."

"Your topic on Jiangxi's ancient academies of learning is a good one. If you write something up for us, we'll put things in motion, and you won't have any problems."

"Great. I'll contact you when the need arises."

"So I think we can leave it at that."

At 7:00 that evening, I was escorted to the airport's VIP lounge. Xiao Xiong asked for my ID card to process my boarding pass, and I again requested the return of my cell phone. She said, "I'll check it with your luggage."

I told her sternly, "A cell phone is a valuable item and it can't be checked as luggage. You need to return it to me. It'll be late by the time I reach Beijing, and I don't have warm clothes with me. I need to telephone a friend to pick me up."

"I've prepared some clothes for you. I know you don't have enough money, so I've arranged for your cab fare. Our bureau also prepared some gifts for you, and I'll wrap your cell phone carefully in with them."

"You're afraid I'll make a telephone call and a big welcoming reception will meet me at the airport. It's cold, and my flight gets in late. I won't let a lot of people come to the airport for me, I can promise you."

"We'll still check the phone for you."

"I wouldn't make a promise to you that I can't keep. Please return my cell phone."

The older man spoke up: "Give it back to Ms. Hua. Ms. Hua, since you've spoken frankly, I will also tell you that we do worry about something happening. We wish you well and hope you'll return home safely."

My flight left at 8:00, and at 7:40 I was escorted from the VIP lounge directly to the aircraft. At the boarding gate, I shook hands with the group from the provincial bureau. As soon as I entered the aircraft, I switched on my cell phone and called Teng Biao to tell him all was well.

It was only then that I knew I was really free.

The day after I returned to Beijing, I learned the reason why the Jiangxi police had driven me all over the place just before my release: On the eighteenth, Teng Biao, Xu Zhiyong, Butcher and others had organized a concern group of people from all over China, including four lawyers, with plans to go to Xinyu to rescue me.

Eleven days after I regained my freedom, the bells rang in the New Year, and I wrote this:

I have a dream; I hope that in the not-too-distant future, my friends will no longer be kidnapped, disappeared or imprisoned, and that they will no longer be forced to leave their homes to wander the earth in exile.

INDEX